Managing Institutional Long-Term Care for the Elderly

Maurice I. May, MSHA
President
Hebrew Rehabilitation Center for Aged
Boston, Massachusetts

Edvardas Kaminskas, MD
Physician-in-Chief
Hebrew Rehabilitation Center for Aged
and
Associate Professor of Medicine
Harvard Medical School
Boston, Massachusetts

Jack Kasten, MPH, JD
Lecturer on Health Services Administration
Department of Health Policy and Management
Harvard School of Public Health
Boston, Massachusetts

with
David Allan Levine, PhD
Management Consultant and Writer
South Attleboro, Massachusetts

AN ASPEN PUBLICATION
Aspen Publishers, Inc.
Gaithersburg, Maryland
1991

Library of Congress Cataloging-in-Publication Data

May, Maurice I.
Managing institutional long-term care for the elderly / Maurice I. May, Edvardas Kaminskas, Jack Kasten, with David Allan Levine.
p. cm.
Includes bibliographical references and index.
ISBN: 0-8342-0275-1
1. Old age homes—United States—Management. 2. Aged—Long term care—United States. I. Kaminskas, Edvardas. II. Kasten, Jack. III. Title.
HV1454.2.U6M39   1991
362.1'6'068—dc20
91-18306
CIP

Editorial Services: Lisa Hajjar

Library of Congress Catalog Card Number: 91-18306
ISBN: 0-8342-0275-1

Printed in the United States of America

1 2 3 4 5

For Barbara

Ethicists . . . do not adequately respect or protect the moral being of client/patients or residents of facilities if they simply clear out a zone of indeterminate liberty for them while remaining indifferent to its particular uses. A liberty merely patronized is a moral being denied. Respect for the patient demands more than giving him berth, licensing him to do, say, or be whatever he pleases. Respect must include an additional moral give-and-take, a sometimes painful process of mutual deliberation, judgment, and criticism, and an occasional accounting for one another's views and deeds.

William F. May

"The Virtues and Vices of the Elderly."
In *What Does It Mean to Grow Old? Reflections from the Humanities*, edited by Thomas R. Cole and Sally A. Gadow. Durham: Duke University Press, 1986.

Table of Contents

Acknowledgments

Some books may be conceived and written in solitude, but this one was not. Rather, it is the product of sharing ideas with hundreds of talented and dedicated people over many years, adapting their suggestions, monitoring the results, making modifications, testing again, and ultimately learning how to do somewhat better what we all care about so deeply—ensuring the delivery of quality long-term care services to infirm elderly residents, their families, and communities.

My collaborators in this project, Edvardas Kaminskas and Jack Kasten, have been actively involved at every step, sharpening my thinking and offering their unique perspectives on clinical and legal issues. In our ongoing dialogue, which began long before we decided to put pen to paper, we have disagreed often, only to pause, reconsider, and sometimes to cast out long-held beliefs as no longer apt. I have relished and benefited from these exchanges greatly. I trust that Ed and Jack feel the same.

I owe an enormous debt of gratitude to my employer since 1962, Hebrew Rehabilitation Center for Aged, and to its staff and trustees for providing such a wonderful environment for learning and growing. My friend Arnold Wolf, a former chairman of the board (1984–1987), has been especially encouraging. In addition to his unceasing support, it was he who established as one of the goals of the organization the writing of this book.

As for others whose incisive minds and good hearts I am more grateful for than I can say, they include R. Hopkins Holmberg, formerly head of the health care administration program at Boston University, who is now living and working in Nairobi, Kenya; David B. Starkweather, professor and director of the graduate program in health services management at the University of California, Berkeley; Kurt Darr, professor of health services administration at The George Washington University; Seth B. Goldsmith, professor of health sciences at the University of Massachusetts at Amherst; Hiram J. Friedsam, professor and director of the program in long-term care administration at the University of North Texas;

Herbert Shore, executive vice president of the North American Association of Jewish Homes and Housing; Carol Lockhart; and Sidney Lee.

Finally, I want to thank my brother Glenn for his constant support and lifelong influence. My greatest source of inspiration is my wife Barbara, and it is to her that this book is dedicated.

Maurice I. May

Chapter 1

Beliefs Narrowly and Widely Held

A PRELIMINARY LOOK AT STANDARDS AND QUALITY

"How long is a second? Certainly we ought to know that," wrote Vannevar Bush, pioneer in computer design, administrator of wartime scientific research, and guiding force behind the creation of the National Science Foundation, in 1966. Do we, he asked, just take the time for the earth to revolve on its axis and divide this by 86,400? But the earth does not turn uniformly. Shall we use the time required for the earth to complete a path around the sun? But this depends, to a slight degree, on what other planets are doing in the meantime. How about the time required for light to travel a measured distance? But this would require a perfect vacuum, and the technique is difficult, to say nothing of the possibility of becoming involved in questions of special relativity. Shall we use the time necessary for some specified atom to emit a certain number of vibrations? This is a sounder approach, but we have to be sure that we have the right atom and that we can count correctly. "I am not of course attempting in this example to really explore this problem," wrote Bush. "I merely wish to indicate how deep an apparently simple question can lead."[1]

In his charming and rhetorical way, Bush was of course asking some very important questions that impact virtually every sort of complex human activity. What should be the standard against which performance is measured? How should the standard be arrived at? Where does the need for further definition lie? What hard and complicated work attends the answering of even the simplest of inquiries?

Such a philosophical thicket lurks behind every bit of conventional wisdom relating to "assurance of quality" in long-term care (LTC) of the infirm institutionalized elderly. Here, as in few other human endeavors, the issues quickly transcend "simple" questions akin to Bush's "how long is a second?" and involve concepts that are so inherently slippery, so resistant to precise definition—concepts such as satisfaction, dignity, and safety—that rational analysis though the application of universally accepted standards would seem to be impossible.

Take, for example, a question that might be found on any quality survey of LTC institutions: What is the incidence of fractured hips due to falls among ambulatory residents? Fractured hips are bad things, right? So falls that produce fractured hips ought to be prevented, right? So the standard of excellence on the fractured hips due to falls scale may be assumed to be zero, right?

Maybe, maybe, and maybe. The ambivalence turns on whether an absence of fractured hips due to falls is itself a valid indicator of good care. Or, to put it in the more abstract language of the assurance sciences, whether the standard as defined constitutes a useful measure of global reality. The standard might be entirely apt—sometimes. For a particular place, it might be one more bit of evidence that wonderful care is being provided. That building corridors are wide and spacious, minimizing the likelihood of collisions and falls. That the floors are maintained properly by the custodial staff. That nurses are well trained and always vigilant.

But zero fractured hips may also be a warning that something less than wonderful is going on. That residents are being wheeled when they might otherwise be walking. That too much restraint is being administered by medical and nursing staff. That an institutional mentality of risk avoidance is fostering dependence and thereby diminishing quality of life among residents.

Same standard. Same results observed. Yet two entirely different sets of conclusions.

This is not to suggest that simple tests of conformance—the sort of picking and probing in the name of objective reality that characterizes the *Standards Manual* of the Joint Commission on Accreditation of Healthcare Organizations (Joint Commission) and constitutes the investigatory approach of various state regulatory authorities —ought to be dismissed as ill conceived and irrelevant. A lot of very bad care is being provided out there in the world, the actuality of which is reflected in buildings that are found to be unsafe, in hot water that is found to be cold, in food that is found to be inedible, in infections that are found to be rampant. A system of regulatory surveillance is necessary to identify the truly bad places and to thwart the avaricious and dangerously incompetent.[2]

But what about the rest of us? For us, the great cost of this find-the-bad-apple approach to quality assurance is twofold. First, as suggested, the standard that is applied may fail to approximate the reality that is being measured. The no-fractured-hips-due-to-falls standard is one example. Another might be this often-asked survey question: What is the incidence of urinary tract infections among a particular class of residents over a given period of time? The physician in charge may be spending very little time with her patients, may have poor relations with residents' families, may be personally difficult or uncommunicative with staff, and may be slovenly in her recordkeeping. Yet she may happen to have a splendid record of accomplishment as regards the incidence of urinary tract infections among her patients. Would you want this physician caring for your frail elderly parent?

The second, even greater cost of the traditional approach to monitoring quality in long-term care institutions is that it actively discourages any systematic attempt at self-improvement. The police officer as inspector enters the premises and says, in effect, "I will find out if you are deficient." The person (or department) being scrutinized quite naturally responds defensively, saying "I will prove to you I am not deficient," and then, as often as not, proceeds to distort the data or subtly alter the inspection mechanism or otherwise divert the attention of the inspector in order to demonstrate his or her purity and thereby escape citation for noncompliance. The nature of the system thus encourages individuals operating within it, including the highest levels of executive management, to ignore or even conceal defects rather than actively participate in their discovery. But only when a defect is discovered does it become useful, for only then can it be made to yield information on how a change in job design or in organization or in procedures or in internal communication can remedy the problem and thereby improve the entire health care delivery process.[3]

"Quality," then, ought to be more than conformance to arbitrary standards. It ought to be more than visiting armies of inspectors conducting orgies of measurement. Rather, quality should—indeed, must—be something that is internally driven. It must embody a strategy for (1) discovering what is truly important to the infirm elderly who are in the care of the institution, their families, and the community; and (2) effecting ongoing, incremental, systematic improvements in the delivery of services to these various constituencies. It requires the LTC institution to develop standards of care that go far beyond minimal thresholds of structure, process, and outcome. For, as quality engineers in every industry know, such floors quickly become ceilings, and a long-term care institution that seeks merely to meet minimum standards can never hope to achieve excellence.

Instead, the management and staff of the LTC institution must seize responsibility for defining what is quality. First, by making a clear statement of the institution's mission—how it intends to behave, how it intends to serve its targeted constituencies. Then, by delineating the process by which it intends to deliver its product. Then, by optimizing the process through the continuous introduction of well-considered incremental changes. Then, when they are satisfied with performance results in test, by committing the process to operation. Then, by striving for excellence by demonstrating to residents, families, employees, and the community that the long-term care product being delivered is indeed reliable and "noise-resistant" over time and under all the widely divergent conditions encountered in the real world. Finally, when feedback from various internal and external constituencies (including regulators) suggests the need for modifications, by considering and testing these modifications and, if they are found worthy, integrating them into the process flow.

All of which is to say, the delivery of quality care to the institutionalized elderly is more than a problem in political control. It is a problem in management. As such, it involves all the things that managers must learn how to do: think innovatively; develop a business strategy that is consistent with the goals and mission of the institution; structure the organization; manage financial resources; assess and manage risk; improve marketing effectiveness; and conduct public relations.

In the pages that follow, all of these issues will be addressed. The questions to be asked are, like Vannevar Bush's query, deceptively simple. How to create a quality institution or setting? How to sustain it? How to nurture it in the face of pressures from within and without?

Yet the point of view offered here is quite different from the traditional approach of how-to-manage manuals. The world of the long-term care administrator—indeed, the world of any general manager of a complex organization—is not definable in terms of static situations and thumb-indexed responses. Rather, it is full of messy problems, where the right thing to do from one perspective all too often seems the wrong thing to do from another perspective.

If one talent, above all, is necessary to do the LTC administrator's job effectively, it is the ability to strike delicate balances everywhere between legitimately conflicting positions. For example, how should the need for resident independence be weighed against the ethical and legal and economic responsibilities of the institution? How can the institution function not only as a home or hotel for some of its residents but as a hospital or hospice for others? How can legitimate societal goals, as expressed in regulatory standards, be balanced against the fiscal imperatives of daily operations? How can the LTC institution address and meet the needs of its staff, its residents, the families of its residents, and the community at large and resolve or balance any antagonisms inherent therein?

Often, in the discussion of these and other matters, the limits of prevailing wisdom on what is quality care of the institutionalized infirm elderly will be severely tested. But that is to be expected, given the complexity and transcendent importance of what LTC administrators do. For no profession is more exposed to the infinite variety of human emotion and capability and foible. To experiment is to learn, and the work of the LTC administrator is nothing less than a sobering and endlessly educational lesson in life.

THE LONG-TERM CARE ADMINISTRATOR'S JOB

The job of LTC administrator involves active participation in two worlds: (1) the world inside the walls of the institution, where it is necessary for the administrator to define the organization's mission, set goals, and bring his or her various technical, human, and conceptual skills to the task of management, and (2) the world outside the walls of the institution, where it is necessary for the administrator to involve him- or herself actively in public relations, the regulatory environment, reimbursement mechanisms, and community interests.

In both of these worlds, the LTC administrator's job is defined—sometimes formally, sometimes not—in terms of various responsibilities and relationships. It is essentially the same job as general manager and has many similarities to executive management positions in complex organizations of every type.[4] "It never ceases to amaze me how many people want to see me each day and how many different problems they come up with," is one familiar refrain. "It never ends. There is always something," is another verse of the same song.

Hardly ever does the door open and someone—a resident, a family member, a staff member, a community person, a local official, a representative of the news media—enter with a question or problem that neatly fits within traditional textbook categories. A controller's question about finances almost always has implications bearing on the regulatory system, reimbursement mechanisms, marketing, or operations. A social worker's question about family contact almost always relates in some way to medical care or admissions policy. A news reporter's question about some event almost always suggests considerations of law, ethics, and public perception.

Yet at the risk of oversimplifying the maelstrom that is the typical workday of the LTC administrator, the responsibilities and relationships inherent in the position can fairly be summarized in terms of six challenges.

Challenge Number 1: Setting basic goals, policies, and strategies despite great uncertainties. A confident forecaster is a foolish forecaster, for the future has ways of surprising everyone. Nevertheless, the LTC administrator must gaze into an often murky crystal ball and try to arrive at satisfactory answers to the following:

- Will any technological or medical breakthroughs fundamentally alter the way we do things?
- How will projected changes in demographics (of the elderly, of the labor force, of the family) and personal income impact the long-term care industry in general and our LTC institution in particular?
- Will there be any substantive changes in the nature of our competition?
- How will changes in the political climate and the local economy affect the availability of money from the public sector?
- As regards proprietary institutions, how will the future financial health of a corporate parent affect the scale and quality of operations? As regards

nonprofit institutions, how will projected economic change impact sources of funding or contribution?

Challenge Number 2: Achieving a delicate balance in the allocation of scarce resources among a multiplicity of interests. As an example, the LTC administrator must become adept at distinguishing between short-term concerns and long-range needs and must make allocation decisions without destroying the enthusiasm and productivity of impacted individuals or departments.

Challenge Number 3: Keeping close tabs on a very large and diverse set of activities. The LTC administrator must create formal and informal mechanisms for gathering information so that he or she will know—either from objective evidence or through intuition—that something is out of control and must be attended to. The administrator must then create—or better yet, will have already created—an organizational structure for examining the problem, arriving at a means of resolution, assigning task responsibilities, and monitoring progress toward the goal.

Challenge Number 4: Getting information, support, and cooperation from the boss (i.e., the board of directors, the corporate parent, the managing public authority, etc.) in order to do the job effectively. The LTC administrator must learn to be demanding of the boss without appearing to be uncooperative or intransigent. Success in this relationship presupposes that the following issues have been resolved satisfactorily:

- Does the institution have an updated mission statement that clearly specifies constituencies, services, and organizational direction?
- Are the responsibilities of the boss and the LTC administrator clearly delineated so that the administrator understands the limits of his or her autonomy?
- Do performance criteria exist for the LTC administrator's position?
- Where the boss is a board of directors, are board members selected on the basis of their interest, willingness to work, community influence, and areas of expertise? Do their areas of expertise fit the needs of the LTC institution?
- Are lines of communication to the boss established, known, and followed?
- Are the boss and the LTC administrator in agreement on new directions? Is the boss willing to risk more creative and forward-looking programs and services?
- Where the boss is a board of directors, are board members sensitive to potential conflicts of interest when nominating new members?

Challenge Number 5: Eliciting the cooperation of important groups or constituencies despite the LTC administrator's lack of any formal authority over them. The LTC administrator must learn to get things accomplished working with a multiplicity of constituencies, despite the existence of differing perspectives, bureaucratic intransigence, mistrust, or even animosity. Included among the groups and constituencies with whom the LTC administrator must deal are families of current and prospective residents, local physicians and hospitals, other community representatives and interests, the news media, and various public regulatory authorities.

Challenge Number 6: Motivating and controlling a large group of subordinates with widely divergent interests and agendas. The LTC administrator must define job responsibilities, develop feedback and control mechanisms, and deal with inadequate performance and interdepartmental conflict.

Each of these six challenges and the range of situations they encompass represent a significant demand on the LTC administrator's time. Taken together, they can be—and often are—overwhelming because of the attention to detail they require and the frustration they evoke.

This is one important reason why LTC administrators tend, as a group, to be risk averse. Why inject more uncertainty and the possibility of deleterious consequences into a workday that is already full and complicated enough?

Another reason, and one that frames all of these considerations, is the nature of the system under which most LTC administrators operate. The rules of the game, as promulgated in Washington and administered by the various state regulatory authorities, have become so cumbersome and are interpreted so rigidly as to actively discourage bold and innovative approaches to the organization and delivery of long-term care services. Instead, they encourage LTC administrators, and everyone else operating within their construct, to be accommodationist. Given the severe penalties for noncompliance to regulations, coupled with the customary forewarning from the boss (in the person of the board of directors or the corporate parent)—"I don't want to hear about any complaints from the state, so just stay legal"—it is little wonder that most LTC administrators opt for the path of least resistance.

How did such a situation come to be? A bit of history will shed some light on this particular impediment to good management.[5]

Prior to the passage of the first Social Security law in 1935, disabled old people were generally kept at home. If there was no room for them or no one to look after them, their options were severely limited: the local poor house, a state hospital (often a mental hospital), or some charitable private home supported by an immigrant self-help organization or religious group.

In 1935, in the midst of the Great Depression and widespread public suffering, the assistance titles of Social Security were enacted, providing for payments of federal money to the aged, the blind, and dependent children. The disbursements under the law were unconditional, meaning they could be used for anything the recipient required—food, shelter, medical care, amusement, or whatever. Thus, if the recipient was in need of nursing home care, he or she (or the family) would locate a home, evaluate it according to personal circumstances, and pay for services rendered in a simple two-party transaction.

In 1950, the innocence of those arrangements were forever altered. In that year the Social Security Act was amended to include the Aid to the Permanently and Totally Disabled category and to allow direct payment of federal money to particular providers of care, such as the nursing home, *on behalf of the recipient of services.* This change was fundamental. Whereas previously the elderly person needing care was the direct purchaser of services and therefore entitled to the usual considerations accorded principals in the marketplace, now under the new law he or she had been reduced to an object of an accounting transaction between the nursing home and the federal government.

At that symbolic point, the nursing home "industry" sprang full-blown upon the stage, and the mating dance between it and the custodians of the public treasury began. Now the operative question for nursing home operators was simply, "What do I need to do to ensure reimbursement?" and quality of care issues came to be filtered through the regulatory standards that currently applied.

Two landmarks thereafter are critical. In 1953, the Social Security Act was amended to require that as a condition of federal assistance the states must have an agency to establish and enforce standards for nursing homes and other medical institutions. Some state legislatures enacted strict legislation; others chose to adopt a more laissez-faire attitude.

In 1965, direct federal regulation of nursing homes was promulgated. In that year, in response to widespread concern over growing medical costs for the elderly, the Social Security Act was amended to provide medical payments for those age 65 and over (Title XVIII) as well as for those receiving income support from public assistance programs (Title XIX).

These amendments, which went into effect in 1967, were followed by a series of complex regulations intended to control costs and improve care. A two-tier classification was created, which borrowed heavily from the medical model of the acute care hospital. Under it, long-term care institutions were designated either as skilled nursing facilities (SNFs) or as intermediate care facilities (ICFs).

SNFs are the more medically oriented of the two kinds of facilities, and their standards for staffing and services are stricter and more detailed. The language used in the regulations suggests the operative distinction: The SNF criteria refer to the elderly receiving services as "patients," whereas the ICF criteria refer to them as "residents." The most important difference between SNFs and ICFs pertains to nurse staffing. SNFs must have a nurse on duty 24 hours a day, whereas ICFs are required to have a nurse on duty only during each day shift.

The nursing home industry responded predictably to this codification of rules by organizing its institutional long-term care services according to the sanctioned SNF-ICF classification. Two problems quickly became apparent, and they persist to the present day:

1. The latitude given to the states under Title XIX of the Social Security Act (Medicaid) in interpreting the regulations has led to substantial differences in how SNF and ICF facilities are defined. For example, in Oklahoma, 98 percent of licensed nursing homes are ICF; in Connecticut, about 90 percent are SNF; in Arizona, 100 percent are SNF. Why the divergence? Certainly it is not because the service needs of each state's elderly residents vary so widely. Rather, different states have dissimilar attitudes about Medicaid funding, and they choose to make different judgments about how much nurse staffing they are willing to pay for under their participation in the program. Medicaid reimbursement rates must, by law, be higher for SNFs than for ICFs. If the rate differential in a given state is large, there is an incentive for the state to control nursing home costs by licensing more ICF beds than SNF beds.

2. Even if the two-tier SNF-ICF structure was consistently applied across state boundaries, as an organizing principle it is inherently unable to reflect all relevant variation (or heterogeneity) in the patient care mix. Elderly people requiring long-term care services do not necessarily fit neatly into one or the other of these two administrative classifications. As a consequence, residents of long-term care institutions often receive—or are indirectly charged for—categories of care that are either unneeded or inappropriate for their individual situations.

That the system was born of good intentions—to control excesses of incompetence and greed and to impose some minimal standards on institutions receiving public monies to care for the infirm elderly—is no doubt true. But if its great strength was to be conformance to standards, so too has conformity become its greatest cost. Predictably, many LTC administrators, already grappling daily with the various and sizable challenges involved in being a good general manager, have responded by endeavoring to "game" the system and thereby minimize the risk of confrontation with the regulators and escape the wrath of the boss.

An example: Every state uses decubitus ulcers (bed sores) as one indicator of quality care. If a resident has decubiti, what is the incentive for the LTC administrator not to transfer this person as quickly as possible to an acute care hospital and thus avoid a bad report card on outcomes? From an accommodationist point of view, there is none. Similarly, if the resident is being returned from an acute care hospital with decubiti, what is the incentive not to send him or her back immediately? Again, none.

But such a course of administrative action carries two enormous price tags. First, the transfer-of-costs game adds greatly to society's total health care bill, because treatment of decubitus ulcers in an acute care hospital is on the order of six times more expensive than equivalent treatment when provided in an LTC institution. Second, the toll on the elderly person who is the object of the game is devastating. To uproot and reinstitutionalize the patient unnecessarily, and perhaps shuffle the patient among a succession of skilled nursing facilities if a bed cannot be held during a hospital stay, is far more than a "sad but necessary consequence" of the rules that govern the game. It is an affront to the patient's dignity.

The premise underlying this book is that, with courage, energy, and deliberation, long-term care administrators can do much better. Caring for the infirm elderly in institutions is a complicated matter, but reduced to its essence, the only meaningful product of effective long-term care administration is a group of residents who are content, fulfilled, and in reasonable control within the limits imposed by their life circumstances.

It is a goal that is much easier to articulate than to achieve. Providing consistently high quality care to a varied group of frail, very old residents, many of whom have severe mental impairments as well as physical disabilities, requires that the functional, medical, social, and psychological needs of residents be individually determined by careful assessment and responded to by comprehensive planning. Also crucial are small and consistent acts of kindness by staff at all levels; the availability of places of privacy for intimate conversation with family or friends; and opportunities for the exercise of personal choice regarding activities, food, and even medications.

In order to fashion such an institution, the LTC administrator must be willing to think very differently about the business he or she is in. Ask what is that business, and the typical LTC administrator will reply that it is a service, something invariably and undeviatingly personal, something that is performed by individuals for other individuals, something that is hard to define, much less to measure.

It is a nice, humanistic image, but one that is severely limiting. For it virtually guarantees that all solutions to improving quality in institutional long-term care of the infirm elderly will be cast in terms of individual performances, that is, upgrading the skills and attitudes of those persons performing the tasks under scrutiny rather than altering the systems and procedures within which the caregivers operate. The content of jobs within the organization is accepted as static. The best any general manager can do is attempt to motivate.

For the long-term care product to be significantly and permanently improved, it is necessary that the LTC administrator become more technocratic in his or her approach to management. Much like the manager of a manufacturing facility, whose product is "things" rather than "people," the LTC administrator must articulate a quality standard that is at once comprehensible, measurable, and achievable and must define in detail the job processes and routines that will yield the intended results.

A new mindset quickly begets new questions. What kinds of tools (old or new) and what kinds of skills, incentives, controls, and audits might be enlisted to accomplish the outcomes that are sought? What alternatives to the present organizational structure exist, alternatives that will allow motivated people to function smarter?

Thoughtful answers to these questions can result in significant improvements in the quality of care provided by the LTC institution. Failure of the LTC administrator even to ask them virtually ensures that things will get no better.

NOTES

1. Vannevar Bush, "Foreword," in *Measures for Progress: A History of the National Bureau of Standards*, Rexmond C. Cochrane (Washington, D.C.: U.S. Department of Commerce, National Bureau of Standards, 1966), iii–iv.

2. On investigatory approaches, see Joint Commission on Accreditation of Healthcare Organizations, *Long Term Care Standards Manual, 1988* (Chicago, Ill.: Joint Commission on Accreditation of Healthcare Organizations, 1988); U.S. Department of Health and Human Services, Health Care Financing Administration, "Medicare and Medicaid Programs; Requirements for Long Term Care Facilities; Final Rule with Request for Comments," *Federal Register* (February 2, 1989) vol. 54, no. 21, pp. 5316–73.

3. On assessing quality in health care, see Donald M. Berwick, "Continuous Improvement as an Ideal in Health Care," *New England Journal of Medicine* 320 (January 5, 1989): 53–56; James S. Roberts, "Reviewing the Quality of Care: Priorities for Improvement," *Health Care Financing Review,* annual suppl. (1987): 69–74; Avedis Donabedian, "Commentary on Some Studies of the Quality of Care," *ibid.,* 75–85. For examination of quality assurance issues in a broader context, see David A. Garvin, *Managing Quality: The Strategic and Competitive Edge* (New York: The Free Press, 1988); Masaaki Imai, *Kaizen: The Key to Japan's Competitive Success* (New York: Random House, 1986); J.M. Juran, *Juran on Planning for Quality* (New York: The Free Press, 1988).

4. See John P. Kotter, *The General Managers* (New York: The Free Press, 1982), especially 10–33.

5. Institute of Medicine Committee on Nursing Home Regulation, *Improving the Quality of Care in Nursing Homes* (Washington, D.C.: National Academy Press, 1986), especially 69–103.

Chapter **2**

Thinking about Patterns of Care

THE PROBLEM-SOLVING PATH TO INNOVATION

"We have a lot of problems here," said the LTC administrator to the consultant whom he had called in to help. "There are 175 beds in the place, and right now 43 of them are empty. We need about an 80 percent occupancy rate to break even at the current rate of Medicaid reimbursement. But demand has dried up and we're not meeting our expenses, let alone making any money. All of our private pay residents have gone elsewhere. The last one transferred a month ago.

"Look, everyone here wants to give good care, and I've always tried to treat my employees right. When I started hearing complaints about two years ago that people were overworked and overwhelmed by the caseload, we began to add staff everywhere. That boosted our overhead for sure, but it hasn't done much to eliminate the complaints. People still say they can't keep up with the job. Turnover is high and morale is lousy.

"And the regulators who are always coming in don't make things any easier, either. The regulations are difficult enough to understand when you read them in the book, since they don't seem to be talking about the real world of our operation. We try to conform as best we can, but often the interpretations we get from the regulators don't square with our understanding of what's written. So we spend a lot of time playing the game—you know, 'keep the monkey off your back'—and I think that while we're doing that we're mixing residents who shouldn't be together and sending a lot of people out to hospitals for minor things when we really could be taking care of them here.

"I guess I feel like we're out of control. What I'm saying is, we always seem to be reacting to things rather than planning. That's probably one reason why staff say they're running in ten directions at once, and when they can't—or won't—do the job anymore, they leave. With all the rehiring and retraining we have to do, no wonder we're probably giving substandard care."

The administrator, the consultant, and the director of nursing walked around the facility, paying particular attention to the physical layout and to the care requirements of various groups of residents. "How many people do you have like this?" asked the consultant, indicating a woman who was seemingly alert and making her way on a walker toward the dining room. The director of nursing replied with a number.

A bit further down the hall there was a man in bed who was rambling incoherently and obviously incontinent. "How many people do you have like that?" Another number.

Around the corner, they looked into a room where a nurse was helping a female resident get dressed. "How many people do you have like that?" Another number.

After the tour, the LTC administrator, the director of nursing, and the consultant sat down to compare notes on the care needs of the resident population and the current levels of staffing. The consultant sketched the physical layout of the building on a pad. He asked, "If you took all the residents you have who are mostly self-sufficient and assigned them rooms in this part of the building, how many people would it require to take care of them—the day shift, the night shift, everybody?" The administrator and the director of nursing conferred, and they quickly reached agreement on the number of staff it would take to provide direct care services.

"And if you took all your residents needing a somewhat higher level of care and put them in this area over here, how many people would it take to do the job?" Again there was agreement on a number.

"And if you assigned your heaviest care population to this group of rooms, what would be the staffing requirements?" Another number was agreed upon.

When the staffing requirements for each of the three indicated levels of care—limited, moderate, and heavy—were totaled, the sum came to six fewer people than currently were being employed. The arithmetic suggested that the cost of these six extra employees accounted for much of the fiscal deficit the institution was currently experiencing.

"I see where you're going," said the LTC administrator. "You want to concentrate RNs and support personnel into areas where care needs are highest and to allow the more independent residents to do more for themselves. It won't work. It's too radical a departure from the way we have always organized services. The residents might accept it, but the families will scream their heads off."

There followed a lengthy discussion of the existing relationship between the institution and the residents' families. Apparently, the LTC administrator and staff had never made much effort to communicate effectively with this constituency, and as a result there was a general suspicion of motives on both sides, sometimes extending to outright animosity. The consultant, LTC administrator, and director of nursing discussed how to remedy this situation, specifically how to meet with the families, listen to their concerns, and convince them that the proposed new method of organizing services was going to improve significantly the quality of care for their aged relatives.

Another consideration was raised by the LTC administrator. "Our policy has always been to try to avoid layoffs," he said. "I think they are destructive of morale, and we have enough morale problems now as it is. How do we get rid of the extra staff?"

"Why not do it over a six-month period?" suggested the director of nursing. "People are leaving anyway. Just don't replace them. Let it happen by attrition."

"The state regulators will object," replied the LTC administrator. "There are minimum requirements for nursing staff under the SNF classification."

"You'll still be within the legal requirements," said the consultant. "You're simply reallocating the bulk of your resources to the service of those who need them the most."

This imaginary conversation reveals an interesting mindset that people in difficulty often manifest. Even when confronted with a messy, ill-defined, dangerous problem—"Demand for beds is down, we're losing money, quality of care has become poor, what's WRONG?"—any suggestion there is a need for structural change (as opposed to procedural change within an existing system) is almost always met with resistance. As in the above example, the full range of traditional objections are trotted out.

"It's against policy."
"We've never done it that way."
"It won't work."
"No one will accept it."
"It's too radical."
"It's probably against the law."

That mindset is hardly unique to LTC administrators. Much of it, probably, is culturally derived. We Americans tend to resist any suggestion that the core of a problem may be more hidden than obvious, that it may be systemic, and that a solution cannot be immediately forced by the marshalling of vast financial, human, or technological resources. The "shoot first, ask questions later" gunslinger did not become part of our national mythology for no reason.[1]

Other cultures look at the problem-solving exercise quite differently. For them, the implementation of a solution has no transcendent urgency. It can wait until the problem is defined, and redefined, and redefined yet again. To the uninitiated this approach sometimes seems endless, but it is part of the process of building a consensus.[2]

This latter method of problem solving has two clear advantages:

1. The chances of solving the wrong problem, or some manifestation or subset of the "real" problem, is greatly reduced.

2. When it finally comes time to implement the solution, those who were intimately involved in the lengthy process of problem definition have become shareholders. That is, they now have a personal stake in seeing that the solution that finally emerges is implemented successfully.

Problems are unavoidable, and in one sense they are beneficial, for they provide an opportunity for individuals within the organization to upgrade quality continuously. Indeed, the greatest danger confronting any organization is consistent failure to recognize and to act upon problems decisively, to identify what the problems really are and not just what they appear to be, to diagnose and correct.[3]

Unfortunately, not all LTC administrators are successful problem solvers. Problems are tiring and time consuming and spirit deadening, and when they occur day in and day out in any organization there is the understandable instinct to seek some mental short cut. So, knowingly or unknowingly, the LTC administrator often engages in what Nobel laureate Herbert Simon has called "programmed problem solving."[4] This is the application of either standard operational procedures (SOPs) or solutions that worked in years past in similar but not identical situations as a means of solving current problems.

There is nothing wrong with programmed problem solving in certain situations, such as when the problem is repetitive, routine, and well defined. When a pipe bursts, throw a wrench on it, take out the faulty section, and get a new piece in place quickly. There is no need—and no time—for "reinvent the wheel" creative thinking and consensus building.

But the limitation of the SOP approach is that it is nondiscriminating. It treats all problems as routine, even when they are not. Sometimes a pipe bursts not because it is faulty but because a flaw somewhere else in the system is causing it to fail. What is the consequence of focusing only on what is immediately understood, of picking and choosing those pieces of evidence that confirm the belief that a problem is entirely ordinary, and of ignoring any data that suggest that what is happening may be unprecedented, elusive, and ill-defined?

This may all seem quite obvious, yet our society tends to hold in very high regard the class of managers who instinctively substitute programmed problem-solving skills for critical problem-solving skills. They are often given that supreme accolade of management: "He's fast on his feet." If the honoree happens to make the mistake of using a routine solution to deal with a novel problem, by the time the organization begins to show signs of illness due to cumulative neglect, the individual is likely either nowhere in sight (having job hopped or been promoted to greener pastures) or is safe from blame because his or her superiors are likewise incapable of assessing the complex relationship of cause and effect over time.

Of course, what constitutes an ill-defined mess for one manager may be legitimately routine for another, so a good deal depends on how often the manager has faced the problem at hand or one that is comparable. In time, many ill-structured problems become well-understood—the so-called wisdom of experience—and useful SOPs may be developed. But because general managers, such as LTC administrators, operate in an environment that is complex, uncertain, ambiguous, and often chaotic, they are quite likely to encounter problems that resist easy definition.

Sometimes, a knotty problem faced by an LTC administrator may involve operations. Other times it may involve strategy. Operational problems are usually repetitive on a daily or weekly basis. Strategic problems impact the future well-being of the institution and typically involve analysis of actions taken, resources committed, or precedents set.

Often the distinction can become blurred, such as when an operational problem left unattended becomes a strategic problem of the first magnitude. For example, chronic shortages of ostomy supplies can directly impact resident care, which can lead to complaints by residents to their families, which can generate adverse publicity, which can result in increased regulatory scrutiny, which can stimulate political ax grinding, which can adversely impact admissions, which can lead to reduced cash flow, which can endanger the financial stability of the institution.

While every crisis may be a problem, not all problems are crises. Some are opportunities, requiring solutions that will enable the institution to exploit new markets or build on fundamental organizational strengths. Sometimes in the process of resolving a crisis, new capabilities are created or discovered, thereby transforming the situation into an opportunity with its own set of problem-solving imperatives.

All of which directly relates to the dialogue between the LTC administrator, the director of nursing, and the consultant that began this chapter. Implicit in it was a challenge: How to understand the difficulties facing the LTC institution in question, and, having done so, how to begin to do a better job of organizing and delivering services. Or, to put it in the context of problem solving, how to discern the differences between types of problems and, where appropriate, to think creatively beyond the constraints of old, comfortable, timeworn channels.

A REHABILITATIVE MODEL

One precept of geriatrics is that while accurate diagnosis of illness is important, it is nevertheless an inadequate criterion by which to judge the health care needs of an individual.[5] In the long-term care setting especially, the diagnostic label is less useful than a fully documented understanding of how the resident behaves and how effectively he or she is able to function.

The "typical" resident with cancer, or psychotic illness, or Alzheimer's disease, or virtually any other chronic affliction cannot be defined with precision. A woman with cancer might be mentally alert and socially active or be bedridden, delirious, and in the final stages of the illness. A manic depressive might be hopelessly erratic in behavior at all times or might remain mostly on an even keel except for occasional and transitory episodes of dissociation. The Alzheimer's patient might be in the early stages of the illness and therefore mobile and sometimes lucid, or he or she might be in an advanced stage and therefore contracted, incontinent, and totally incapable.

For purposes of organizing services in a long-term care institution, therefore, it would be extremely inappropriate — indeed, cruel — to group residents in living units on the basis of medical diagnosis alone. A person who is immobile and vulnerable ought not to be living with, or in proximity to, someone who is mobile and aggressive, even if the medical origins of their disabilities are the same.

To be sure, "health" considerations are important in assessing the amount and skill level of nursing care required. But other factors, such as mental status, behavior, and the degree of ability to conduct activities of daily living, are of much greater consequence and must therefore be given primary consideration in assessing the needs of the individual resident and in allocating the human and capital resources of the LTC institution.

In the dialogue between the LTC administrator, the director of nursing, and the consultant, the consultant suggested segregating residents according to predefined classifications of functional need. He said that when the arithmetic was done—so many residents requiring lighter care over here, so many residents requiring heavier care over there—it was likely that better care for all could be achieved, and at a savings.

That is the premise underlying the organization of services in place at Hebrew Rehabilitation Center for Aged (HRCA) in Boston. Each resident is evaluated, then grouped with others who have like or compatible functionality in a particular nursing unit. At HRCA, which is a large institution (currently 725 beds) and has a resident population whose level of functionality ranges from the very alert to the extremely debilitated, three "patterns of care" (PI, PII, PIII) are defined, and within Pattern III, the most debilitated group, six subpatterns are identified.

The idea of grouping residents according to their functional needs and allocating resources accordingly was born of practical necessity. In 1963, HRCA had just completed a major building program, expanding the facility to 475 beds, and it had almost run out of money. At the time, the state of Massachusetts was paying $8.25 per day per resident for care.

Question posed by the LTC administrator: How to do a good job with $8.25 per resident per day?

Answer: By creating a resident population not disproportionately represented by the extremely debilitated.

Question: How to accomplish that?

Answer: By controlling admissions.

Question: Then what?

Answer: By organizing services for residents according to the special needs of discrete groups.

So the LTC administrator looked closely at the physical layout of the new facility—the number of floors in the building, the number of corridors on each floor, the number of rooms on each corridor, and so on—and asked the nurses, "If you had 40 residents in this area of the building, and all of them had these sorts of functional and behavioral characteristics, how much staff would you need to take care of them around the clock?" And then, "If you had, over on that side of the nurse's station, 40 residents who were more severely disabled and had these sorts of functional and behavioral characteristics, how much staff would you need to take care of them?"

The answers received suggested that a cost savings might be achieved if aggregate care was substituted for skilled nursing care wherever possible. For example, if an activities person was hired to work with groups of residents for a total of four hours a day, the expense of the new position could be justified by the savings achieved through reducing the scheduled time of nurse's assistants.

Though controlling costs had been the initial stimulus for this thinking, the broader implications soon became apparent. The additional benefits realized were these:

Improved Efficiency. Under the previous model, LTC management tended to believe the larger the staff, the better the care. Accordingly, it staffed to the maximum, and as costs inevitably rose it tried to admit more ambulatory residents yet cared for them as if they were highly dependent. Under the new pattern-of-care model, staff allocation was far more efficient, and the inevitable conflicts between personalities on the job were greatly reduced.

Improved Quality of Care. Under the previous model, where residents of all levels of functionality were commingled, nurses tended to give disproportionate attention to those individuals who required the most care and sometimes too little attention to those whose needs were, or appeared to be, less compelling. Under the new pattern-of-care model, where residents were brought together on the basis of like or compatible functionality, all individuals living on a nursing unit tended to have the same basic set of needs, and so nursing staff could concentrate their efforts on meeting the collective requirements of the group without feeling they were giving less than complete care to any particular individual.

Improved Quality of Life. Under the previous model, residents were encouraged to be dependent and to cede primary responsibility for their care to doctors and nurses. Under the new pattern-of-care model, residents were encouraged to take as much responsibility for their own lives as they were able to handle. Also, because living arrangements were organized by level of functionality, residents were more likely to find companionship, form associations, and otherwise develop an abiding sense of community.

The basis for organizing resident care services under the rehabilitative model in use at HRCA is the functional assessment patterning system. Each resident is evaluated using seven functional assessment scales, which measure (1) mobility, (2) dining, (3) dressing and hygiene, (4) toileting, (5) mental status, (6) behavior, and (7) health. On each of these scales, impairments requiring nursing care to compensate for the resident's disabilities are quantified, and by employing a simple multistep formula the resident's functional impairment scores are translated into an overall pattern of care.

Other LTC institutions, depending on their size, floor plan, logistics, and strategic mission, may not require so comprehensive a patterning system. For small institutions, it may make sense instead to divide residents into just two groups: "alert" and "not alert." In any case, what is important is that the LTC institution follow some systematic procedure of evaluating residents, then organize services based on the cumulative results of the evaluations.

The operative distinctions between Patterns I, II, and III—the three major classifications of resident functionality at HRCA—can be summarized as follows:

Pattern I services those elderly who have experienced some degree of physical or mental deterioration but who are nevertheless independent and require very little staff intervention except during occasional episodes of acute illness. These residents are mobile, perhaps with walkers. They are alert. They take all their meals in a main dining hall. They spend a substantial amount of time engaged in recreational activities.

Pattern II services those elderly who have experienced more physical or mental deterioration and who, therefore, have greater need for staff care. Pattern II residents are less independent than Pattern I residents but more able to carry on activities of daily living than Pattern III residents. Typically, they have decreased mobility, experience some toileting difficulties, need assistance in dressing, have episodes of disorientation, or require observation and assessment of chronic medical symptoms. A Pattern II resident may come to a main dining hall for one or more meals per day or, for extended periods, may take all meals in his or her room.

Pattern III services those elderly who are severely debilitated physically and mentally and, therefore, have the heaviest staff care requirements. Six identifiable subpatterns (A–F) are defined within Pattern III.

Subpattern IIIA services persons who do not have important intellectual loss. Incontinence can be tolerated, provided the incontinent resident can announce his or her need or accidents promptly and be changed before any unpleasant odor develops. Major behavior disorders cannot be tolerated because of the potential for disruption of what is intended to be a harmonious, socially interactive unit.

Subpattern IIIB services persons who have moderate intellectual loss but do not have uncontrollable incontinence or severe behavior disorders. It is believed that these residents make the most compatible floormates for those with IIIA characteristics.

Subpattern IIIC services persons who have moderate intellectual loss, do not have severe behavior problems, but who do have uncontrollable incontinence. They are segregated from IIIA and IIIB residents in order to protect these from the inevitable odors of uncontrollable incontinence.

Subpattern IIID services persons who have severe intellectual loss but do not have severe behavior problems. It is believed that these residents make the most compatible floormates for those with IIIC characteristics, because with limited cognitive function they are least likely to be bothered by proximity to those with severe incontinence.

Subpattern IIIE services persons who have severe behavior disorders and are mobility dependent or otherwise defenseless and unable to escape attack. In order to protect these residents from any violence that their behavior problems might provoke, they are segregated from mobile residents with severe behavior disorders. It is believed that those with IIID characteristics are the most suitable floormates for those with IIIE behavior disorders.

Subpattern IIIF services persons who have severe behavior problems, pose a significant threat to self or others, and cannot be managed on any other unit. They may or may not have severe intellectual loss and they may or may not be incontinent. Residents with IIIF characteristics are segregated from other residents in order to maximize their quality of life and to minimize negative impact.

FUNCTIONAL ASSESSMENT SCALES

The seven functional assessment scales are used to evaluate a resident's usual and customary pattern of functional ability over the two weeks immediately preceding the assessment.

Every resident living on a nursing unit is assessed on the first day of alternate months (February, April, June, August, October, December). In addition to these regularly scheduled evaluations, testing may be done whenever the need is indicated, such as when a resident's functional status appears to have changed or after a resident has been transferred to a higher pattern of care as a verification of placement.

On the basis of functional assessment scores for all categories, a composite evaluation of the resident's current status is made. (See "Translating Functional Assessment Scores into a Pattern of Care" below). The data are then used as an aid in deciding whether any change in pattern-of-care assignment is warranted.

Evaluating Mobility

There are five standards against which the mobility of residents may be evaluated: independent, some assistance, daily light assistance, substantial assistance, and dependent. Definitions and examples are given below. For the scoring of typical cases, see Appendix A.

Independent

Definition: Resident can independently and reliably travel around the entire facility. Repeated trips possible.

Example: Resident may use assistive devices such as cane, walker, or wheelchair but requires no staff assistance.

Some Assistance

Definition: Resident can sometimes, but not always, leave the unit on own.

Examples: Resident independently goes to the main dining room for all meals but needs assistance to go to clinics or special events.

Due to low stamina, resident is capable of independently making only one or two short trips off the unit (e.g., to main dining room).

Resident gets tired in late afternoon, resulting in difficulty in ambulation.

Daily Light Assistance

Definition: Resident requires staff assistance to leave the unit; needs little or no assistance on the unit (assistance provided less than three days a week).

Examples: Resident transfers independently or with minimal help, and ambulates independently.

Resident gets lost when off the unit.

Resident must be accompanied by staff member when leaving the unit.

Substantial Assistance

Definition: Resident requires regular limited assistance on the unit.

Examples: Resident always requires supervision, limited assistance, reassurance, or verbal cueing for bed mobility, transfers, or ambulation.

Resident transfers independently or with minimal help and needs limited assistance when moving about the unit.

Dependent

Definition: Resident is immobile without physical assistance; requires continuous physical contact and guidance in all transfers and ambulation.

Examples: Resident is lifted from bed to Geri-chair.

Resident is transferred via Hoyer lift.

Resident needs help repositioning in bed.

Resident walks but must always be assisted.

Evaluating Dining

There are five standards against which the dining capability of residents may be evaluated: independent, some assistance, daily light assistance, substantial assistance, and dependent. Definitions and examples are given below. For the scoring of typical cases, see Appendix B.

Independent

Definition: All meals eaten in the main dining room.

Examples: Resident goes to the dining room without assistance for all three meals.

Resident is capable of preparing a meal or taking diet supplements on the unit independently.

Some Assistance

Definition: Some meals eaten in the main dining room, but resident needs to receive some meals on the unit.

Examples: Resident eats breakfast on the unit, lunch and dinner in the main dining room.

Resident takes diet supplements on the unit, provided and monitored by staff.

Occasionally (once a week or less) resident needs assistance going to the main dining room.

Daily Light Assistance

Definition: All meals eaten on the unit. Resident may need limited staff assistance.

Examples: Resident needs reminder to come to meals.

Resident must be brought to the dining area on the unit.

Resident needs staff assistance to organize tray but eats independently (e.g., cuts food, butters bread).

Resident needs reminder to eat during meals.

Substantial Assistance

Definition: All meals eaten on the unit. Resident requires significant assistance during meals.

Examples: Resident must be brought to the dining area on the unit and given reminders to eat.

Resident requires constant coaxing or assistance during meal.

Resident requires supervision because of possible aspiration.

Dependent

Definition: Resident requires continuous staff assistance.

Examples: Resident must be fed.

Resident must be tube fed.

Evaluating Dressing and Hygiene

There are five standards against which the dressing and hygiene capability of residents may be evaluated: independent, some assistance, daily light assistance, substantial assistance, and dependent. Definitions and examples are given below. For the scoring of typical cases, see Appendix C.

Independent

Definition: Resident dresses, bathes, and grooms self without help of others.

Examples: Resident obtains and puts on clothes independently.

Resident is able to handle all clothes, including zippers, buttons, laces, and snaps.

Some Assistance

Definition: Help provided is less than daily with no more than two activities or daily (including reminders) with one activity.

Examples: Resident requires some assistance with weekly bath.

Resident dresses completely except for minor omissions (e.g., cannot button all buttons, unable to manage snaps, needs help with shoes).

Resident requires daily assistance in donning and/or removing elastic stockings.

Resident requires assistance putting on a simple leg brace.

Resident requires reminder to clean and put dentures in mouth.

Resident requires reminder to dress, bathe, or groom.

Daily Light Assistance

Definition: Help is provided daily with one major activity or any two or more minor activities.

Examples: Daily laying out clothes is required.

Resident needs help pulling garment over head or legs and help in grooming.

Resident needs assistance in shaving and in putting on a simple leg brace.

Substantial Assistance

Definition: Resident is totally dependent in some areas or at some times during the week.

Examples: Staff assistance is required in all areas of bathing, grooming, and dressing one or two days a week.

Resident grooms and dresses self in morning but tires in the afternoon, requiring total assistance.

Dependent

Definition: Resident is totally dependent three or more days a week.

Examples: Resident requires total assistance, but can move parts of body (arms, trunk, head).

Dressing and hygiene is entirely done by staff.

Evaluating Toileting

There are five standards against which the toileting capability of residents may be evaluated: independent, some assistance, daily light assistance, substantial assistance, and dependent. Definitions and examples are given below. For the scoring of typical cases, see Appendix D.

Independent

Definition: Resident performs self-care in all toileting areas, including managing ostomy care or incontinence without help.

Example: Resident changes own ostomy bag and cleans equipment.

Some Assistance

Definition: Resident needs assistance with self care less than daily, and incontinence episodes occur no more than twice a week.

Examples: Resident needs reminders less than daily.

Resident needs ostomy care less than daily.

Bedpan or urinal must be provided.

Daily Light Assistance

Definition: Resident needs daily toileting program, and incontinence episodes occur no more than twice a week.

Examples: A regular reminder program is required.

Resident needs assistance in the toileting room.

Resident needs assistance in going to the toileting room.

Resident needs partial daily help with ostomy care.

Resident needs total routine ostomy care.

Substantial Assistance

Definition: Continence is partially maintained, and incontinence episodes occur three or more times a week.

Examples: Staff support is required no more than twice a week on day and/or evening shift, although during night shift resident may be incontinent more frequently.

Resident needs total routine and nonroutine ostomy care (e.g., special skin care).

Dependent

Definition: Resident is totally incontinent and requires substantial assistance with hygiene.

Examples: No self-control is possible.

Incontinence incidents requiring staff support occur three or more times per week on each shift.

Evaluating Mental Status

There are four standards by which the mental status of residents may be evaluated: normal, mild impairment, moderate impairment, and severe impairment. Definitions and examples are given below. For the scoring of typical cases, see Appendix E.

Normal

Definition: Resident is oriented to time, place, and person (short-term and long-term memory are intact) and is able to reason, plan, and organize daily activities.

Example: Memory is intact; patient is oriented and lucid.

Mild Impairment

Definition: Memory loss is present, but resident is able to reason, plan, and organize daily activities.

Example: Orientation is adequate (time of day, meals, and season are remembered, but day and date may be forgotten).

Moderate Impairment

Definition: Memory loss interferes with resident's daily life.

Examples: Resident may get lost off the unit.

    Resident may need time to adjust to routine of a new environment.

    Resident is not able to remember names of others.

    Resident may not remember where personal articles are located.

Severe Impairment

Definition: Resident has severe memory loss, has little (if any) comprehension, and is unable to follow directions.

Examples: Resident has little, if any, ability to express own needs

    Resident may identify a familiar face but cannot maintain interpersonal relationships.

    Resident understands little of what is said.

Evaluating Behavior

There are seven categories of behavior by which residents may be evaluated: noisy, bizarre, physically abusive, verbally abusive, wandering, depressed, and agitated. Each category is independent of the others.

The following scale of severity is applied to each:

1. Behavior disorder is not present.
2. Behavior disorder occurs less than once a day.
3. Behavior disorder occurs once a day.
4. Behavior disorder occurs more than once a day.
5. Behavior disorder is serious and unresponsive to staff intervention.

For the scoring of typical case examples, see Appendix F.

Noisy

Examples: Resident talks out loud to self.

Resident cries a majority of the time.

Resident constantly bangs on tables.

Resident makes disturbing sounds.

Resident shouts intermittently.

Bizarre

Examples: Resident disrobes in public areas.

Resident engages in unsuitable sexual behavior.

Resident smears or throws food.

Resident spits on the floor.

Resident eats soap.

Resident inflicts injury on self.

Physically Abusive

Examples: Resident strikes or scratches others.

Resident throws objects.

Resident performs aggressive maneuvers with wheelchair.

Resident inappropriately removes restraints from other residents.

Verbally Abusive

Example: Resident uses insulting, threatening, or profane language.

Wandering

Example: Resident disturbs others and/or poses danger to self by roaming aimlessly inside or outside the nursing unit. Resident may attempt to leave the building.

Depressed

Example: Resident is withdrawn, sad, and persistently miserable.

Agitated

Example: Resident shows physical manifestations of distress, including hand-wringing, nervousness, pacing, and repetitive complaining and questioning.

Evaluating Health

The health category is used as one indicator of a resident's need for light care (Pattern I) or medium care (Pattern II). In HRCA's experience, health is not a valid indicator of Pattern III status, and so for Pattern III residents it is used mainly to confirm the results of the various functionality, behavior, and mental status assessments.

Seven nursing treatments are identified in the health assessment category:

1. drug regulation
2. vital sign monitoring
3. special skin care (e.g., turning schedules, application of special lotions or creams, etc.)
4. observation and assessment for acute medical symptomatology
5. decubitus care or wound care
6. irrigation or catheter care
7. sterile dressing care (as distinct from decubitus care)

For each of the seven treatments,

- if the treatment is provided to the resident less than daily, score as zero (0)
- if the treatment is provided to the resident daily, score as one (1)
- if the treatment is provided to the resident more than once a day, score as two (2)

Add up the scores for the seven treatments, and correlate health to nursing requirements as follows:

Light nursing care (Pattern I indicator)	Sum of score = 0 to 5
Medium skilled nursing care (Pattern II indicator)	Sum of score = 6 or more
Heavy skilled nursing care	Continuous monitoring for acute medical symptomatology by licensed nursing staff around the clock

TRANSLATING FUNCTIONAL ASSESSMENT SCORES INTO A PATTERN OF CARE

The first step in the scoring procedure is to assign each resident to one of the three defined patterns of care—PI, PII, or PIII.

Each functional assessment category (mobility, dining, dressing and hygiene, toileting, mental status, and the various components of behavior except "depressed" and "agitated") serves as an independent indicator of pattern-of-care placement. Therefore, if a resident scores as a PII in one category, with all other categories indicating PI, he or she is considered to be a PII. Similarly, if a resident scores as a PIII in one category, with all other categories indicating PI or PII, he or she is considered to be a PIII.

The scores and suggested pattern indicators (PI, PII, and PIII) by functional assessment category are as follows:

Function	Assessment	Pattern Indicator
Mobility	Independent	PI
	Some assistance	PI
	Daily light assistance	PII
	Substantial assistance	PII
	Dependent	PIII
Dining	Independent	PI
	Some assistance	PII
	Daily light assistance	PII
	Substantial assistance	PIII
	Dependent	PIII
Dressing and hygiene	Independent	PI
	Some assistance	PI

	Daily light assistance	PII
	Substantial assistance	PII
	Dependent	PIII
Toileting	Independent	PI
	Some assistance	PII
	Daily light assistance	PII
	Substantial assistance	PIII
	Dependent	PIII
Mental Status	Normal	PI
	Mild impairment	PI
	Moderate impairment	PII
	Severe impairment	PIII

Behavior	*Assessment*	*Pattern Indicator*
Noisy	Not present	PI
	Less than once a day	PI
	Once a day	PI
	More than once a day	PII
	Serious and unresponsive	PIII
Bizarre	Not present	PI
	Less than once a day	PI
	Once a day	PII
	More than once a day	PIII
	Serious and unresponsive	PIII
Physically abusive	Not present	PI
	Less than once a day	PI
	Once a day	PII
	More than once a day	PIII
	Serious and unresponsive	PIII
Verbally abusive	Not present	PI
	Less than once a day	PI
	Once a day	PI
	More than once a day	PII
	Serious and unresponsive	PIII
Wandering	Not present	PI
	Less than once a day	PI
	Once a day	PII
	More than once a day	PIII
	Serious and unresponsive	PIII

"Depressed" and "agitated" are scored according to the same scale of severity as the other components of behavior, but are not used as independent determinants of pattern-of-care placement. Rather, they are treated as significant states of being that the primary care team must be alert to in order to intervene appropriately. (See "The Primary Care Team" below.) Sometimes this will require reassigning a resident to a higher level of care, but only after changes in the resident's functionality or behavior (perhaps as a consequence of the "depressed" or "agitated" states) are manifested and have been evaluated using all functional assessment test categories.

The second step in the scoring procedure is to assign those residents identified as Pattern III to one of six subpatterns (IIIA–IIIF). The suggested indicators for each subpattern are as follows:

IIIA	Mobility	Any
	Toileting	Any
	Mental status	Normal or mild impairment only
	Behavior	Any rating of 1 through 4 on severity scale
IIIB	Mobility	Any
	Toileting	Any but dependent
	Mental status	Moderate impairment
	Behavior	Any rating of 1 through 4 on severity scale
IIIC	Mobility	Any
	Toileting	Dependent
	Mental status	Moderate impairment
	Behavior	Any rating of 1 through 4 on severity scale
IIID	Mobility	Any
	Toileting	Any
	Mental status	Severe impairment
	Behavior	Any rating of 1 through 4 on severity scale
IIIE	Mobility	Dependent
	Toileting	Any
	Mental status	Any
	Behavior	Any rating of 5 on severity scale

IIIF	Mobility	Any but dependent
	Toileting	Any
	Mental status	Any
	Behavior	Any rating of 5 on severity scale

For typical case studies and suggested pattern-of-care assignments using all functional assessment categories, see Appendix G.

THE PRIMARY CARE TEAM

At HRCA, the responsibility for administering care to each resident under the pattern-of-care model belongs to a primary care team, which consists of a physician, a head nurse, and a social worker. The team members act in concert and as equals.

A primary care team is formed for each nursing unit. The team meets a minimum of once a week in order to discuss changes in any resident's status and to formulate plans of action. There is sometimes heated disagreement among team members, as might be expected in the dynamics of small-group interaction. For example, the physician may insist on a strict salt-free diet for a particular resident with severe hypertension. The social worker may counter with the view that being forced to break a lifetime habit of eating heavily seasoned food can be more debilitating to the resident than beneficial. The nurse may offer insight into the resident's present outlook and demeanor and predict the response to the proposed change in diet regimen.

Or there can arise disagreement among team members as to who is first among equals. The nursing staff has 24-hour-a-day, 7-day-a-week responsibility for the unit. The social worker's obligations may be divided between two or three other teams, and he or she is on call 8 hours a day, 5 days a week. The physician may be responsible for all residents in several nursing units and have professional obligations outside the LTC institution as well. In such situations, the team quickly learns to agree in advance which member is to make what decisions in the event the other two are absent or unavailable.

When there is a disagreement or when problems arise due to unforeseen or unpredictable circumstances, team members are expected to explore and resolve any difficulties for the good of the team and the residents in its care.

All decisions regarding the transfer of a resident to a higher pattern of care are made by the primary care team, with a majority of two out of three prevailing in the unusual event of an inability to reach consensus. The team is also empowered to approve out-of-pattern placements where special circumstances warrant, so long as other residents on the nursing unit are not jeopardized by the arrangement. Such special circumstances may include, but are not limited to, the following:

- A married couple with different care needs, where the better functioning partner is willing and able to assume a major role in caring for the more debilitated partner.

- A resident with a serious personality or behavior problem, where the transfer is expected to trigger or significantly worsen the situation.

- A resident who temporarily requires greater than usual care due to an acute illness, with recovery of normal function expected when the acute illness subsides.

- A dying resident who staff and family agree should be maintained in familiar surroundings as part of an overall attempt to maintain comfort.

- A resident who is functioning better than required for the nursing unit but would be expected to decline functionally if transferred to a lower pattern of care where the accustomed supports are not available.

- A resident whose family requires additional time to accept a transfer decision to a higher pattern of care, which will be effected within 60 days regardless.

- A resident for whom a special, temporary rehabilitation program is being tried in the hope of improvement.

Clearly, these pattern-of-care decisions impact not only the resident being evaluated but also staff, the resident's family, and other residents living on the nursing unit. It is, or can be, an extremely difficult balance for the primary care team to maintain—to be an advocate for each resident, to determine what is best for the resident being evaluated given the unique circumstances of his or her life, and yet to recognize at the same time that in an institutional setting the interests of other persons are equally worthy and must also be considered.

The primary care team does not resolve such quality issues easily, and sometimes the solution it arrives at satisfies no one fully. Nevertheless, the team concept is a crucial component of the pattern-of-care system as implemented at HRCA, for it entrusts decision-making responsibility to those individuals who must live with the consequences.

There is, of course, a chain of authority to review patterning and related decisions. The director of nursing and the director of social services are jointly accountable for all decisions made by the primary care teams. On some occasions, such as when the LTC administrator or the director of nursing believes a team's decision will adversely impact the functioning of the unit or other residents on the unit, the decision will be reversed. The LTC administrator retains ultimate responsibility for setting up controls, for monitoring outcomes, and for assisting team members in their understanding of what is or is not a good decision. But it is the primary care team that is initially and principally responsible.

STRUCTURE, OUTCOMES, AND PUBLIC POLICY

The functional assessment patterning system accommodates expected changes in resident condition through the transfer process. Once in a higher pattern of care, an individual with severe impairments, such as dementia, a behavior disorder, crippling arthritis, or incontinence, may benefit from specialized care delivery techniques that were unavailable at the lower level. For example, unlike many SNFs and ICFs, HRCA rarely uses catheterization for incontinence. Because residents who share this problem are grouped by pattern of care, alternative methods, such as bowel and bladder training programs, can be used successfully.

Similarly, under the pattern-of-care system, it is not necessary to sedate some residents with drugs in order to protect others. Instead, the nursing staff can use behavior modification techniques and individual programs of care to help severely impaired individuals.

Take, for example, the case of Esther K., who suffered from a neurological disorder and psychosis as well as myriad physical problems, including diabetes, anemia, arthritis, and gastrointestinal disease. Esther K. was continually demanding attention from the doctors and nurses and interrupting at the nurse's desk to describe her physical status, bowels, headache, stomach, and so on. Her complaints and inquiries were incessant and repetitive and the responses were never satisfactory to her.

It is easy to imagine what the fate of Esther K. might have been in an SNF institution where residents are commingled without regard to specific differences in their functionality. Her disruptiveness and insatiable demands on the time of nursing staff would almost certainly have been controlled by medication.

Under the pattern-of-care system at HRCA, however, a different approach was taken. First, she was placed in a pattern of care where staff members were experienced in these kinds of problems. Ninety-five percent of residents in Pattern IIIE and Pattern IIIF have major behavioral disorders, compared with one-third to one-half of other Pattern III residents. (For a distribution of major identifying characteristics by pattern of care in a typical resident population, see Appendix H.)

Once Esther K. was situated in the appropriate group, a program of behavior modification was developed in which the nursing staff set up planned interaction times for her of no less than 15 minutes. At 7:30 A.M., the nurse or aide discussed with Esther K. all the problems of the previous night and those encountered upon awakening. When medication was administered at 8:30 A.M., any changes in regimen or routine were reviewed. On the afternoon shift (3:00 P.M. to 11:00 P.M.), Esther K.'s scheduled interaction times were 4:30 P.M. and bedtime. On the night shift (11:00 P.M. to 7:00 A.M.) the nurse made herself available at 11:00 P.M. or whenever Esther K. awakened. These planned, round-the-clock sessions greatly reduced the resident's incessant demands without neglecting her or resorting to medication.

The success of the functional assessment patterning system with this type of resident stands in sharp contrast to the unwillingness of many SNFs and ICFs to accept such individuals at all. Given the prevailing rates of Medicare and Medicaid reimbursement, most LTC institutions prefer to accept residents who are in better health, because they are less costly to care for.

But what happens when someone who is already a resident develops pneumonia, suffers a stroke or a fracture, or deteriorates mentally? These are hardly uncommon occurrences in an elderly population, yet most LTC institutions are unprepared for them.

The typical SNF or ICF responds to a resident's increased level of need in one of two ways. Either the resident is not moved, which creates an imbalance in service such that the individual is either neglected or else takes up such a large percentage of staff time that other, less needy residents feel the effect, or the resident is expelled through temporary or permanent discharge to an acute care hospital. Whatever the disposition, the cost to all involved parties—the individual, the other residents, the staff, and society at large—is considerable.

There is, obviously, a powerful fiscal imperative at work here. LTC institutions are caught in a bind. Skilled nursing care is expensive to provide: The more of it that is required, the more the institution has to pay. Yet our society is already bumping up against the limits of its ability to fund long-term care of the infirm elderly, and the demand for institutional services continues to grow.[6]

So what structural changes in the organization of services in LTC institutions might be made to help alleviate this fiscal "crunch" and also improve quality of care?

One possible approach, which is suggested by the preceding discussion of HRCA's rehabilitative model, is to look more critically at the conditions of participation for Medicare and Medicaid that currently prevail. Under these criteria, SNFs and ICFs are required to maintain certain levels of skilled nursing staff. But depending on the functional requirements of the resident population of the particular LTC institution, these requirements may be excessive. For example, if an LTC institution is structured to care mainly for Pattern I residents or their equivalent, it does not need as many skilled nurses as do LTC institutions caring for a more debilitated Pattern III population.

The logic of this perspective can be argued in many ways. At present, SNF regulations hold that one licensed nurse must be on duty every night on each nursing unit. For heavy care populations, this requirement may be entirely appropriate. But for independent, alert, reasonably healthy populations (such as residents on a Pattern I nursing unit), it may be unnecessarily costly. For Pattern I residents, one licensed nurse might provide ample coverage for two or three units, with qualified nurse's aides taking responsibility for the bulk of the routine night duty.

Another possibility involves the administering of medications. Under the law, this activity must be supervised by a licensed nurse, who is responsible for ensuring that the medication given to a resident is actually swallowed. Question: Is this a reasonable statutory requirement as applied to a Pattern I or even a Pattern II setting?

On a 40-bed Pattern I unit, a licensed nurse, in order to dispense medications accurately, must be familiar with the regimens of some 40 residents. If several nurse's aides were permitted to perform or assist in this task, they would need to be familiar with the regimens of perhaps 7 residents each. Who is more likely to make a medication error, the licensed nurse or the several aides?

It might be justifiably argued that a distinction should be drawn between prescription and nonprescription drugs, that the administering of a beta blocker is a more significant nursing activity than the administering of an antacid. However, no such distinction exists in the regulations. Assuming, therefore, that nurse's aides are able to read and understand simple directions, how can it be argued that they are incapable of dispensing an aspirin or a spoonful of milk of magnesia? Do they not dispense such medications at home with perfect accuracy when tending to their children or their own aged parents?

The law regulating the dispensing of medications is extravagantly wasteful of the time of licensed nurses in Pattern I or Pattern II settings. Furthermore, it conveys a demeaning message to nurse's aides: "There are limits to our trust. You can bathe a resident, but you cannot give her an aspirin." So, as an alternative, why not make the dispensing of nonprescription medications one of the responsibilities of aides? This could have several salutary effects. First, there would probably be a significant reduction in the incidence of medication errors, because, as already noted, the present system places an unreasonable burden on licensed nurses. Second, there would likely be an increased commitment to caregiving among the aides, because management would have signalled that they are truly trusted.

Indeed, the entire scope of medical recordkeeping in SNFs and ICFs should be reexamined. Currently, the regulators expect LTC institutions to maintain medical records comparable to those of acute care hospitals, despite the fact they have one-fourth the staff. This expectation is neither reasonable, nor cost-efficient, nor necessary. As an alternative, why not make entries into the resident's chart "by exception" only? For example, if a resident is scheduled to receive a medication daily at a particular hour, a written entry into the record would be made only when, for whatever reason, the medication is *not* given. The savings in time achieved would enable skilled nurses to do more of what they were trained to do—skilled nursing—and free them from the obligation of performing high-cost clerical chores that add nothing to quality of care and serve mainly the convenience of the regulators.

All of these suggestions—and many others that will be forthcoming in these pages—are offered in the spirit of "continuous quality improvement." They are predicated on the belief that quality is more than conformance to a set of arbitrary standards. It is an ongoing process of thinking, testing, implementing, and refining that has as its goal the building of a structure that is able to deliver better care more efficiently to an increasingly needy resident population.

NOTES

1. For insight into this American mindset, see Henry Nash Smith, *Virgin Land: The American West as Symbol and Myth* (Cambridge: Harvard University Press, 1950); Walter Van Tilburg Clark, *The Ox-Bow Incident* (New York: Knopf, 1940).

2. For discussion of this approach to problem solving among the Japanese, see Robert C. Christopher, *The Japanese Mind: The Goliath Explained* (New York: Simon & Schuster, 1983); Richard T. Pascale and Anthony G. Athos, *The Art of Japanese Management* (New York: Simon & Schuster, 1981).

3. See Harvey J. Brightman, *Problem Solving: A Logical and Creative Approach* (Atlanta: Georgia State University, 1980); Arthur B. VanGundy, *Techniques of Structured Problem Solving* (New York: Van Nostrand Reinhold, 1981); Richard O. Mason and Ian I. Mitroff, *Challenging Strategic Planning Assumptions* (New York: Wiley, 1981).

4. Herbert Simon, *The New Science of Management Decisions* (Englewood Cliffs, N.J.: Prentice-Hall, 1977).

5. Testimony of John W. Rowe before the U.S. House of Representatives, Committee on Energy and Commerce, Subcommittee on Health and the Environment, *Long Term Care Services for the Elderly*, 99th Cong., 1st Sess., October 18, 1985, 5–10, 25–37.

6. William J. Scanlon, "A Perspective on Long-Term Care for the Elderly," *Health Care Financing Review*, annual suppl. (1988): 7–15; Pamela Doty, Korbin Liu, and Joshua Wiener, "An Overview of Long-Term Care," *Health Care Financing Review* 6 (Spring 1985): 69–78.

Chapter 3

Building an Organization

EMPLOYEE MOTIVATION: MYTHS AND REALITIES

It is one thing to advocate risk taking and the exercise of imagination in the organization of long-term care services for the elderly. It is quite another to create an institutional environment within which such modes of behavior can take root and flourish. Even the most casual reader of the literature of management knows there is no more predictable and incessant refrain among general managers everywhere than "Why are we not as innovative here as we want to be?" The issue transcends the world of LTC administration. It affects organizations of virtually every type, regardless of size or field of endeavor.

It is hardly unreasonable for managers to want their employees to function more intelligently and enthusiastically on the job. Yet all too often, when reflecting upon the lack of innovative spirit in their organizations, managers tend to cast the problem solely in terms of employee motivation, that eye-of-the-beholder analysis of a given individual's intensity of purpose in confronting daily challenges at work. Hardly ever is this scrutiny accompanied by a systematic analysis of the organizational *structure* within which employees are expected to function or of the *content* of the jobs which are being performed in a less than satisfactory manner.

As suggested, American managers—LTC administrators among them—share a predisposition to act (i.e., to impose solutions on sometimes poorly understood problems rather than analyze first). As a result, when confronted with an individual or group whose motivation is suspect, or in an attempt to engender a higher level of satisfaction among employees, the general manager often finds him- or herself choosing from the options immediately at hand. Usually, the recourse is to some form of deal making, in which the general manager says in effect, "Behave in this way or perform in this manner, and in return I will see that you get a reward." The reward may be permission to keep the job, or if the employee's performance is above minimal standards and the incentive arrangement is subtler, it may involve the promise of more money or more status. But whatever the specifics, the nature of the quid pro quo and the power relationship underlying it are entirely familiar to all parties.[1]

As an approach to problem solving, however, deal making is both dangerous and flawed. Not the least of its difficulties involves inherent confusion as to who exactly is doing the controlling, the manager or the employee. When the employee responds to the deal by performing the job somewhat better than before, there is evidence of *movement*, and perhaps the manager experiences a momentary flush of success. But was any *motivation* actually instilled in the newly rewarded employee? Is the process of improvement going to continue? Is the improvement that was observed going to last?

To all questions, the answer is "not likely," for the motivation problem almost always resurfaces, though sometimes in other guises. And assuming the LTC administrator recognizes it and can find the time once again to address it, he or she usually has little choice but to return to the same carrot-and-stick options. Often a new deal is cut, but now with a tightened set of expectations and, probably, more limited results.

The failure of this strategy—not to mention the cost in terms of time, effort, and lost opportunity—derives from management's inability to understand the essence of the problem. Workers on the job are hardly ever motivated by considerations such as administrative dicta, working conditions, the salary structure, titles, or fringe benefits. To be sure, the neglect or absence of these considerations can be a powerful motivation inhibitor, as when management is blatantly indifferent to its employees' health and safety, is insensitive to the petty tyrannies or abuses of incompetent supervisors, or is unwilling to devise and administer fair and reasonable wage and benefit programs. But employees are not motivated by the absence of dissatisfaction. Even when their working environments are cleansed of all secular problems, they still have other, extremely powerful needs that must be met in order for them to be willing to go the extra mile on behalf of the organization.

These needs relate to the job itself—what the person does—as opposed to the situation in which he or she does it. They are based on an innate yearning for a sense of personal achievement, for work of inherent importance, for recognition, for responsibility, and for psychological growth. All the love, safeguards, incentive, rewards, and personal instruction in the world will not be enough to engender devotion to the task and creativity in its execution unless the jobholder sees the task itself as something worth doing.[2]

For LTC administrators, as indeed for general managers of any organization, this conclusion presents some important conceptual difficulties. There is nothing intrinsically compelling about emptying bedpans, washing bedclothes, scheduling nursing coverage, or entering purchase orders for ostomy products. Some jobs by their very nature would seem to be beyond enlargement. How might the content of these and other positions within the typical LTC institution be defined so that those who perform them will feel a greater sense of responsibility and personal achievement?

Some specific recommendations were made in Chapter 2, as part of the discussion of the organization of services in the functional assessment patterning system and the division of responsibilities among members of the primary care team. Other suggestions will be offered later in this chapter, when various staff functions are discussed. Yet as a framework for thinking, the LTC administrator may find the following points useful.

1. Employees everywhere, in organizations of every type, complain of constant evaluation by supervisors without commensurate opportunities to exercise their own professional judgment. In effect, they are saying to general managers, "Ask us what we should do, and take our answers seriously. Otherwise, we will stop taxing ourselves and will partially withdraw." As a corrective for employees at higher levels within the organization, try relaxing some audit controls while enabling the employees to retain full accountability for the job to be done. Similarly, at lower organizational levels, try increasing individual accountability for specific tasks or assignments.

2. Give employees a complete natural unit of work (a nursing unit, a group of residents, a designated area, a departmental function, etc.) within which to operate. Do not spread their effective range so wide as to make measurement, monitoring, or appreciation of the quality of their work meaningless.

3. Grant additional authority to employees in their activities. Introduce specialized or more difficult tasks not previously handled. Enable people to become experts at what they do.

4. Make periodic reports of progress to the employees directly rather than to their supervisors. This bypassing of the chain of command represents an important form of internal recognition for the employees involved. It will likely elicit anxiety and even hostility from the supervisors, probably due to fear that they are being rendered superfluous. Perhaps they are, in which case an important cost savings will have been discovered. More likely, however, the supervisors will turn to other tasks that have been neglected because of the time required to check and report on the work of subordinates.

INTERPERSONAL COMPETENCE

If the keys to building an effective organization are (1) systematic analysis of the structure within which employees function, and (2) careful evaluation of the content of the jobs that are to be performed, then the process of change for the LTC administrator must begin with a severe and candid self-scrutiny.

The basic question is this: How well do you function as a general manager? There is scarcely an LTC administrator anywhere who would not, when asked this question, commence to speak with deep conviction of the importance of such factors as "openness," "individuality," "risk taking," and "concern for truth." Who has not heard him- or herself (especially when interviewing candidates for staff positions) speak solemnly of the importance of trusting creative people and leaving them alone in their work?

In responding almost reflexively in this way, LTC administrators are not being intentionally deceptive, much less intentionally self-deceptive. But the truth of the matter is, what one says and how one behaves under the daily pressures of the job can be two entirely different things.

Think back to your last staff meeting. As the LTC administrator, you probably ran the meeting from your accustomed position at the head of the table. While the individual presentations were, in theory, made to the group and were nominally open to group comment, in all likelihood they were directed primarily to you for your approval. This is not to say that many "ideas" were not tossed onto the table, usually when a subordinate wanted to learn your viewpoint or when you decided to straighten out a subordinate by asking questions in such a way as to demonstrate the inconsistency of his or her thinking. But beneath the surface of collegiality, of free and open interchange, there were layers of meaning and undercurrents of emotion that remained entirely unexplored.[3]

If this depiction rings true, it is virtually certain that in this typical staff meeting some types of behavior were conspicuous by their absence, including[4]

- expressions of positive or negative feelings
- risk taking
- trust
- mistrust
- overt refusals to give one's point of view
- overt refusals to listen to someone else's point of view

Clearly, a value structure is at work here, one that gives to the organization's meetings a quality of ritual theater. Its premises may be summarized as follows:

1. Rationality must prevail. Intellectual discussions are seen as "good" and "relevant," while emotional and interpersonal discussions are considered "irrelevant," "immature," and "not related to work."
2. Human relationships are influenced most effectively through unilateral direction, coercion, and control by the general manager as well as by the rewards and penalties that sanction these approaches.

Guided by these tacit rules and by the example of the person in charge, the members of the LTC institution's management team quickly learn to play it safe. They sense an incongruity between the LTC administrator's stated values (i.e., his or her advocacy of risk taking, openness, innovativeness, and truth telling when discussed in the abstract) and actual behavior. They can see no advantage in pointing out this inconsistency, nor in expressing their vague unease at what it might portend for the organization or for them personally. Given the implicit strictures against raising issues pertaining to feelings, they choose to maintain a "businesslike" veneer and to avoid any possible confrontation, embarrassment, or career damage.

Once a manager who reports directly to the LTC administrator decides to pursue a strategy of emotional containment, that manager also begins to behave in an incongruent manner vis-a-vis his or her own staff or department. Whereas once the manager validated the goals of the organization through deeds, he or she is now more isolated, less communicative, more self-consciously manipulative. Moreover, the manager begins to wonder, "If I am hiding feelings and concerns that I think might make others uncomfortable, perhaps my people are doing the same to me. Perhaps what I am hearing in my own department meetings is not how my people truly feel about difficult issues. How can I function, or survive, if they won't tell me the truth?"

In such a dynamic, it is not long before there exists a predisposition toward mistrust up and down the chain of command. People will mistrust each other's behavior if not necessarily their motives. The world of work, which was once congenial despite the multiplicity of daily problems, has now become inhospitable. What was once touted as an organizational virtue—being left alone to do the job—has now, in the absence of any meaningful feedback from others, become a source of dread.

In extreme situations, seeking after trustworthy answers to unarticulated questions drives individuals to expend vast amounts of energy looking for clues, especially clues that others—colleagues, superiors, subordinates—may be unaware they are disclosing. Every cough, every grimace, every sideways glance is assumed to be laden with import and is therefore subjected to extended, whispered analysis by political allies, almost always on company time. The potential for exaggerating the meaning of such "hidden signals" is immense, and soon hardly anyone within the organization is able to differentiate valid from invalid information, honest from dishonest communication.

Once formed, the dysfunctional organization creates its own energy. The divergence between stated values and objective reality continues to grow, and what emerges is a culture based not on risk taking and innovation but on hidebound conservatism, mistrust, and survival conformity—all factors that clog the arteries of organizations. Since the cause of the problem cannot ever be discussed (because of the unspoken rule against disclosure of feelings), the situation can only breed more distrust, more conformity, more playing it safe.

What can the LTC administrator who finds him- or herself enmeshed in this seamless web do to break free?

First, it is important to understand what will not work. Lectures, articles, and management self-help books may be useful in posing the issues and getting thought processes started, but they are not likely to alter anyone's behavior. As industrial psychologist Chris Argyris has written regarding his own extensive research into the interpersonal behavior of executives:

> I [know] of no case where managers were able to alter successfully their behavior, their group dynamics, and so forth by simply realizing intellectually that such a change was necessary. . . . What kind of thin-skinned individuals would they be, how brittle would their groups and their organizations be if they could be altered that easily?[5]

What the LTC administrator must do is to vow not to accept group ineffectiveness as a fact of organizational life. But to increase effectiveness requires more than wishful thinking. It requires a structural change in the way staff meetings are conducted so that honest communication between managers is not only solicited but institutionalized.

INSTITUTIONALIZING INTERPERSONAL COMPETENCE THROUGH ORGANIZATIONAL RESTRUCTURING

The institutionalization of interpersonal competence properly begins with a joint planning exercise. Once a year, the LTC administrator and management staff should go on a "retreat." The purpose is to develop an agenda of projects to be accomplished during the coming year.

The first rule is to limit discussion to those projects that cut across departmental boundaries and that therefore require the assent and active participation of at least two managers in order to be completed successfully. Items that are wholly within the province of a single department (e.g., a fiscal services department goal to reduce outstanding accounts receivable to an average of 45 days) are excluded from consideration, because they can generally be handled by the department manager and staff alone.

The yearly planning exercise need not be in a sumptuous setting; it need not even be held outside of the LTC institution. The meeting is just as effective when convened in an onsite conference room over several evenings or on a weekend. The point is to assemble the best strategic thinkers of the organization and to encourage them to examine common needs at a somewhat longer range and with a broader angle of vision than they might otherwise be accustomed to. In larger organizations, participants might include the LTC administrator and five or six vice presidents, each with responsibility for one or several departments. In smaller organizations, participants might include the LTC administrator; the heads of nursing, social work, food services, and maintenance; and one or two others.

As the planning exercise progresses and the brainstorming becomes heated, a list of projects—important to some, unimportant to others, but all germane to the institution and its mission—begins to emerge. Typical projects on the preliminary list might include the following:

- Design a systematic plan for moving residents and staff into a newly renovated area at a minimum disruption to residents' lives and services.
- Install telephone service in residents' rooms.
- Ensure widespread resident participation in leisure activities.
- Develop and implement a plan for more effective utilization of storage space.
- Develop and implement a plan to improve resident area cleanliness and appearance.
- Reduce the number of special diets while maintaining good nutrition and attention to residents' medical needs.
- Develop and implement a plan to ensure continuity of nursing management staff while maintaining appropriate performance levels.

The list of proposed projects should be lengthy, far exceeding the capability of the organization to accomplish all of them within a year's time. This "overloading" is an important part of the process, for it requires the group to establish its priorities and pare down the list to a manageable number of items.

When the participants in the planning exercise agree that they cannot think of any more projects, they are encouraged to mingle among themselves (perhaps over libations or a buffet dinner), to politic, and otherwise to lobby for their choices. The LTC administrator, who has been running the meeting, engages in these informal deliberations but does not attempt to unduly influence the fashioning of a final agenda. Certainly, the LTC administrator may push for consideration of pet projects, but the major goal is to develop a staffwide consensus on what needs to be done.

When the informal deliberations are completed, the participants are asked to vote for their choices. This may be a relatively simple procedure or somewhat more complicated, depending upon the size of the organization and the number of candidate projects on the list. In any case, each participant in the meeting should rank the most important project (i.e., the one he or she believes must be started or completed in the next year) as number 1, the next most important as number 2, and so on. To show relative weight in a group tally, it may be useful to assign a point value to each choice (10 points for a number 1, 9 points for a number 2, etc.). The votes are counted, the projects are listed in descending order of popularity, and a final agenda for the upcoming year is drawn.

The first phase of the yearly planning exercise is now finished.

Each week thereafter throughout the year the group reassembles. It is preferable that the meetings be held after normal business hours, when the participants are better able to draw a deep breath and look beyond the bustle of the day's activities to the agenda at hand.

At the first meeting after the yearly planning exercise, each project on the listing is assigned. Usually, the person who suggested the project initially is given responsibility for its completion. The LTC administrator, who runs the meeting, is not exempt from these proceedings. The administrator participates as a member of the group and, like the others, is assigned (or volunteers for) responsibility for those projects that are most appropriate given his or her office or special area of expertise.

In undertaking an assigned project, the first task of the manager is to formulate, in writing, a careful statement of (1) the project's objective, and (2) the indicators that should be used to determine that the project has been successfully completed. This written document, which ought to cover no more than a single page, is distributed to the group at the next weekly meeting.

A sample managerial objective format is shown in Exhibit 3-1.

Several things regarding this managerial objective format ought to be noted. First, it does not endorse an elaborate and costly ritual of data gathering in conjunction with the project implementation process. This is not to suggest that numbers are not useful aids to understanding. For example, "improvement" in

Exhibit 3-1 Sample Managerial Objective

Project:	Evaluating and improving therapies.
Objective:	To evaluate the work of the therapy departments and initiate improved programming for all residents by [date].
Indicators:	1. By [6 months after objective completion date], 80 percent of administrative staff should agree that significant improvement has been achieved in all therapy departments and that quality-of-life concerns of residents will be better met in the foreseeable future.
	2. By [6 months after objective completion date], 80 percent of administrative staff should agree that changes in therapy programming will not negatively impact the institution's operations, finances, or resident care.

the therapy departments might well be monitored using increases in the number of residents participating in various programs or increases in the number of staff hours per week spent in direct service to residents. But these yardsticks do not tell the whole story, and they should not be assumed to do so. They provide no meaningful definition of the quality of services that are rendered, nor do they say anything insightful about the subtle yet substantive improvements in residents' quality of life that occur (or ought to occur) as a result of the efforts being made.

The point is, if managers were clever enough to devise realistic ways of quantifying ongoing progress in the implementation of programs involving two or more departments and hundreds of elderly residents and their concerned families, the problem under consideration would be understood so well as to cease to be a problem. In real life, when new paths are being explored, many cause and effect relationships are not immediately apparent. So the managerial objective format usually postpones judgment of a project's success until it is completed, or even for a considerable time thereafter, and then measures success according to the perceptions of key people who are known to share the values of the institution.

Three specific criteria are usually applied in this regard: (1) A sizable percentage of the group must agree that the stated objective has been reached; (2) the achievement of the objective has not had negative consequences in unforeseen areas; and (3) the achievement of the objective has not had unplanned budgetary impacts. In the interim, the LTC administrator might ask for project updates and offer suggestions as to how to clear bottlenecks, but otherwise he or she is compelled to trust management staff members to exercise their good judgment, expend their fullest energies, and work together toward the common goal.

A crucial aspect of the discussion of each managerial objective at the weekly staff meeting involves role-playing. Every project is assigned not only a presenter but also a responder, who acts as the boss. Together they must develop the managerial objective statement to the point where it is acceptable to both of them. Any member of the group may be selected to act as responder for any project. The LTC administrator may nominate someone, or the presenter may do so, saying something like, "I haven't worked with Susan lately. I think she would be a good person to respond to this project." Just as the LTC administrator is eligible to take on any project as a presenter, he or she may also assign him- or herself to be a responder or may be selected for that role by another member of the group.

At the weekly meeting, each project team is allowed 20 minutes—no more—for discussion. The presenter reads each section aloud, pausing to comment on the wording of a sentence, the implications of a phrase, questions regarding methodology or consequences, and so on.

The responder listens carefully and is encouraged to interject thoughts or concerns at any time during the presenter's discussion. The presenter responds to the comments as they are made, and a conversation ensues regarding the statement of the objective and the proposed indicators. Expressions of feelings, emotions,

intuition, and prejudices are not only permitted during this conversational exchange, they are actively encouraged.

After 20 minutes, the conversation between the presenter and the responder
stops, even if in midsentence. Sometimes, total agreement is reached between the
two participants on the statement of the objective and indicators, in which case
the statement of the managerial objective is finalized. Other times, disharmony
prevails, in which case the statement is rewritten by the presenter to reflect
concerns expressed during the discussion, and the process begins again between
the same two parties at the following week's meeting.

Following the interchange between presenter and responder, each and every
member of the group is required to comment candidly on the quality of the
interaction between the participants. Observations such as "I don't think John
was listening carefully to what Susan was trying to say. She was really concerned
that . . . " are typical. Because this audience is generally friendly, and because
each participant shares the goals of the LTC institution, ulterior motives are not
(usually) suspected. As the weeks go by and the group grows more trusting of the
exercise, interactions between once-cautious individuals invariably become less
stilted and more incisive.

Clearly, the purpose of these meetings is not just to articulate specific objectives
regarding LTC operations. It is also to institutionalize communication among
members of the group. By virtue of the stylized format, intelligent people who
might otherwise be unaware of, or even indifferent to, each other's world views
are encouraged to cooperate in the resolution of important organizational concerns. No one is exempted from consideration of knotty problems and proposed
solutions, and everyone has a vested interest in building a consensus so that the
implementation phase of problem solving can proceed as smoothly as possible.

The weekly meetings have additional virtues as well. They demonstrate to
each member of the group that other good minds exist within the organization.
They allow participants to discover in their colleagues abilities and competences
that complement their own, encouraging them to work together outside the weekly
forum on matters of mutual concern. And perhaps most important, when the spirit
of interchange and collegiality exists among department managers, it is virtually
certain to spread to lower levels throughout the organization, for the departmental
managers themselves will come to insist upon it.

Also, the weekly staff meetings provide a unique opportunity for the LTC
administrator to see subordinates in action, to watch how individuals react to the
comments of others, to learn how they think. In this way, the managerial objective
format is a management tool for evaluating people as well as for bridging barriers
that exist between departments. The LTC administrator is, in effect, saying to all
staff managers, "This group must function, and I am so anxious for it to do so, I
am willing to go through this elaborate, time-consuming, weekly ritual to ensure
that it happens." The implication for careers is clear.

Finally, because he or she is an active participant in the group, the LTC administrator finds the weekly meeting extremely useful as a means of gaining feedback regarding his or her own performance. As time goes on and participants become more comfortable and more trusting of the role-playing format, they will say to the chief as they say to each other, "You weren't listening well. Andrew is very concerned about . . . " Such openness from the LTC administrator's staff can only be a source of strength for the organization. When authority rests on absence of feedback from below, it is always brittle, never viable.

CHOOSING THE RIGHT PEOPLE

Regardless of how innovative the organization is in communicating its values and eliciting the best efforts of its members, it is not a structure made of granite. Rather, it is a fragile thing, fashioned of feelings and spirit, nothing more. This reality places a special burden on the LTC administrator when choosing people for various positions within the organization. He or she must select wisely, looking for those qualities that are consistent with the long-term care mission. People with such qualities, when safely on board, will themselves select good people, and the organization will soon be populated by caring individuals who subscribe fully to its goals.

In some respects, of course, the process of hiring people for employment in a long-term care institution is identical to the process of hiring people to work in a machine shop or a restaurant or a bank. It involves, first, giving careful thought to the reasons for adding someone to the payroll, including the specific tasks to be accomplished. Therefore, always begin by writing a complete, realistic job description in which you differentiate between your minimum requirements and what you would be delighted to find. Always consider your financial resources so that you do not skew your salary structure or spend extravagantly on unnecessary recruiting.

The usual caveats apply to hiring for long-term care institutions. Resist the temptation to fill a position quickly in order to meet short-term needs. Pay heed to your vague apprehension regarding inconsistencies in a candidate's presentation or record. Do not flatter yourself by thinking that mere exposure to your energy and success will galvanize a chronic underachiever. Recognize that people are acquisitions, much like capital equipment, except that their influence, for better or worse, is felt far more widely. The cost to any organization of hiring the wrong person or failing to hire the right person is incalculable in terms of damage to morale and lost opportunity.

Yet the focus here is on the staffing requirements of long-term care institutions, special places devoted to servicing the many needs of the frail elderly. In the pages that follow, some detailed suggestions will be given regarding the qualities to look for in candidates who apply for membership in your organization. Much the easiest part of the process is looking at credentials (i.e., a candidate's record of education and work experience, as well as recommendations written by individuals with whom you are personally or professionally acquainted) and verifying them. The far more difficult task is to discover and illuminate that human core that suggests here is a person who is not only eager but well suited to working with and for the infirm elderly.

To begin, a few things to look for when interviewing candidates:

1. Look for people who will instinctively be advocates for the elderly, who like them as people, and who can see the world from their perspective. This applies not only to candidates who are applying for caregiving positions, such as nurses, social workers, and therapists, but to candidates for all positions, including applicants for purchasing, food service, and maintenance.

2. Look for people who make easy connections between things they have done and what they perceive as the new job's requirements. No position is exactly the same from one organization to another, even if it is called the same, described the same, and paid the same. People who say things like "I have never done exactly this sort of work in the way you describe, but I have done this and this, and I think that experience gives me a certain insight" are worthy of a closer look.

3. Look for people who have a need for discovery—who do not know everything about the job being applied for and *know* they do not know everything. So ask, "What is important for you to learn here? What abilities do you want to develop?" and listen closely to the answer for evidence of intellectual curiosity.

4. Look for people who will fit easily into your existing group. Do you really trust this person to do his or her part in advancing the mission of the institution?

Beyond these several points, there is a full range of personal characteristics and qualities that generally apply to people who find satisfaction and purpose in working with the elderly in long-term care settings. The LTC administrator, whether interviewing for upper level management positions or for jobs deep within the organizational structure, should screen for these attributes.

Eight attributes are defined in this regard: dependability, common sense, allegiance to the work ethic, integrity, initiative, orientation toward teamwork, caring, and humor. Sample interview questions are given, and suggestions offered as to what the interviewer ought to look for in order to gauge the existence and intensity of each attribute.

Dependability

Dependability is the constancy with which a person performs the tasks and assignments of the job. It is characterized by low absenteeism, an ability to self-motivate, and a willingness to respond to extraordinary circumstances for the sake of the greater good.

Sample Interview Questions. "When was the last time you came to work sick?" Then, as a follow-up, "Why was it so important for you to do so?"

What the Interviewer Ought to Listen for. Some indication that the responsibilities of the job transcend issues of personal comfort. However, be aware of the fine line between devotion and martyrdom. Impassioned statements regarding dedication to duty in the face of a common cold ought to be as much cause for suspicion as a consistent record of absenteeism.

Common Sense

Common sense is the ability to exercise sound judgment. It is based on life experiences and an intuitive sense of what is correct in a given situation.

Sample Interview Questions. Try a case study, such as the following: "You're out of the office for three days. When you return, you have telephone messages on your desk from the president of the board of directors, the state department of public health, a long-time member of your department, who says she is resigning, and a family member calling about a resident's complaints. Which telephone call do you return first, second, third, fourth, and why?"

What the Interviewer Ought to Listen for. Some indication that the candidate is alert to the values of the institution and has the self-confidence to follow his or her convictions. Accordingly, the rationale given for the order of the return telephone calls is more important than the actual priority. Generally, the resident and the resident's family must come first, then the valued staff member, then the state regulators. But an excellent candidate might say, for example, "I already know about the situations that are troubling the resident's family and the staff member and the regulator. I'm not aware of any current matter involving the board of directors, so it makes sense to call the president first and find out if anything is wrong."

Allegiance to the Work Ethic

The work ethic is characterized by the belief that work is important and meaningful in itself. It is associated with pride of accomplishment and is characteristic of those who are personally productive and unfailingly cooperative in meeting departmental and institutional goals.

Sample interview questions. Try a case study, such as the following: "The family of a resident come into your office at 4:55 P.M. with what they think is a problem, but it really is not all that important. How would you handle the situation?"

What the Interviewer Ought to Listen for. Some specific indication of awareness that the family's perceptions are legitimate even if largely uninformed and that the time of day of the meeting is irrelevant. The tenor of the candidate's response is as crucial as its content. Is the candidate sympathetic to the family's position or does he or she dismiss their expressions of concern with some easy categorization, such as "They are probably feeling guilty." Give high grades to a candidate who is willing to acknowledge that the information provided by the family, however lacking in substance, may indeed point to something important that needs to be corrected. Likewise, look favorably on someone who stresses the importance not only of gathering facts but also of getting back to the family promptly with details or a plan of corrective action.

Integrity

Integrity involves strict adherence to a moral or ethical code of conduct. It is the force within a person compelling him or her to do the right thing because it is, plainly and simply, the right thing to do, even though expediency might suggest some easier course of action.

Sample Interview Questions. "In your last job, did you ever make a really difficult moral choice?" If that question draws a blank, try "Did you ever know of anyone who knowingly did substandard work? What did you think about that? How did you handle it, or how would you handle it if it occurred?"

What the Interviewer Ought to Listen for. Some quiet evidence that the candidate possesses a moral code that guides his or her passage through life. Beware the preachy response, however, for it may betray a rigidity that is apt to rupture in time of crisis. Rather, give high marks to someone who appears to be honest, straightforward, and true to his or her beliefs, even when those beliefs prove to be inconvenient or a source of personal discomfort.

Initiative

Initiative is the ability to take positive action for the good of the organization without prodding or special instruction from a supervisor.

Sample Interview Questions. Try a case study, such as the following: "You have an employee who has been a good worker for a long time. One day, while helping a resident on a walker down a corridor, she turns to avoid a wheelchair, stumbles, and falls into the person she is assisting, knocking him to the ground.

The man bangs his head, briefly loses consciousness, and sustains severe bruises to his arm and shoulder. He is frightened and agitated and is rushed to the hospital for evaluation. What would you say to the family? What would you say to the employee?"

What the Interviewer Ought to Listen for. Any indication that the candidate is willing to address the problem directly rather than see it shuffled off to someone higher in the organization. For example, it is neither brave nor helpful to say, "It is really up to the LTC administrator to notify the family, tell them the details, and take it from there. So if they came to me to ask what happened, I'd say, 'it was an accident and I'm sorry about it,' and then refer all their questions to him."

Instead, a candidate with initiative might reasonably respond, "After making sure I had all the facts, I would write an incident report on how the accident happened and get it to the boss immediately. Then, unless I'm told otherwise, I'd call the family, since I'm the one who is responsible for what happens on the unit. If the family has already heard from the hospital and calls me first, I'd tell them how the accident happened and how sorry I am."

As for what the candidate should say to the employee, give highest marks to the person who says "I'm sure she feels terrible about it and needs to know that she is not blamed. But in that context, I'd also stress once again the importance of being extra careful at all times." Any candidate who sees an immediate need to make a speech or to distribute a memo to all unit personnel about accident prevention is probably more concerned with self-preservation than with supporting individual staff members in time of trouble.

Orientation toward Teamwork

Being team oriented involves being committed to work with other people, valuing their contributions, and helping to develop their talents in order to accomplish shared objectives.

Sample Interview Questions. Try a case study, such as the following: "A family member comes in and complains to you about a black nurse who is caring for her mother. The mother is not happy, saying she has never liked or trusted black people, though no specific instances of substandard treatment are cited. Give me several approaches to handling this situation, the pros and cons of each, and tell me which one you would choose and why."

What the Interviewer Ought to Listen for. The response will say a great deal about how much the candidate trusts staff, how much he or she thinks about the resident's (and the family's) needs, and—most important—how he or she balances those two considerations. It is insight into the quality of mind that concerns the interviewer, not the solutions offered to the hypothetical problem. Reject, of course, any candidate who is unaware of the conflicting issues involved—team morale versus resident's needs (however laced with prejudice). Also, be wary of any candidate who can propose only one solution, no matter how insightful. A team orientation requires skill in people development. If others get accustomed to going to a staff member for the one "best" answer, they will cease to think for themselves, and the loss to the organization will be profound.

Caring

Caring is genuine concern, compassion, and respect for others, especially (in a long-term care setting) for the elderly. It is evidenced in countless daily acts of kindness, of compassion, of empathy, in taking satisfaction in a job well done.

Sample Interview Questions. Try a case study, such as the following: "A child of one of our residents dies or is extremely ill. The family is very reluctant to share this information with the elderly member for fear it will upset or even kill her. What should you do?"

What the Interviewer Ought to Listen for. As in the previous example, you should be interested primarily in the quality of mind and heart at work. What is key are the questions posed by the candidate in groping for a response. "What if the child dies and the resident finds out about it? Will she ever trust the staff again if she suspects we knew and did not tell her?" "Does the family have the right to make that sort of decision for the resident, however well intentioned their motives?"

Probably the best answer the candidate can give is that death is a part of life's experience, which the elderly understand better than we may think, and that it is important we do nothing to betray their trust, even if the consequences are painful. "Try to convince the family they should tell her," said a young woman interviewing for a nursing position, "but if they do not, it's up to us to do so. Otherwise, we are in danger of falling into the trap of too much caring in the short term, which makes us ineffective in the long term."

Humor

A sense of humor includes the ability to laugh at ourselves and at the situations in which we find ourselves. It is a measure of personal security, perspective, and nondefensiveness. At work (and in life), it is used as a communication technique, as a tool to deal with stress and anxiety, as a method to defuse tense or unproductive situations, as a means to gauge the seriousness of situations, and as a way to humanize working relationships. In psychologically healthy people, humor is never indulged in at the expense of another.

Sample Interview Questions. "What is the funniest thing that happened to you on your last job?" "Did your last boss ever make you laugh?"

What the Interviewer Ought to Listen for. Is the candidate so taken aback by the questions that he or she is unable to answer? If so, perhaps a sense of humor is totally lacking or the candidate is too defensive to acknowledge it. If the candidate responds with an anecdote, does it reveal a caustic, biting side to his or her personality or does it show an appreciation for human foible in the face of difficult or ridiculous circumstances?

LOOKING AT THE DEPARTMENTS

Thus far, the discussion regarding the staffing needs of long-term care institutions has focused on those qualities and attributes that are desirable in individuals.

By extension, the departments within which people work must also develop "personalities" that are consistent with their mission in the organization.

The therapy departments, food services, and maintenance and housekeeping will be spotlighted in the sections that immediately follow. In each instance, the importance of advocacy will be stressed. Specifically, departments, like individuals, must instinctively be advocates for the elderly, and communication between the staff of different departments must be encouraged in order that together they can determine what is in the best interest of the residents in their care.

Therapy Departments

The therapy departments, which include physical therapy, occupational therapy, and leisure activities, are the rehabilitation advocates for all the residents. In addition to carrying out recommendations made by physicians, they are also responsible for advising the nursing staff on how to maximize the physical and mental potential of the residents.

Cast in this light, the charter of the leisure activities staff, for instance, goes far beyond providing activities and games to residents as a way to pass the hours whenever the schedule of the nursing staff permits. It is also to ensure that residents get sufficient "mind" and "fun" time—if need be, by negotiating with staff nurses on the residents' behalf.

So too with the occupational therapy and physical therapy departments. In addition to performing specific therapeutic tasks, they are responsible for helping to train nurses and aides in how to continue a resident's treatment. For example, an aide who is dressing or bathing or feeding a resident can also stimulate muscle tone or otherwise help the individual toward some higher level of self-sufficiency. It does no good if an occupational therapist spends hours retraining a stroke victim to be able to button a shirt and the nurse or aide on the unit fails to allow the resident to help to put on the shirt.

As regards specific duties under this rehabilitative model, the imperative of the leisure activities function is that every resident be involved in some form of leisure activity every day. For those residents who are intact cognitively, large group participation, and the social interaction it provides, is generally indicated. For those residents who are not intact cognitively, smaller groups, or even individual attention, are warranted.

In formulating a treatment plan for each resident, it is important that the leisure activities staff not only know who the person is now (medical history, physical or mental deficits, etc.) but also attempt to learn from consultation with the family who the person used to be. For example, at HRCA, the staff discovered that listening to opera was once an important part of the lives of many residents. When recordings of famous operas were played to leisure activities groups, people with ostensibly low cognition would remember words or begin to sway to the music. Obviously, the sounds had touched them in ways that could not have been predicted had there not been an investigation of their past interests.

Smaller LTC institutions may not be able to afford large numbers of leisure activities personnel to provide a wide range of treatment for their residents. They may, instead, have to rely on part-time staff, volunteers, or nurse's assistants. Nevertheless, the organizing conception of the program remains the same.

Because leisure activities are so important to the quality of life, the daily programs should not be interrupted by the arrival of the doctor making rounds except in case of emergency. If interruption is routinely permitted, the subliminal message to residents is that dependency (on physicians) takes precedence over activities intended to reverse helplessness and create independence. For this reason, clinical staff and leisure activities staff should attempt to coordinate schedules and avoid unnecessary overlap.

The purpose of the physical therapy and occupational therapy functions is, likewise, to increase residents' control over their lives and give them a sense of well-being. To some extent, increasing the degree of control is simply preventive maintenance. For example, the charter of the physical therapist should include development of individual programs for residents to build muscle strength, one effect of which may be to reduce the number of falls.

Another focus of physical therapy and occupational therapy is to restore lost function where at all possible. Thus, active physical therapy intervention is indicated when a resident returns from an acute care hospital with a broken hip or another skeletal problem or after a stroke. Occupational therapy is used in retraining individuals how to perform activities of daily living, such as cutting food, positioning an arm to avoid contractures, dressing with the use of hooks and velcro rather than buttons, and so on. These programs are not only extremely valuable in terms of improving quality of life, they can also be cost-effective. For example, because many of the elderly in long-term care institutions suffer from disabling arthritis, programs of therapy to maintain or improve range of motion may significantly reduce the need for nursing assistance in dressing and bathing.

As suggested, for the therapy departments to reach their full potential within the LTC organization, there must be ongoing communication between their staff and the members of the primary care team. The recreation therapist, who works with residents every day, might be the first to notice "a weakness in Mrs. Johnson's left side" and so recommend that the physical therapist challenge her a little more. Such interdepartmental communication may be formalized by written reports from the therapy departments to the primary care team. Or, better yet, it can be done verbally whenever the occasion requires. However the sharing of information between departments is accomplished, it reflects all parties' commitment to quality care and a recognition of their mutual dependence in striving to achieve that goal.

Food Services

Food is sustenance. Also, consuming it is a social event with broad cultural implications. All of which is to say that for elderly residents in LTC institutions, food is resonant of feelings and memories that range far beyond the realm of nutrition to thoughts of past family gatherings and to when the world was young. It is a thing intimately connected to quality of life.

Because residents have such an interest in the occasion and presentation of the day's meals, much happiness can be added to their lives by personalizing the service as much as possible. For those who take their meals in the dining room, this may mean serving food at the table from a cart so that they can choose items or portions. Or it may mean offering beer or wine in moderation. Or it may mean assigning waitresses to particular stations for a month or more before rotating so that they can become fully familiar with each resident's likes and dislikes and provide feedback to management on which menu items are being well received and which are not. Similarly, for residents who take their meals in their rooms, the people who serve them ought to be assigned permanent routes.

A focus group—that tried-and-true tool of advertising agencies and media consultants—can also be used to increase resident participation in food preparation activities. Before the kitchen decides to change the menu (by offering a new recipe, a new type of pastry, a new flavor of soup), it might invite a group of residents to conduct a taste test. The information derived may well be useful ("It would have more flavor if you added garlic, the way I used to when I was cooking for my husband") but even if it is not, the residents are made to feel that their opinions are valuable, that they are looked upon by the institution as something more than the recipients of assembly line meals.

There is also the advocacy obligation. If a doctor has ordered a very bland diet for a resident and the food service department is aware that the individual is unhappy with it, the dietitian is obliged to alert the primary care team and recommend substitutes. Perhaps the new diet would not be exactly as prescribed, but if the resident is more content and has agreed to the change, there is a gain.

The hiring of food service personnel must be consistent with this advocacy perspective. "Do you like working with old people?" is an entirely appropriate question to ask of dietitians and kitchen help, since elderly residents often like to wander into the food prep area to see what is going on or to ask for a snack.

Because of the traditionally high turnover of personnel (not only in LTC institutions but in the restaurant business in general), LTC management should make a genuine attempt to provide career ladders. Many people in food services begin employment as unskilled laborers, and when trapped in static positions for too long, they leave merely for the sake of change. As a corrective, try giving dishwashers some training in salad prep. Enable waitresses to spend some time in the diet office so that they can learn about diets and nutrition and direct patient care. Also, keep a sharp lookout for individuals in any department who appear to have supervisory potential, and provide the necessary training.

Such tactics will encourage the flow of new ideas and new techniques to the food service department and will result in good sanitation, good storage practices, and the presentation of a consistently satisfying product to the resident clientele.

Maintenance and Housekeeping

The maintenance and housekeeping employees, who install shelves, erect walls, replace light bulbs, fix toilets, repair the heating system, clean the rooms, and change the linens, impact residents' quality of life greatly.

Often this occurs on the most personal level. Older adults who have left a house or apartment for a single or shared room in an institution understandably take great comfort in small material possessions, such as a radio, television, clock, pictures, jewelry, bric-a-brac—the remembrances of a lifetime. Without these things, their habitat would be sterile and their lives, in important respects, devoid of meaning.

Maintenance and housekeeping employees must be extremely sensitive to this, not only by being especially careful when working in residents' rooms but also by understanding that an occasional five or ten minutes spent in repairing a resident's clock, fixing the heel of a shoe, or hanging a picture "just right" is not time away from a more important project but is hugely important in itself. These little services for residents can be the very things that turn the LTC institution into a home.

As with every other department, a caring perspective can be achieved only if the right sort of person is hired. "How do you feel about elderly people?" "If you are hounded by an old person who wants you to do something for him *right now*, how would you feel about it?" "What was your relationship with your own parents? Your grandparents?" These are very appropriate questions, not only when interviewing candidates for a supervisory position, but also applicants whose job will be to perform general maintenance or housekeeping chores.

The maintenance department must be especially aware of the impact its various projects will have on other departments (nursing, housekeeping, food services, etc.) and must recognize its obligation to communicate what is going to happen well in advance of the event. In this sense it too becomes an advocate for the residents' interest. For example, maintenance might announce to other departments, "Next Thursday there will be an electrical shutdown at 11:00 P.M. We expect it to last until 5:00 A.M., possibly until 8:00 A.M. What problems do you foresee? Will you need emergency power?" Or, if there is going to be a water shutoff for several hours, "Is laundry aware that there is a possible rust scale problem for a while after the water comes back on?"

Such interdepartmental communication is most effective when formalized, ensuring that everyone gets the message. Therefore, the LTC administrator ought to mandate a monthly meeting between department heads or their representatives to discuss upcoming projects and their possible impact. Not only will this head off some potentially dangerous situations, but the discussion may also result in large cost savings to the institution. For example, when maintenance is asked to evaluate the proposed purchase of a new type of wheelchair, it may be discovered that one model of chair will require rebuilding almost every ramp and doorway in the institution but that another will fit existing structures quite nicely. Or when looking at the need to upgrade the laundry room, it may be discovered that one approach to the problem will require major plumbing modifications but that another can be easily accommodated using the existing hookups.

Mostly, the creation of effective maintenance and housekeeping operations requires that the LTC administrator regard these departments as something more than "those people down there in the cement block office next to the boiler room." The administrator must take care to select individuals who understand the unique needs of a long-term care institution and, when staffing supervisory positions, to choose people who can communicate the caring perspective to their employees and converse with counterparts in other departments on an equal footing.

Since the administrator is not likely to have vast experience in maintenance or housekeeping operations, he or she will be best served by individuals who can think in terms of available options. People who say, "I've chosen to do it this way for these reasons," are always more valuable than those who ask, "I can do it either one of these ways, so which one do you want?" or insist, "It just can't be done."

OPINION AND ATTITUDE SURVEY

Development

Periodically, it is important to obtain an objective assessment of employee opinions and attitudes. Many LTC administrators fail to do so, however. They believe it is quite beyond their ability to gather the information themselves, and they consider the alternative, the hiring of professional consulting services, too expensive and not appropriate to the long-term care environment.

There is no valid reason why management of an LTC institution of any size cannot devise and administer a useful opinion and attitude survey, one that will provide baseline data for comparison with surveys taken in years to come. Indeed, there may be important advantages to doing it in house. Primary among these is that it offers the opportunity to involve your employees in the process from the beginning and thereby reinforce the basic message of the exercise, which is "We are extremely interested in your opinion, and we value it greatly as a basis for understanding what we as an institution must do to improve."

At HRCA, for example, management relies on a representative group of employees from various departments (an employees' council) to help formulate the questions to be asked in the survey. In this way, the survey is accepted as a normal part of work life. The thrust of the questions will have been discussed among employees in advance, and the tendency to think in terms of "us" versus "them" will be reduced.

What sorts of questions should be asked in the survey? They should be broad enough to address the key issues of employee morale, productivity, and perception of management. Some of these questions are commonly used in opinion and attitude surveys for other types of businesses. "How do you rate the pay schedule here?" "Are you satisfied with the benefits program?" "Does your supervisor let you know what is expected of you in your job?" "Do people who get promotions here usually deserve them?"

Other questions are more specific to LTC institutions. "Rate the care given to our residents." "Do residents always ask staff to do things they could do themselves?" "Do you ever feel in danger working here?" "Is management really concerned about providing quality care to the residents?"

Administration

Whether management of the LTC institution decides to administer a standardized opinion and attitude survey or one of its own devising, several caveats apply:[6]

1. Take absolute safeguards to preserve the appearance as well as the fact of confidentiality. Administer the survey to large groups simultaneously so that completed questionnaires cannot be attributed to specific individuals or small groups. Be sure the person administering the survey is someone who is trusted by all to maintain the anonymity of the respondents.
2. Give the survey on the company's time and at a time that is convenient to all participating. The survey should take no more than 20 minutes for anyone to complete.
3. Do not ask questions about subjects that you do not intend or cannot afford to change. For example, in almost every company anywhere, just about everyone complains about parking lots and the cafeteria. These perennial areas of dissatisfaction rarely undergo improvement. Therefore, when employees see questions about them on the opinion and attitude survey, they tend to give them even worse grades than they may deserve, not only to voice unhappiness in the hopes that an extreme response will finally spur management to action but also as a test of management to see if the survey itself is a valid exercise or only a charade. When nothing is done to add more parking spaces or improve the food, this tends to discredit other areas of opinion and attitude measurement in which improvement can and will be made.

The attitude survey questionnaire in use at HRCA is given in Appendix I. It may be modified for use at virtually any size LTC institution.

Evaluation

The results of any survey of employee opinions and attitudes will be useful to management only if they are summarized in a clear, concise fashion. The following approach is suggested.

1. Make each survey question the headline of a single 8½-by-11-inch sheet. Or use larger sheets for ease of data entry and then reduce to 8½ by 11. At the top of the sheet, summarize the responses of all employees to the given question. For example:

	Yes	*No*
Do the people who get promotions here usually deserve them?	76%	24%

2. On each sheet, classify the responses to the question according to identified employee subgroups. Subgroups may include categories of age, gender, shift, full- or part-time employment, length of employment, department, supervisory

responsibility, direct contact with residents, and education required for the job. List all subgroups on each sheet. For example:

Age	Under 20
	20 to 29
	30 to 49
	50 or older
Gender	Male
	Female
Shift	Day
	Evening
	Night
Employment Schedule	Full-Time
	Part-Time
Years Employed	Less Than 1 Year
	1 to 4 Years
	5 or More Years
Department Groupings	Nursing
	Other Health Services
	Medicine
	Medical Records
	Pharmacy
	Dentistry
	X-ray
	Laboratory
	Audiology
	Social Services
	Therapy Services
	Occupational Therapy
	Physical Therapy
	Leisure Activities
	Expressive Therapy
	Respiratory Therapy
	Food Services
	House Services
	Engineering/Maintenance
	Laundry
	Materiel

	Other
	Administration
	Personnel
	Fiscal Services
	Switchboard
	Security
	Auxiliaries
	Volunteer Services
Supervise One or More	Yes
	No
Direct Contact with Residents	Yes
	No
Education Required for Job	Less than High School
	High School
	College

3. Enter the responses to each question according to the subgroups that have been identified. For example:

Do you feel there is cooperation between departments?

Department	Usually (Percent)	Sometimes (Percent)	Almost Never (Percent)
Nursing	32	57	11
Therapy Services	50	47	3
House Services	50	44	6

When done in this fashion, anomalies in the reported data will be immediately apparent and inquiries by management leading to possible corrective action can be initiated. As an example, consider the data received in response to the following question:

Have you been made aware of what the benefits programs provide?

Years Employed	Very Aware (Percent)	Somewhat Aware (Percent)	Unaware (Percent)
Less than 1	8	34	55
1 to 4	25	53	22
5 or more	44	47	9

The data show that a combined 91 percent of all persons employed five or more years consider themselves either very aware or somewhat aware of what the benefits programs provide but that more than half of all persons employed less than one year consider themselves unaware.

Why should this be so? Is it because the various in-house publications and bulletins explaining how the benefits programs work have remained unread during the past year? Are employees acquiring their understanding (or misunderstanding) of the programs over time by the expedient of explaining them to each other in the absence of any useful information from management?

Since the total employee benefits package represents a sizable expense to the institution and one of its collateral purposes is to encourage employees to stay on the job and thereby reduce the enormous cost of labor turnover, effective communication of what the package provides is extremely important. The survey data clearly suggest the need to reevaluate the structure of internal communications and perhaps schedule a series of departmental meetings so that the benefits programs can be explained in detail, especially to newly hired employees.

When the opinion and attitude survey is formalized and administered routinely every three or four years, the trends revealed can be very useful in pinpointing emerging difficulties. As an example, consider the data recorded over several surveys in response to the following question:

In general, my supervisor really tries to find out my
ideas and suggestions for improvement.

		1981 (Percent)	1985 (Percent)	1989 (Percent)
All Employees	Agree	66	68	58
	Disagree	34	32	42
Nursing	Agree	67	64	46
	Disagree	33	36	54
Administration	Agree	83	76	80
	Disagree	17	24	20

The data show that, for all employees, there was a 10 percent shift between 1985 and 1989 from agree to disagree, indicating a growing dissatisfaction with this aspect of supervisor performance. Was this slippage general throughout the organization? Apparently not. Employees working in administration continued to give their supervisors high marks, but nurses were now indicating a high level of discontent. Clearly, the surveys jointly disclosed a problem that requires the immediate attention of management.

Whatever the results of the employee opinion and attitude survey, they should be shared widely throughout the organization. All department heads should receive a full set of summary data sheets, with the expectation that they will (1) review the findings with their own staff and (2) issue plans and timetables for corrective action where warranted.

In this way, the feedback loop is closed and a formal mechanism established for ongoing evaluation of all departments and functional areas within the LTC institution.

EMPLOYEES' COUNCIL

Management systems are never perfect, because the people working within them are not perfect. Everyone makes mistakes. Everyone is subject to erratic behavior due to stress. Everyone has personal blind spots, quirks, and failings.

For this reason, in those LTC institutions large enough to warrant it, thought should be given to the creation of an employees' council. This body, which functions like the safety valve on a boiler, comprises departmental representatives chosen by their peers from throughout the organization. It meets regularly with the LTC administrator to advise him or her of emerging or existing problems, to offer opinions on a variety of subjects pertaining to administrative policy, programs, and procedures, and to assist in the formulation of questions for the employee opinion and attitude survey.

A model for the organization of an employees' council is given in Appendix J. Under this structure, any employee with more than one year of service is eligible for election by a constituency of 50 persons from his or her department or area. Larger departments (of 100 or more employees) may elect more than one representative. Smaller departments may combine for voting purposes into groups of 50.

Once the council is chosen, its members elect the officers. The chairperson is responsible for setting the agenda for each meeting. The council convenes, usually on a monthly basis, to discuss any issues it considers important to the work environment at the institution. Nothing is exempt from consideration, including wage and salary structure, benefits programs, or administrative dicta or procedures.

A member of the administrative staff, usually the human resources representative, attends each council meeting as an ex officio member. This person is given the courtesy of the floor when recognized but enjoys no voting privileges.

At HRCA, where an employees' council has been in existence for many years, the council by tradition creates a yearly "priorities" list containing what it believes are the principal issues the administration ought to consider. This list is not created in a moment. Rather, it is the result of an extended dialogue within the council and between each council member and his or her constituency. The list is refined, prioritized, and presented to executive management at a yearly meeting, and it forms the basis for discussion as to what courses of administrative action are possible and reasonable in the upcoming year.

The employees' council, through its elected members, may also function as a facilitator of communication between individual employees and the organization. For example, when an unhappy employee is reluctant to discuss a work-related problem with his or her supervisor for fear of repercussion, because of a language difficulty, or for whatever reason, the council representative can step in and serve as an intermediary. Meetings are quickly arranged to include the human resources manager, the supervisor's supervisor, or the LTC administrator if necessary. Usually, the result is mutual agreement on what the issue at hand really is, so that a troublesome situation that might otherwise have been left to fester is resolved with few adverse consequences.

The creation of an employees' council is not something to be undertaken hastily, for once done it is extremely difficult to undo without great suspicion and a residue of mistrust on the part of employees. Nor should the LTC administrator expect the council concept to receive universal approval from everyone within the organization. First-line supervisors especially tend to resent any circumvention of the traditional chain of command.

Also, the warnings of the legal profession ought to be carefully considered. Legal opinion generally is that, because an employees' council is closely akin to an in-house union, its existence sets a dangerous precedent and is therefore best avoided.[7]

Yet the gain to be derived from an employees' council is often worth the risk of its creation. Having the information which only an employees' council can provide is far better than not having it, and the feedback received constitutes an important internal check on quality in its many dimensions.

Perhaps the greatest difficulty in establishing a useful and productive employees' council is to draw the often fine line between participation in problem solving and ownership of the problem. On the one hand, it is important to give employees a sense that they are being heard, that their opinions are truly valued, and that their involvement contributes to the well-being of the institution. On the other hand, it is necessary that the employee constituency understand that sharing in the discussion does not imply or confer ultimate decision-making responsibility.

Recognizing this distinction and being able to maintain it, blurring it occasionally and clarifying it when necessary, is probably the hardest single task of general management. When done successfully, however, it can become the source of great satisfaction.

NOTES

1. See, for example, Harry Levinson, "Asinine Attitudes toward Motivation," *Harvard Business Review* 51 (January-February 1973): 70–76; Harry Levinson, "Management by Whose Objectives?" *Harvard Business Review* 48 (July-August 1970): 125–34.

2. Frederick Herzberg, "One More Time: How Do You Motivate Employees?" *Harvard Business Review* 46 (January-February 1968): 53–62; Frederick Herzberg, *Work and the Nature of Man* (New York: World Publishing, 1971); Chris Argyris, *Integrating the Individual and the Organization* (New York: Wiley, 1964); Michael Beer and Richard E. Walton, *Notes on Reward Systems and the Role of Compensation,* Published Document No. 9-485-050 (Boston: Harvard Business School, 1984).

3. See Kotter, *General Managers,* esp. 59–153; George D. Kieffer, *The Strategy of Meetings* (New York: Simon and Schuster, 1988); Antony Jay, "How to Run a Meeting," *Harvard Business Review* 54 (March-April 1976): 43–57.

4. Chris Argyris, *Organization and Innovation* (Homewood, Ill.: Richard D. Irwin, 1965), 193–245; John J. Gabarro, *Understanding Communications in One-to-One Relationships,* Published Document No. 476-075 (Boston: Harvard Business School, 1975); Louis B. Barnes, *Managing Interpersonal Feedback,* Published Document No. 9-483-027 (Boston: Harvard Business School, 1982).

5. Chris Argyris, "Interpersonal Barriers to Decision Making," *Harvard Business Review* 44 (March-April 1966): 93–94.

6. See Fred K. Foulkes, *Personnel Policies in Large Nonunion Companies* (Englewood Cliffs, N.J.: Prentice-Hall, 1980), 259–75; Dale A. Rublee, "Predictors of Employee Turnover in Nursing Homes," *Journal of Long-Term Care Administration* 14 (Summer 1986): 5–8.

7. Foulkes, *Personnel Policies,* 276–98.

Chapter 4

Family Ties

"How am I doing?"

It is a dangerous question for any manager to ask, because the answers received may be too full of candor and not especially welcome. No one enjoys being audited, and "shoot the messenger" feelings lurk not far below the surface in almost everyone.

Yet having acknowledged that, the fact is that it is always better for the LTC administrator to know what his or her constituents are thinking than not to know, and for the most pragmatic of reasons: Sooner or later, you are going to find out anyway, and probably from a source that is noisy, insistent, and entirely lacking in perspective. Bad news—if that's what the messenger brings—may arrive as a letter from an attorney representing an angry, frustrated family of a resident; or as a telephone call from a regulator acting on a complaint; or as a visit from a union representative informing you of the results of an employee organization drive. In any case, the opportunity to correct problems or miscommunications in an ordered and thoughtful way may have long since been lost.

A more prudent course is to institutionalize feedback and control mechanisms by incorporating them into the structure of the organization. Systematic solicitation of constituents' opinions serves two closely related purposes:

1. It is a critical aspect of an LTC institution's quality assurance program, enabling the administrator to find out what is going wrong in the organization and also what is going right, so that programs for correction or improvement may be conceived and implemented.
2. It is the essence of risk management, establishing a framework for communication with all constituents for the lifetime of the relationship so that any problems may be resolved internally rather than through the intervention of outside agents.

In the previous chapter, feedback and control mechanisms were discussed with regard to the employees of the institution. In this chapter, the focus is on how to manage interaction with another internal constituency, the families of residents.

THE DECISION TO ENTER AN INSTITUTION

There is no universal story that neatly summarizes the ferocious assault that aging can unleash upon the family unit. Rather there are countless stories, as many as there are families to tell them.

The experience of gerontologist, social worker, and author Elaine Brody testifies to the enormous variety of life circumstances that can lead families to the doors of long-term care institutions. Among the people who called the Philadelphia Geriatric Center one "typical" day were the following:[1]

- An exhausted 70-year-old woman who could no longer go on caring for her disabled 93-year-old mother.
- A recently widowed 50-year-old who had just completed her education in preparation for a return to work but found that her mother had Alzheimer's disease and could not be left alone.
- A couple in their late 60s with three frail parents between them.
- A divorcee of 57 who was caring for two disabled sons, a 6-year-old grandchild, and an 87-year-old wheelchairbound mother.
- A young couple in their early 30s, about to have a first child, who had taken into their home the wife's terminally ill mother and the confused, incontinent grandmother for whom the mother had been caring.

Two points are immediately suggested by Brody's enumeration. The first— and it is sustained by numerous intergenerational studies, including Brody's own research—is that most children do the very best they can for their aged parents and grandparents, and they are doing it for more years than ever before (often into their own old age) because their parents and grandparents are living longer than ever before.[2]

The second—also well-documented in the social gerontological literature and verified by the experience of LTC administrators everywhere—is that many families eventually bump up against limits beyond which they simply cannot go.[3] It is at that point that they begin to investigate the nursing home option.

Such families can be in desperate need of help, often in ways they do not fully realize. Consider, for example, a typical situation: Mother, 90 years old, is suffering from some cognitive impairment, periodic episodes of angina, diminished vision and hearing, and sporadic incontinence. She lives in the home of her eldest daughter, who is 66 years old, and her daughter's 70-year-old husband, who has recently undergone coronary bypass surgery and is now retired. Her grandchildren are grown and married and have children of their own.

Despite the daughter's responsibilities to her husband, children, and grandchildren, she has assumed the role of her aged mother's primary caregiver. The bundle of tasks involved constitutes virtually a full-time job.[4]

Specifically, the daughter must be available to her mother whenever needed. She must supervise prescribed treatments, evaluate options for further treatment, monitor the course of various conditions, and evaluate the significance of changes. She must provide structure to her mother's daily activities, cope with upsetting behavior, maintain open communication, and assist in the performance of basic activities of daily living.

The daughter must also attempt to heal herself. She must try to compensate for the emotional drain of constant responsibility, for the loss of personal time and space, for the loss of sleep, for the restrictions imposed on her future plans and perspectives, and for the loss or reduction of physical and emotional intimacy with her husband and other family members. She must avoid a severe drain on her own strength and health and accept the likelihood of a progressive downward course in her mother's condition. She must attempt to work through changes in the life-long mother-daughter relationship, separate feelings regarding her mother's condition from feelings regarding her mother as a person, resolve uncertainty about her own skills as a caregiver, and confront the possibility of institutionalization.

The daughter must also negotiate with the family. She must maintain communication and exchange information with her siblings, designate other "responsible" family caregivers for those times when she is unavailable, and manage feelings toward family members who do not regularly help. She must maintain the family as an effective decision-making group, give reasonable consideration to her mother's opinions and preferences, and as a family member, help to evaluate the need for institutionalization.

The daughter must also negotiate with society. She must interact with medical and social services personnel and familiarize herself with the service system and its various options. She must act as an advocate or third-party negotiator for her mother and develop a knowledge of state and federal reimbursement mechanisms.

The obligations of affection are seemingly endless, and they are draining. For some adult children of aging parents, there arrives ultimately the quiet realization that limits have been reached, that the personal cost has simply become too high. "What do I owe my mother?" a 65-year-old woman asked an HRCA social worker during the application process. "I owe her my love, my understanding, my caring. But do I owe her my life? Must I give up the living of my life and my obligations to the rest of my family to pay off some silent debt I owe from childhood?"

For other adult children of aging parents, the path to the door of the long-term care institution is less easily negotiated. "I could have done more for her, I should have done more for her" is the bitter self-appraisal often heard by social workers during the intake interview. This despite a level of physical and emotional exhaustion that is palpable.

If these are the two poles of the independence-dependence dichotomy — one adult child who is able to distinguish the things she can do for her parent from the things she cannot do and another who sees institutionalization of her parent as a personal failure of love and caring—what is clearly true is that our culture tends to celebrate the latter position as selfless, even heroic, and to disparage the former as selfish, even blameworthy. Institutions are perceived as cold, whereas families are unfailingly warm. "Putting" an aged relative into a nursing home is akin to spurning and summons images of a family unit that is, at root, insufficiently familial.

Of course, the reality of the matter, known to every social worker who works with families of the aged, is that many elderly people actively participate in the decision to enter a nursing home;[5] that many families continue to care for an impaired older person under conditions of such severe strain that there is deprivation and suffering for the entire family unit;[6] and that whatever the family dynamics at work in the individual instance (symbiotic ties, the gratification of being the "burden bearer," a fruitless search for parental approval that has never been received, expiation of guilt for having been the favored child, or whatever), excessive caregiving may represent not emotional health or heroism or love but pathology.[7]

Just as some elderly persons need more help than their children can provide, so too do some children of aging parents need to be helped to reduce the amount of care they provide. They need to be shown that the emotional distancing of children from parents at this stage of their lives is part of a process of personal growth and maturation and does not represent a savage cleaving of ties. Helping families achieve this perspective is, or ought to be, a vital part of any LTC institution's mission.

The primary care team concept, with its emphasis on family interaction and involvement in life cycle decisions, is one way to address some of these special needs. Other programs and approaches, which will be discussed below, include (1) family seminars, which focus on interfamily dynamics and the psychosocial issues relating to institutionalization; and (2) family days, in which families are asked to respond to the "How are we doing?" question and thereby join staff in defining what constitutes quality of care for their infirm elderly relatives.

MANAGING THE ADMISSIONS PROCESS

Sensitivity to the needs of the family begins when someone approaches the long-term care institution worried or in trouble.

Usually, there has been a precipitating incident. Mother has fallen. Mother has become incoherent. Mother is terrified because her daughter and son-in-law are being transferred out of state and will no longer be there to care for her. Mother has telephoned her daughter once again at three o'clock in the morning to describe some symptom real or imagined, and the daughter's husband says he cannot tolerate the turmoil anymore.

So the call goes out to the LTC institution. Sometimes the individual making the call is the elderly person him- or herself. Sometimes it is the spouse or a child or grandchild. Sometimes it is a social worker from an acute care hospital acting on behalf of an elderly patient who is being discharged, is in decline, and has no place else to go. In any event, a balance has been tipped in some significant way, so that the life circumstance of the elderly person is now, suddenly, less tenable.

Whether the LTC institution gets 1,200 of these initial inquiries each year or 120, whether the institution employs ten social workers to manage the application process or just one, there is a fundamental truth that applies. It is that when the telephone rings or someone appears in person seeking information, it is a potential customer calling, a person with needs. The needs may be well defined or poorly understood by the caller. The exchange that follows may conclude to everyone's satisfaction in just a few minutes, or it may mark the beginning of a relationship between institution and family that will last for years, even decades. But whatever the circumstances or eventuality, the caller is entitled to receive what every person wants in an initial inquiry to any LTC institution, indeed to any firm purporting to provide service to its customers:

- answers to questions
- solutions to problems
- a sense of commitment
- empathy
- truthfulness

Good customer service embraces all of these things. It is an *attitude* conveyed to the caller by the institution's representatives. It is the caller's *perception* of helpfulness and of caring on the part of the representatives. It is an *aura* that pervades the transaction from beginning to end.

It is, however, also something more than that. Good customer service is tangible, rooted in rationality, the end result of creative administrative thinking about how to organize, who to hire, how to train, how to proceed. Only when the customer service *process* has been well defined and closely followed will attitude, perception, and aura be correct.

Whether the long-term care institution has 700 beds or 70, the procedure for managing the application process ought to go like this:

Step 1: The Initial Inquiry. The telephone rings, the mail is opened, or an elderly individual or family member arrives in person at the LTC institution seeking information. The receptionist responds to the call or visitor by asking the person's name and, after receiving it, notifies the social worker on duty. Each such event constitutes an "initial inquiry," and the name of the person calling, writing, or arriving is logged by the social worker onto a preapplication inquiry sheet (see Appendix K for sample format).

This clerical entry is done for two reasons. First, it provides a written record that can subsequently be used by management as a double-check to ensure that each inquiry and any follow-up actions taken have been pursued to a satisfactory conclusion. Second, the cumulative historical data provide strategic information that can be of great value to the LTC administrator. Who have been asking for information? What are their needs? Were appointments scheduled? Were applications taken? Is the applicant mix changing over time? If so, why? Is the ratio between initial inquiries and applications taken changing over time? If so, why?

At a large LTC institution, such as HRCA, there might be 1,200 initial inquiries in a typical year. At smaller places, the number will obviously be far fewer. But whatever the size of the institution, the inquiries received are characterized by the wide variety of personal situations being described. Some people are clearly in need of immediate help. Others acknowledge they are not yet ready for institutionalization but instead are seeking information for use at some later date, or they need guidance, empathy, or details on in-home services locally available.

If a caller (either the elder, a relative, or a referring social worker) is inquiring about admission to the institution, the social worker receiving the call must first determine whether the person qualifies. To do so, reference is made to the institution's application and admissions policies. Every institution's admission standards are its own. They derive directly from the formal statement of strategic mission (Who do we intend to serve? What levels of care do we intend to provide?), and they effectively distinguish one long-term care institution from another. But regardless of how the institution chooses to position itself in the marketplace, certain categories of information must be provided and written as policy. A sample application and admissions policy statement, reflecting the strategic mission of one type of long-term care institution, is given in Appendix L.

The social worker must try at this point to screen out potential applicants from those callers expressing only psychosocial needs. "I am lonely." "My husband died yesterday so I have to come to your place." In such instances, the social worker has a moral obligation to empathize with the caller, express concern for the situation, but indicate that institutionalization does not seem to be the answer to the caller's problem at the present time. Then the social worker should direct the caller to whatever agencies or community-based services are most appropriate to the indicated need.

If the caller (either the elder, or a relative, or a referring social worker) describes a person who sounds like a viable candidate for residency, the social worker receiving the call responds that it *appears* the person is a potential applicant. When speaking to a relative of an aged person needing care, the social worker should always inquire, for example, "Have you asked your mother if she herself is interested?"

The experience of HRCA, which is confirmed by findings frequently reported in the social gerontological literature, is that adjustment to institutionalization is most often successful when the elderly applicant has been involved in and supportive of the nursing home decision from the outset.[8] Hence the inquiry about whether the aged person is interested. The reply given is duly noted by the social worker on the preapplication inquiry sheet.

Step 2: The Preapplication Questionnaire. In response to inquiries from or about seemingly viable candidates for residency, the social worker immediately sends to the initiator of the inquiry a preapplication questionnaire (Appendix M) with cover letter (Appendix N). As the social worker explains to the visitor or caller, "This questionnaire is not an application for admission. It is not a legal document, and by filling it out you are not obligated in any way. It is just a way for us to begin to gather information so that we can help you make the right decision."

Depending on the circumstances, the social worker might also say, "This preapplication questionnaire is a good vehicle to begin discussing the situation with your mother. It is a nonthreatening document, and it might serve to break down some barriers to communication. Remember, when you fill out the questionnaire with your mother, we would like her to sign it, not you. Okay?"

Whenever a questionnaire is sent out by the social worker, the date is logged on the caller's preapplication inquiry sheet.

Step 3: The Intake Interview. When the preapplication questionnaire is completed, signed by the prospective applicant, and returned, the social worker schedules the elderly person and a family member for an intake interview. Almost always (at HRCA, more than 95 percent of the time) this interview is conducted at the institution regardless of the medical condition or functionality of the prospective applicant.

Going to the elder's residence for the interview is discouraged for several reasons. First, it is not a cost-effective utilization of staff time. Second, the elder's intimate familiarity with the home surroundings may mask the existence of significant functional impairments. Third, and primarily, it is extremely important for an elder in need of care to physically cross the institution's threshold, even as only a prospective applicant. This symbolic journey enables the elder and accompanying family member to experience the sights, sounds, and feel of the place itself and therefore to consider the prospect of institutionalization in a realistic rather than an abstract context.

In the course of the intake interview, the social worker (1) sees the elder alone, (2) sees the elder and the family member together, and (3) sees the family member alone. One social worker does all three interviews.

There are several reasons for conducting separate interviews. In preliminary stages of senile dementia, the family may be able, consciously or unconsciously, to "cover" for the elderly member. In one-on-one interaction with the prospective applicant, the social worker is more apt to discern the true level of functionality.

Also, by conducting separate interviews the social worker is more likely to learn what are the attitudes of the prospective applicant and the family with regard to living at the institution. Is the elder ambivalent or opposed? Is there agreement or conflict within the family?

During these several interviews, the social worker takes notes and begins to formulate an opinion as to the prospective applicant's eligibility for residence. As a guide to organizing thoughts and observations, it is helpful to use an intake interview form (Appendix O). Data categories typically include the prospective applicant's name, age, marital status, appearance, and personality; the reason for the application; and the family situation and relationship.

In the course of conducting the intake interviews, the social worker attempts to share as much information as possible with the prospective applicant and the family member. If resident care services at the institution are organized around a pattern-of-care concept, the patterning system is explained. Where appropriate, details regarding Medicaid eligibility requirements are provided. If there is a lengthy waiting period for a bed at the institution, the best possible prediction as to time frame is given and the importance of interim planning is emphasized. If it is apparent that the elderly person can no longer live in the present circumstances and no bed is currently available, alternative placements or temporary services are discussed.

For a prospective applicant who is not immediately in need of a bed, the existence of a waiting list can, in fact, be beneficial. It encourages the elder and the family to think through needs carefully and to explore other, perhaps more suitable, options. In this way, the intake interview functions as a screen, separating those who truly require the LTC institution's services from those whose needs may be better served elsewhere.

When the interviews are finished, if the elderly person is not already exhausted, the social worker gives a brief tour of the institution. If a pattern-of-care system is in place, the pattern unit to which the potential applicant would likely be assigned is visited.

At the end of the session, the elderly person faces the decision whether to apply for residence. Some elders are unwilling to apply and fairly flee out the door, saying "I can't, I won't." Others take the pen eagerly. Still others need more time to make up their minds.

Occasionally, a family dispute will ensue at this point, or soon afterwards, regarding the proper course of action. Family member A will say, "I want Mom in a nursing home. This is a good place. I think she should apply." Family member B will say, "She doesn't belong here. I want her to come to Virginia to live with me." It is an impasse, and perhaps only the latest chapter in a family dynamic that has been ongoing for many decades. But whatever its origins in history, the role of the institution is neither to adjudicate nor to take sides. Rather, the correct response of the social worker is to say, "You two must reach a consensus. When you do, tell us which one of you will be spokesperson for the family. But whoever you choose, please realize that it is your mother, and not you, who must make the decision to come live here."

If the policy of the institution is that applicants be admitted in chronological sequence, the date of the signed application fixes the position on the waiting list. When a subsequent decline in functionality necessitates a change in the applicant's pattern slotting, the original date of application should hold, though the effect will likely be to lengthen or shorten the waiting period depending on bed availability in the new pattern unit.

When the elderly person and the family member have departed the premises, the social worker completes the "intake dictation" section of the intake interview form. This is done whether the person has formally applied for residence, has refused to apply, or is in the process of deciding. The social worker enters observations regarding the individual's social history, health, and financial status; interim planning; the projected pattern of care (if appropriate); and the projected waiting period for the pattern indicated.

Step 4: Staying in Touch with Applicant and Family. From a customer service perspective, it is virtually impossible to contact applicants and their families too frequently. Periodic telephone calls or correspondence from the social worker have the effect of letting the elderly individual and the family know that "we are thinking about you and we care about your situation." They are valuable information-dispensing opportunities, allowing the social worker to update the applicant or family member on waiting list status, new programs or services offered, and any other matters pertaining to the pending application for residence. Also, they are important information-gathering opportunities, enabling the social worker to learn of any changes in the applicant's living arrangements and to gauge any decline in functionality that might impact pattern slotting and, therefore, time remaining on the waiting list.

While some contact between the LTC institution and applicants and their families is imperative, the frequency of contact is obviously limited by the number of social services staff available for the task. Many LTC institutions have only one social worker, and if that person's responsibilities include all interviewing of prospective applicants and all interaction with families of current residents, there may be time for little else.

One solution is to invite the applicant and family to initiate the contact with the institution. "Call us as often as you want with any questions. Let us know immediately of any changes that might impact the application," should be the social worker's often repeated encouragement.

Beyond that, the social worker should also maintain a "tickler" file of all applicants to ensure that either the elder or the family member is contacted at least once every six months. The file need be nothing more than a box of 4-by-6-inch index cards, each card referencing an applicant's name and telephone number, family member's name and telephone number, date of application, and projected pattern assignment. Or, in more automated office environments, the file can be maintained on a personal computer, and be programmed to show the names and numbers scheduled to be called each day. In any case, the date of each call made or received by the social worker should be noted in the applicant's record, along with any changes in status or situation.

Two external events require prompt follow-up correspondence by the social worker. If the applicant or family withdraws the application for any reason, a letter confirming the fact and stating that the applicant's name has been removed from the waiting list is sent (Appendix P).

If follow-up contact with the family reveals that the applicant has died, a letter of condolence is sent (Appendix Q).

Step 5: The Reevaluation Interview. As the date of admission draws closer, the social worker contacts the applicant and family and arranges for a reevaluation interview. Because of inherent difficulties in predicting the exact date of bed availability from a waiting list (the social worker's intuitive forecast may be right on target or wide of the mark in any given instance), the reevaluation interview can occur any time from a week to several months before actual placement.

The reevaluation interview is conducted much like the intake interview. In LTC institutions where services are organized according to a pattern-of-care system, the social worker now does a formal pattern assessment. If the intake interview or any follow-up discussions have indicated the need for specialized evaluations for services offered by the institution (e.g., occupational therapy, physical therapy, psychiatric services, etc.), the social worker will arrange for the appropriate evaluations at this time.

Such evaluations aside, the essential purpose of the reevaluation interview is to say to the applicant and family, "After today, begin to get ready." This does not mean, as the social worker should take great pains to explain, that the elderly person must immediately sell the house or vacate the apartment and get rid of all belongings. Rather, the "get ready" message means that the soon-to-be resident must be prepared to come into the institution with a suitcase, with medications, and with a plan as to how he or she wishes to dispose of living quarters and distribute household items.

However much the applicant and family have prepared for this moment, the message is startling. For those who have been experiencing first-hand the many insidious encroachments and losses associated with old age, the prospect of giving up the material possessions of a lifetime takes on enormous symbolic importance. It is, perhaps, the harshest truth regarding institutionalization—that not all of your lifelong treasures will be able to fit there.

For this reason, the social worker advises the applicant not to take any definitive action concerning household and possessions for at least a month after becoming a resident "because you might not like it here and wish to leave."

Step 6: The Information Brochure. At the reevaluation interview, every LTC institution regardless of size ought to provide the soon-to-be resident and the family with a packet of information that explains what they need to know or do in order to facilitate entry. This information may be in the form of an expensive full-color booklet or may consist of photocopied sheets in a simple file sleeve. The style of presentation will depend on the particular market the institution is serving and the image it wishes to convey.

Whatever the approach, the prospective resident and family are entitled to receive clearly worded information about the following sorts of topics:

Building Guide. Description of the institution and map showing what activities or departments are located on each floor.

Clothing. Advice to the residents to label all garments to prevent loss. Information as to the size of closets. Recommendation (where appropriate) that clothing brought on the day of admission be seasonal and request that families take responsibility for storing any additional clothing for later use. Notification of availability of laundry service. Description of any in-house clothing programs for residents who are incontinent or require frequent changes.

Fiscal Information. Payment schedules for private pay residents, including any monies due on the day of admission. Enumeration of services that are included in the basic per diem rate and services that are extra. Billing procedures. Financial guarantees required by the institution pending approval of the resident's Medicaid application.

Medicaid Information. Details regarding who is eligible (extent of personal assets), who should apply, where to apply, when to apply, and required verifications.

Medical Care Services Provided. How service is structured (in-house medical staff, outside physicians, etc.). Hospital and clinic affiliations. Dental programs. Ophthalmology programs. Audiology programs. Transportation services.

Therapeutic Services. Description of physical, occupational, and recreational therapy departments.

Religious Services. Description of programs, location, and schedule.

Electrical Safety. Policy regarding the use of personal electrical appliances.

Furniture and Bedding Guidelines. Description of what the institution provides and what items the resident may (and may not) bring.

Dietary Information. Time and place of meals. Description of in-room meal services. Physician-ordered dietary restrictions. Rules governing families' presence at meals.

Hairdressing and Barber Shop Services. Location, menu of services, times, and prices.

This listing is hardly exhaustive, and the content of the information package may vary greatly depending on the LTC institution's size, scope, and market. In any case, what is important for the social services staff and the management of the institution to recognize is that they are in the business of admitting into residence real people with real personalities who have had real life experiences. These individuals are not blank slates. Some are greatly embittered by their life's course. Some are resigned. Some are contented. But all of them, if adjustment to institutionalization is to proceed successfully, must prepare for the move, and the key to adequate preparation is useful information.

Step 7: Medical Record Release. In LTC institutions where medical treatment of residents is the partial or complete responsibility of an in-house medical staff, it is important to solicit a summary of the prospective resident's medical records. Accordingly, at some step in the application process—perhaps at the initial inquiry, during the intake interview, or just prior to admission—the social worker asks the elderly person to sign cards authorizing the release of medical records.

A medical release request form (Appendix R), accompanied by a signed card, is sent to all appropriate physicians, hospitals, or clinics.

Step 8: The Preadmission Review. When the reevaluation interview is concluded, the social worker presents the file to the social services supervisor or LTC administrator for review. This step constitutes a check and balance, ensuring that any recommendations made by the social worker regarding placement, pattern assignment, and so on, are valid and appropriate.

In larger LTC institutions, the primary care team (nurse, social worker, and doctor if available) to whom the resident will be assigned may also convene to review the assignment. If there are issues in question, the file is returned to the admitting social worker for rework.

When the applicant passes the preadmission review procedure, he or she is officially approved for a bed according to the set chronological sequence.

THE FLAWED LOGIC OF THE ADMISSIONS PROCESS

The logic of the admissions process that has been described is, in several significant respects, flawed. One problem involves the existence of a lengthy waiting list.

A waiting list for residence in an LTC institution represents something of a public endorsement. It shows that people are attracted to the enterprise rather than to its competitors and so implies that management must be doing something right, at least for the moment. Of a place with no waiting list, the son or daughter of an aging parent can justifiably ask, "Since you show no surplus of demand for beds at this time, what other evidence can you offer that this is the best place for my mother to be?"

Most businesses are able to predict with reasonable certainty how long a customer's wait will be. A manufacturer, knowing the backlog of orders and the production capacity, can commit to delivery in, say, 20 weeks, and assuming there is no catastrophic breakdown of equipment or juggling of the queue, this estimate will be accurate. A restaurateur, knowing the hour a party was seated and the approximate time required to complete a meal, can usually predict table turnover to within 10 or 15 minutes.

By contrast, an LTC administrator finds it virtually impossible to predict bed availability with any accuracy. How to foresee when an episode of acute illness is going to necessitate a resident's transfer to hospital and, from there, to a facility providing a higher level of care? How to forecast the occurrence of sudden death or when a terminal illness is going to reach its inevitable conclusion?

Because such circumstances are beyond anyone's control and therefore beyond prediction, the waiting applicant and family are placed in a state of great uncertainty. "How much longer will it be?" they reasonably ask the LTC administrator or social worker. "Can we continue under the present circumstances a little longer?" they wonder to themselves.

As a consequence, some elderly people attempt to "game" the admissions process by applying for residence in advance of anticipated need. It is a kind of insurance they seek, a comfort in knowing that someone will be there for them in the future in case they are unable to continue under present circumstances. As such, it is an entirely rational (if unacceptable) response to the problem of the waiting list. A list cluttered with names of persons who have no need, now or perhaps ever, for the LTC institution's services can only drive away potential customers whose needs at the time are legitimate and urgent.

So, as noted above in the discussion of the initial inquiry and intake interview steps, the social worker must make swift judgments about the applicant's current suitability for residence. But in doing so, he or she is acutely aware of the classic bind in which people are being placed: "You cannot apply here until such time as you have a demonstrable need. But when the time comes that your need is manifest, you may not be able to get in."

For those elderly individuals whose applications are accepted and who take their place on the institution's waiting list, life goes on, complicated by the sometimes accelerated consequences of whatever events precipitated the initial inquiry. How should the LTC administrator and social services staff respond to these people and their families?

Part of the answer, as has been suggested, lies in open and forthright communication. Let them know as frequently as possible what is happening with regard to the status of their application. If the waiting list has not shown any significant movement in six months, say so. If every predictive remark must be prefaced with a cautious "Our best guess is . . . ," don't be reluctant to use this phrase.

There is also, as has been noted, a larger obligation. It is to provide assistance and direction to people in need, even if there is no direct benefit to the institution itself. Such activity may involve gently steering an elderly person or the family to a community agency that can assist with interim planning. Or, where the elderly person or the family are at the edge of a crisis, it may involve directing them to another nursing facility, perhaps as a temporary placement until a bed at your institution becomes available.

This sort of assistance obviously may result in a potential customer gone forever or, at the least, long postponed. The other side of the ledger, however, is more significant. By broadening the definition of its obligation to elderly applicants and their families in need, the institution solidifies its reputation in the community as a humane and caring place, which, in turn, creates a measure of good will among those who would be customers.

MANAGING THE MOVE TO A MORE INTENSIVE LEVEL OF CARE

The entry of a relative into a long-term care institution represents an enormous change for all family members.[9] For some, relationships improve significantly, as adult children no longer panic at the ring of the telephone, knowing that their aged mother or father is safe and well cared for. Children may have the first opportunity of their adult lives to see their parent make a successful adjustment to entirely new and unfamiliar circumstances and may marvel at the existence of an inner strength and resiliency they never knew was there. In other families, relationships rupture entirely, and children withdraw emotionally or physically or both. In some families where affective ties have lessened, the children become more important to their parent in different ways and are now seen by the parent as symbols of success and as bearers of the family's tradition and values.

In all instances, a new equilibrium of sorts has been reached. Substantive family issues may remain, to be sure. Long-thwarted interpersonal relationships, failure to come to terms with life as it was, may create an awful underlying tension. But on the surface, at least, there is the calming effect of a new daily routine that has taken hold and replaced the untenable situation of before.

The need of the elderly parent for a more intensive level of care, a need that may arise gradually or abruptly, shatters the equilibrium and brings powerful emotions once again to the fore. For the LTC administrator and staff, this creates a whole new set of communication challenges.

As with any managerial task, defining the proper procedure for managing internal transfers begins with understanding the situation and then asking the right questions.

A typical instance: Using the functional assessment patterning system, a primary care team has identified a female resident on a unit who is badly out of pattern. The situation is not only negatively impacting her quality of life, it is also creating a high level of stress among the nursing staff, who, in struggling unsuccessfully to provide care to the out-of-pattern resident, are neglecting the needs of many of the other residents on the unit. Transfer to a more intensive level of care is clearly indicated, but the family is very reluctant. Indeed, in response to news of her mother's latest functional assessment test score, the daughter states, "You can't move my mother to Pattern IIIE. She's not as bad as the people on that unit. Move her there and it will kill her."

Given that a resident needs to be transferred for the good of herself, the unit staff, and the other residents, how should the need be viewed? Is it a *fact* that management ought to communicate to the family? Is it an *opinion* for which management seeks concurrence? Or is it a *recommendation* that can be accepted or rejected by the family at its whim?

The correct response, the authors believe, is none of these. Rather, the need for transfer to a more intensive level of care ought to be viewed as a *fact for which management seeks the family's concurrence.*

How is this possible? How can the institution involve families so that the need for transfer is perceived neither as a command, nor as an abdication of decision-making authority, but as a solicitation of cooperation?

Answer: Trust does not occur in an instant but is the byproduct of experience. From the very beginning of the admissions process, through the months and years when the resident's functionality is stable and all is well, the family must have confidence that the people of the institution truly care about their aged relative. If that trusting relationship has existed over time, when the need for transfer to a higher level of care arises, the family will feel free to share its upset, to begin its mourning for losses observed, and to accept change. If, however, the relationship between the family and the institution has long been characterized by suspicion or neglect, the game has already been lost, and it is a virtual certainty that the family will not take the news of an impending transfer well.

Several red flags alert the social worker that the family is going to resist the transfer to a more intensive level of care. The evidence for these is entirely impressionistic but nevertheless is consistent with HRCA's experience over the years.

- When an adult child (usually a daughter) previously cared for an aging parent up to, and even exceeding, the limits of her own endurance and is still struggling with guilt over the decision to institutionalize, he or she will find it especially hard to accept a transfer to a unit that is perceived to be dramatically worse than the home environment. "Mother looks so much better than the other people on this floor," is the typical reaction on visiting the new unit for the first time, though in fact mother looks quite the same as the other residents there and functions at very much the same level.

- When the rate of the aged relative's decline is slow but perceptible, the family begins its grieving process early and suffers the anxiety of endless anticipation. When the time for transfer to a more intensive level of care finally arrives, it is all too easy for them to deny the reality and to insist that things today are no worse than they were yesterday.

- When a resident is admitted on the line between one pattern and the next (for example, a Pattern II rating, but mentation at Pattern III), the change to the more debilitated status will usually come quickly, and the family, unless educated from the outset about what is likely to occur, will be caught unprepared. "For now, we can provide your father with the care he needs on Pattern II, but you ought to be fully aware that . . ." must be the social worker's explicit message from the beginning.

- When an adult child never enjoyed a close relationship with the parent, a decline in functionality necessitating a transfer to a more intensive level of care can sometimes provoke a huge, angry reaction. The child can become obstreperous, protective, and accusatory, perhaps as a way of hiding what he or she felt and may still be feeling after all these years.

Involving the family in the decision-making process regarding transfer and soliciting their concurrence while avoiding catastrophes of miscommunication is a crucial part of management's job. Flexibility in approach is key. Where appropriate, say to the family that the institution will gladly provide an objective look by someone other than the primary care team (usually the LTC administrator or the head of social services functions as referee) to ensure that the latest functional assessment testing of their relative has been done accurately. Once promised, see that this review is done promptly, and schedule an appointment with the family as soon as possible to discuss the findings. Emphasize to the family in all of these discussions that the institution also has responsibility for 39 (or however many) other residents on the unit and that staff on the higher level pattern will be better able to meet their relative's daily needs.

Occasionally, the recommendation of the primary care team for transfer to a more intensive level of care is plainly wrong. The team may be suffering from burnout with that particular resident, and a lateral transfer to a different unit within the same pattern may be all that is required. If such a mistake has been made, admit it openly and discuss why staff became exhausted in this given instance.

Most often, however, the assessment of the primary care team will be correct. If so, say so, and try to make the family comfortable with the reality of the impending change. Arrange a meeting with the new primary care team. Encourage discussion of the resident's needs from the family's own unique perspective.

In short, the entire process must not be considered a win or lose game. Rather, management's intent ought to be to create a win-win situation, one in which the family are comfortable with the new primary care team, their feelings are fully considered, and they have confidence that the staff of the LTC institution genuinely care about their aged relative.

THE BED ALLOCATION PROBLEM

That there is a demonstrable need for transfer of a resident to a higher level of care does not necessarily close the case, for that same bed may also be coveted by an aged person in the community who is likewise in a perilous state of decline and who may have been languishing on the institution's waiting list for months or years.

Allocating scare resources to the truly needy is one of the hardest managerial jobs imaginable. To do it, the LTC administrator or the head of social services (or whoever is assigned the task) must possess the wisdom of Solomon, carefully weigh many factors, and recognize that, whatever the ultimate decision, there will be many people who are disheartened or pained or angry.

As regards the applicant from the waiting list, the important questions to be asked are these: Just how needy is this person? Can he or she continue in the present circumstances a little longer, perhaps with additional community support? Or is there now no place left to turn? How long has it been since the LTC institution accepted into residence anyone from the waiting list? Can the institution afford to be known in the community as a place "you can never get into"?

As regards the resident seeking transfer from within the institution, the important questions to be asked are these: How much stress among staff is evident on the unit to which the resident is currently assigned? To what extent has the care of other residents on the unit been negatively impacted? How many residents on the unit are out of pattern? Is this number acceptable or is the intent and utility of the patterning system being compromised?

There may also be other considerations. As part of its application and admissions policies, the LTC institution may give top priority to those applicants who, in the opinion of the admitting social worker or other responsible manager, are completely alone and have literally no one to provide the necessary supervision. Such individuals may move to the head of the waiting list or even into the bed of someone who has been transferred to an acute care hospital for an anticipated lengthy stay, notwithstanding the impact on others who have been patiently waiting their turn.

Or the policy of the LTC institution may be to grant administrative priority to applications for residence of current employees, volunteer staff, trustees, and perhaps also to their spouses, parents, siblings, and other members of their extended families. When such a policy is in effect, the chronological order of the waiting list may again be disrupted.

So, in grappling with the bed allocation problem, there are many considerations—some ethical, some moral, some political, some economic—and there are no easy answers. The initial question eventually becomes the final question: Which elderly person in need shall be rewarded with the available bed? Pick one. Who shall it be?

In this way, the job of the LTC administrator is unlike that of most other general managers. The manufacturer can stick with the production schedule. The restaurateur can adhere to the "first come, first served" list of waiting patrons. Neither document, of course, is immutable. Each can be (and often is) subverted given the proper incentives. But for these managers, there is at least the appearance of a formal process based on principles of equity.

However, for the LTC administrator of an institution that is organized according to a pattern-of-care system, there can be no such illusion. Several aged and infirm people—one or more from inside the institution, one or more from outside the institution, and each with a desperate need for the institution's services—find themselves competing for the same bed. Each is a person whose history and circumstances make his or her case sui generis, and someone must decide which is the most worthy.

Policy statements may facilitate decision making somewhat. But there are no easy guidelines, at least none that are entirely satisfactory, and the choices involved can be heartbreaking.

ENGAGING FAMILIES AS SUPPORT RESOURCES

When a family remains actively involved after their aged relative has taken up residence in the institution, both quality of care and quality of life appear to benefit. Evidence in the social gerontological literature strongly suggests that long-term care residents whose families visit them regularly receive more attention from staff, have more personalized living quarters, have higher morale and life satisfaction, and feel less alone and forgotten.[10]

The immediate and obvious conclusion is that a closer partnership in the caregiving process between each family and the institution ought to be encouraged.[11] Like any such managerial prescription, however, it is easier to assert than to accomplish.

A major part of the problem is the different perspectives of the two groups. Both the institution and the families would tend to agree that institution staff should be primarily responsible for managing large scale, technical aspects of care, including medical treatment, safety and security, housekeeping, food service, and so on. Both would probably also agree that families ought to be actively involved in satisfying the residents' more idiosyncratic needs, such as personalized room furnishings, clothing, and special leisure-time activities.[12]

But beyond that, the definitions quickly become blurred. Who is responsible for the multitude of tasks that seem to fall in the nether world between "large-scale" and "idiosyncratic"? Are they the institution's responsibility? The family's responsibility? A joint responsibility?

Five categories of caregiving tasks have been found by researchers to be most ambiguous in this regard:[13]

1. *Responsibility for personalizing care.* Who should provide special foods? Who should make sure the resident's room is attractive? Who should give a birthday party for the resident?

2. *Responsibility for monitoring and ensuring the provision of care.* Who should monitor and report any abuse or neglect? Who should ensure that drugs or medications not covered by Medicare or Medicaid are ordered? Who should file claims for benefits? Who should provide transportation to the doctor? Who should ensure the availability of adequate supplies (facial tissues, lotions, etc.)?

3. *Responsibility for clothing needs.* Who should launder the resident's personal clothing? Who should mark the resident's personal clothing? Who should keep the resident's clothing inventory up to date?

4. *Responsibility for grooming.* Who should clip fingernails and toenails? Who should arrange for hair grooming?

5. *Responsibility for providing reading materials.* Who should ensure that current newspapers are available? Who should provide a source of books and magazines?

Nor do definitions of responsibility, once arrived at, necessarily remain fixed over time. For example, when does an idiosyncratic need (such as the need for laundry service for a severely incontinent resident) become sufficiently general throughout the resident population to warrant implementation of an institution-wide program administered by the staff?

When no one knows for sure who is responsible for what, there is fertile ground for mistrust and frustration. One group may underestimate its range of responsi-bilities vis-a-vis the other, leading to neglect of the resident's immediate needs, or it may overestimate its legitimate purview, leading to resentment, mistrust, and withdrawal by the other. In either case, the predictable casualty will be quality of resident care.

Each LTC institution must, of course, decide for itself what is the proper role of families as a support resource. The experience of HRCA, for example, validates the findings of the social gerontological literature cited above: Family involve-ment is good for residents and therefore should be actively encouraged. So HRCA has very liberal visiting hours ("Come visit whenever you want, night or day," is basically the message). Also, it provides an ample supply of visitor parking, has comfortable lounge areas where residents and families can gather, and offers a full schedule of special family events.

Such an approach may or may not be consistent with the needs of the resident population of every LTC institution. But whatever is decided regarding the proper extent of family involvement—limited, coequal, or somewhere in between—com-munication of intent and perspective, as always, is the key. Without close attention to possibly incongruent role expectations, neither staff nor families can be ex-pected to carry out their tasks consistently, let alone do so in a shared and balanced manner.

MANAGING THE FAMILY CONSTITUENCY

To residents' families, given the often jagged state of their emotions, any LTC institution at first appears forbidding. As a consequence, they form initial opinions based on small clues, which they gauge on the basis of prior experience with other, roughly comparable institutional entities. Therefore, how the switchboard oper-ator answers the telephone, how quickly the caller or visitor is delivered to the person who can provide needed information, or how rapid the organization's follow-up is can take on transcendent importance, and impressions once formed are extremely difficult to change.

Problems arise when information received by the family of a resident is fragmented, diffuse, or not entirely responsive to what is really troubling them. A typical example: The family comes onto the unit floor to visit Mother. Mother is soiled. Her daughter sees this and becomes extremely agitated. She does not see, and cannot see, that mother was changed only five minutes before. She asks the first person she encounters, a nurse's aide, for an explanation of this outrage. The aide, who is not assigned to the resident's care, does not know the situation and, becoming defensive, summarily dismisses the family by pointing them in the direction of her supervisor. The supervisor, who at the moment is trying to deal with several other matters that seem to her to be more urgent, fails to recognize the underlying problem—the family's fear that mother is being cared for badly— and, responding only to the immediate anger and complaint, takes refuge in the institutional perspective and launches into a discussion on how there are 39 other residents on the unit and all activities must be done according to schedule. By this time, the family is quite convinced that their innermost fears about long-term care of the elderly are valid, and confronted by what appears to be an unfeeling bureaucracy, they begin to think about available options.

There are several steps the LTC administrator can take to minimize the likelihood of such catastrophes of miscommunication. Each involves a conscientious effort to remove the perceived barriers between "us" and "them" so that families (1) are able to know from the very outset who in the institution they can go to for information and (2) are able to voice their opinions and concerns in structured settings, with any changes in policy or procedure resulting from their suggestions reported back to them either in a follow-up meeting or in writing.

In order for such interaction between residents' families and the long-term care institution to be free flowing, no more than one department should assume formal responsibility for facilitating communication. In other types of enterprises, the funnelling of information between the organization and its client constituency is the function of the "customer service" operation. Under HRCA's pattern-of-care model, it is the responsibility of the social services department. Accordingly, every effort is made by the social services staff to explain to the family, at the time the resident enters the institution and continually thereafter, that if they have a problem and do not know what to do about it, the social worker on the primary care team is the first person to go to.

Because the social worker is trained to listen and to understand the issues underlying specific situations or complaints, most of the time he or she will gather the relevant facts and be able to explain the matter to the family's satisfaction. When the social worker cannot, a second organizational premise, which is also advertised extensively, comes into play. It is that everyone in the organization has a boss and that, whenever necessary, families are invited to go up the organizational ladder and give management another chance to respond to the particular issue or problem.

Typically, the LTC administrator and the head of the social services department (if the position exists within the organization) sit as the organization's supreme court. In this role, the administrator's major obligation is to listen to what is being said, not only to the immediate circumstances being recounted but to the undertones, and then to clarify the root issues to the satisfaction of all participants. Usually, the cause of the family's agitation or apprehension is that it has lost contact with or confidence in the primary care team and, in substitution, has taken to directing its queries to whoever else is immediately available. These other staff personnel almost certainly are not directly involved in the resident's daily care, and though they may make every effort to respond to what they think is the family's problem within the limits of their understanding and the time available, they tend to address only collateral issues, thereby frustrating and enraging the family even further.

So the LTC administrator sits, listens, and reaches agreement with the family on the real issues to be investigated. Perhaps most important, the administrator establishes a time frame within which he or she (or some designated person) will get back with answers, a program, or a progress report. Then the administrator must be sure to do whatever is necessary and contact the family *before* the agreed date. This subtly reinforces the truth of the matter, which is that the organization is being extremely conscientious in its investigations on the family's behalf. The administrator must also be sure to communicate all findings, progress, and so on, *in person* and not by telephone. Interaction between people actually present is always more effective, more informative, and ultimately more productive than an exchange of disembodied voices over a telephone line.

Often, in these meetings, the families will persist in their version of what happened, and the institution's staff will continue to see things quite differently. Underlying the differences in perception is, generally, a lack of trust. The LTC administrator must be confident enough in his or her staff and their findings to disclose to the family what they have discovered, either "This is where I think you were right and we were mistaken, and it suggests some problems we have to look at" or "This is where I think your assessment is wrong, and here is why I think so." In either case, the administrator must accompany the evaluation, where necessary, with a revised process or procedure, the implementation of which promises to minimize the likelihood of the chain of events under discussion occurring again. Then the administrator must rehook the family to the primary care team so that any similar miscommunication may be avoided in the future.

THE FAMILY SEMINAR PROGRAM

The family too must make an adjustment to institutionalization, and how well it does so, as the social gerontological literature suggests, can have a major impact on how quickly or how completely the resident becomes acclimated to his or her new surroundings. For some families there may be issues of guilt or resentment involved, and these must be acknowledged and dealt with. For all families there is a need to understand the goals of the institution and to know how they, as individuals, can interact with the institution without feeling or being thwarted.

Part of the job of the LTC institution is to help families of newly arrived residents address these issues. When it does so effectively, everyone benefits: the families, the residents, the institution. At HRCA, for example, the primary vehicle for accomplishing this objective is the family seminar program, which is held several times a year. Each seminar meets for four consecutive weeks, usually on a weekday evening, for two hours per session.

The first session (week 1) consists of a panel discussion followed by a question and answer period. Representatives from administration, nursing, the therapy departments, medicine, dietary, and social services each speak for about five minutes on the services the departments provide. The pattern-of-care system and the primary care team concept are explained, and the point is made clearly, by both the LTC administrator and the social services person, that the social worker assigned to each resident acts as the liaison between the family and the institution. "We need and we want family input" is an oft-repeated theme, as is the promise that the families will be informed of any changes in the primary care team or the composition of any particular unit. The general discussion that follows fills the remainder of the two hours and often continues after the scheduled end.

The second, third, and fourth sessions (weeks 2–4) focus on family dynamics and the psychosocial issues relating to institutionalization. With two social workers acting as facilitators, the members of the seminar discuss questions such as these: "How did you arrive at the decision to institutionalize?" "How did it get played out with your brothers and sisters?" "How are you all handling it now?" Ideally, a bond is created between the participants as they come to realize that others too are experiencing the same feelings of anger, sadness, and resentment at the need for institutionalization or, indeed, at the very process of aging.

Also discussed in these sessions are what to expect as the aging process continues. Topics include how transfer decisions to heavier care units are made under the pattern-of-care system, signs of physical and mental decline, and issues of death and dying.

The social workers are trained as part of their formal education and again at HRCA to lead these groups. They quickly acquire first-hand knowledge of what to expect from families of new residents, the range of emotions existing at or beneath the surface, the fragility of some individuals, the strength of others— knowledge that is extremely useful to them in their daily interactions with individual families. By working in teams, the social workers learn to rely upon each other, which can be a comfort and a protection against the feelings of isolation often created by the daily pressures of their job.

In summary, the family seminar program at HRCA is a time-limited, self-help program facilitated by the social services department. Its overriding purpose is to open channels of communication so that family members of new residents can feel comfortable in their evolving relationship with the center and its staff.

FAMILY DAY

The family seminar orients the families of newly admitted residents to the goals and operations of the institution. Family day, which is held annually at HRCA, addresses a more broadly defined constituency, asking the families of *all* residents "How are we caregivers doing?"

Family day has undergone many changes at HRCA over the years, and that learning experience may be useful to LTC administrators so that mistakes need not be repeated.

When the program was begun years ago, the family day format was much like the initial meeting of the family seminar—staff presentations followed by questions and answers from the floor. Several problems quickly became apparent.

First, some individuals are more disposed than others to raise issues in a large-group setting. As a result, the complaints of certain individuals were given full airing in the sessions, while most of the attendees sat quietly. Could it be assumed that the nonparticipation of the majority meant they tacitly agreed with the points of view being expressed by a few or was their silence merely a polite expression of boredom? How might the institution learn more precisely what was important to the many who were not volunteering their opinion?

Second, the resident population of the institution was becoming increasingly heterogeneous, and the families attending family day reflected that mix. Did the families of residents with full mentation and limited physical disability look at the range of services provided by HRCA from a different perspective than the families of residents with severe physical or psychosocial limitations? If so, how might management separate these equally valid perspectives and respond to each fairly?

Clearly, in order for family day to be truly useful to management, to the families, and ultimately to the residents, some changes in the structure of the program were indicated. Specifically, a formal written survey of family opinion needed to be taken in advance of the event. Once completed and returned, the survey results could be classified, quantified, and used both as a guide to management and as a basis for reporting back to the families at family day what they as a group and as identifiable subgroups considered important.

There was, however, a fine line to be observed here. On the one hand, the intention of the survey was to make families aware that the management of HRCA was genuinely concerned with what they thought or how they felt about issues relating to quality of care and quality of life. The intention was to assure them that their suggestions and criticisms were taken very seriously and that every effort would be made to evaluate their input and to initiate changes based upon the information received.

On the other hand, HRCA's management did not want to give the families the impression that it was in any sense abdicating its responsibilities as the primary decision maker for the institution. The families were being invited to critique the caregivers, to offer their insight into what management was doing well and badly, indeed to define what quality of care and quality of life meant to the family constituency at that particular point in time. But the ultimate responsibility for setting policy and guiding the institution in the months and years ahead remained with the managers, not the families.

The striking of this delicate balance is evident in the letter that is sent to all family contact persons on HRCA's list (some residents specify only one contact person, others give many) inviting them to the annual family day event (Exhibit 4-1). Enclosed with the letter is the survey questionnaire (Exhibit 4-2), which each recipient is asked to complete and return by the deadline irrespective of whether he or she plans to attend.

Exhibit 4-1 Invitation to Family Day

Hebrew Rehabilitation Center for Aged
1200 Centre Street
Boston, Massachusetts 02131

September 6, 1991

Dear Family Member:

Each year, HRCA asks families to join us in evaluating our services so that we can continue to maintain the highest standards of care for your relative.

Please join us for our Family Day Breakfast and Discussion Program on Sunday, October 27, from 8:45 A.M. **to noon.**

Our annual Family Day is an opportunity for you to personally share with us your thoughts on the care your relative receives. We place great value on these discussions, and urge you, if at all possible, to attend.

So that we may plan for your attendance, please return the enclosed reservation form by October 1st.

Included with this letter is a questionnaire. Even if you are unable to attend Family Day, we hope you will thoughtfully complete our questionnaire and return it by October 1st. We study your responses closely and use them as a basis for future planning.

We look forward to receiving your questionnaire and reservation form and to seeing you on October 27th at Family Day.

Sincerely,

In the enclosed questionnaire, three basic questions are implicitly asked: What do you like most about the quality of care being provided to your aged family member? What do you like least? What changes do you suggest?

Respondents are asked to rate departments, services, and conditions according to this scale: excellent (E), good (G), fair (F), poor (P), and don't know or not relevant (DK/NR). Space is provided for additional written comments.

All responses to the questionnaire are tabulated prior to the family day event. The results are arrayed

1. by nursing unit
2. by pattern (i.e., two or more nursing units combined)
3. by total institution (i.e., patterns I, II, and III combined)

With the data presented in this way, many layers of detail are revealed, allowing management to identify not only those problems or concerns that are shared by all families served by the LTC institution but also those problems that are specific to particular locales or circumstances.

As an example of the usefulness of this management tool, some years ago at HRCA there was an apparent anomaly in the questionnaire response data regarding food quality and quantity. At first glance, there seemed to be no problem indicated. Of the 215 questionnaires received for the total institution, 91 percent (196 out of 215) rated the food quality and quantity either excellent or good. Only 9 percent (19 out of 215) rated it fair or poor.

Category: Food Quality/Quantity
Total Institution Questionnaires = 215

Excellent:	116
Good:	80
Total:	**196 (91%)**
Fair:	13
Poor:	6
Total:	**19 (9%)**

Even when the data were sorted by pattern, there was little hint of a problem. Pattern I responses were consistent with the results for the total institution. Of 41 questionnaires received from families of Pattern I residents, 98 percent (40 of 41) rated the food excellent or good.

Category: Food Quality/Quantity
Pattern I Questionnaires = 41

Excellent:	26
Good:	14
Total:	**40 (98%)**
Fair:	1
Poor:	0
Total:	**1 (2%)**

Exhibit 4-2 Family Day Questionnaire

Hebrew Rehabilitation Center for Aged
Family Day Questionnaire

1. Check how long your relative has been at HRCA.
   __ 3 months or less
   __ 3 months to 1 year
   __ 1 year to 3 years
   __ 3 years or over

2. Please rate your experience with the service provided by the departments listed. Please write any comments in the space provided.

	Excellent	Good	Fair	Poor	Don't Know/ Not Relevant
Administration					
Audiology					
Bank					
Barber and beauty shop					
Dental clinic					
Dietary					
Eye clinic					
Housekeeping (cleaning)					
Laundry					
Leisure activities (recreational)					
Maintenance (repairs)					
Medicine					
Nursing					
Occupational therapy					
Physical therapy					
Podiatry					
Religious services					
Security					
Social services					
Volunteer services					

Comments:

3. Please rate your experience in the following areas. This list was developed from our last Family Day discussion. Please write any comments in the space provided.

	Excellent	Good	Fair	Poor	Don't Know/ Not Relevant
Staff attitude (e.g., sensitivity)					
Staff responsiveness and performance					

Exhibit 4-2 continued

	Excellent	Good	Fair	Poor	*Don't Know/ Not Relevant*
Staff familiarity with and knowledge of residents					
Showers/baths per week					
Resident living environment (e.g., atmosphere, comfort)					
Visiting areas					
Food quality/quantity					
Number of recreational activities					
Cleanliness					
Pest control					
Telephone service for residents					
Elevator service					
Supplies/equipment (e.g., wheelchairs)					
Return of resident personal clothing by laundry					
Housecleaning					
Other					

Comments:

Resident's Unit:

Resident's Name (Optional):

Similarly, Pattern II data were consistent with the findings for the total institution and for Pattern I. Of 86 questionnaires received from families of Pattern II residents, 97 percent (83 of 86) rated the food excellent or good.

Category: Food Quality/Quantity
Pattern II Questionnaires = 86

Excellent:	44
Good:	39
Total:	**83 (97%)**
Fair:	3
Poor:	0
Total:	**3 (3%)**

Pattern III responses, however, began to reveal a shift in opinion. Of 88 questionnaires received from families of Pattern III residents, 83 percent (73 of 88) rated the food excellent or good, and the remaining 17 percent (15 of 88) rated it fair or poor.

Category: Food Quality/Quantity
Pattern III Questionnaires = 88

Excellent:	46
Good:	27
Total:	**73 (83%)**
Fair:	9
Poor:	6
Total:	**15 (17%)**

Still, an approval rate of 83 percent might have been considered unremarkable, except that the negative responses were not distributed evenly among Pattern III families but were specific to a particular nursing unit.

The breakdown of Pattern III responses by nursing unit revealed the following situation:

Category: Food Quality/Quantity
Unit IIIB Questionnaires = 15

Excellent:	0
Good:	6
Total:	**6 (40%)**
Fair:	5
Poor:	4
Total:	**9 (60%)**

Unit IIIB comprises residents the great majority of whom are mentally disoriented and require help in ambulation, dressing, bathing, and eating. None of these people are able to go to the dining room for their meals. All take their meals on the unit, and the meals are served from carts.

As the data show, 60 percent of the families of Unit IIIB residents rated the food quality and quantity fair or poor. This number represents 60 percent (9 of 15) of the fair or poor ratings given by all Pattern III families and 47 percent (9 of 19) of the fair or poor ratings for the total institution. Why would this be so? What was occurring on Unit IIIB to account for the evident and disproportionate dissatisfaction?

At this point, the data could yield no further insight. Staff had, however, learned enough to pose some direct questions to the families at the upcoming family day event.

Family day consists of two parts. There is a general session in which topics pertaining to the institution as a whole (renovations, procedural changes, personnel changes, etc.) are discussed. Then those attending break into smaller groups (family forums), which are segregated by pattern, since the individuals so selected presumably have like concerns or at least a common frame of reference.

Each of these family forum sessions is attended by representatives from social services, nursing, and medicine. The results of the questionnaire, especially as they pertain to the group assembled, are given, and this feedback forms the basis of the discussion. One member of the group—a family member, not a staff member—is asked to take notes so that the proceedings can be summarized and incorporated into a general report to the LTC administrator and staff.

At the meeting of Pattern III families, the results of the questionnaire were disclosed and particular attention was paid to the dissatisfaction evidenced on Unit IIIB with regard to food service. "What is the cause of your unhappiness?" asked the staff. Several people responded that the food being served from the carts was cold. This was puzzling. The staff were confident that the food was hot leaving the kitchen, for temperature was constantly monitored by food services personnel as part of their ongoing quality program. If there was a general failure, why was there no complaint from families representing other units that received meals served from carts? The staff were also reasonably certain that HRCA was using the right equipment to maintain temperature during the trip of several minutes (including waiting for elevators) from the kitchen to the unit floor. But again, if there was an equipment problem, why were Unit IIIB families alone in their complaint?

There was nothing further to be learned about the problem from the families attending the Pattern III forum. The staff promised to investigate the matter further and to get back to the families as quickly as possible with the findings.

As often happens when procedures exist to facilitate structured problem solving, the answer to the cold food mystery on Unit IIIB turned out to be simple. The tray-stacking system in use on the carts was being compromised. The stacked trays would keep food hot so long as the trays were removed one at a time from the top. But one nurse's aide on Unit IIIB, in a well-meaning effort to see that some residents were served first, would routinely break the stack and remove those residents' meals, which would allow heat to escape from the other trays. The solution: have the trays for those residents needing to be served first placed on top of the stack. Once the nursing staff on each unit were informed of the situation, and after some instruction to the aides not to break the stacks, the problem disappeared.

Sometimes improvements in services and residents' quality of life result from a more widespread but less well-focused dissatisfaction. Questionnaire data on "laundry" one year revealed that on many Pattern III units there was displeasure with the laundry service, a fact that was subsequently verified in the family day small-group discussions. Basically, the families of incontinent residents were asking, "How can we be expected to provide 3 or 4 changes of clothing per day, seven days a week? That is 28 changes of clothes before the laundry gets done. Can't laundry service be improved?"

The concern was valid, but when questionnaire data and the feedback from the Pattern III small group sessions were reported to the managers of several departments, the solution they found was more imaginative than merely accelerating the laundry schedule for the benefit of selected nursing units. Instead, the managers stepped outside the problem as defined and asked, "What would it cost the institution to provide fresh changes of clothing, including all laundering charges, to those residents in need?" The expense, they discovered, was nominal, and the result was a house clothing program, which was made available at a small additional monthly charge to any resident or family who elected to join.

In this way, the solicitation of feedback from families through the family day questionnaire and small group meetings and the distribution of the results to the various departments constitute a vital component of the institution's quality program. Done in the spirit of improving quality of care, and often quality of life, for the residents, it represents anything but a "report card" on departmental failings. Rather, it is a way to identify what operations or services need to be improved upon and to encourage innovative problem solving and imaginative solutions.

The family day program has been so successful at HRCA that it is augmented throughout the year by "mini" family days, generally involving those nursing units that are experiencing a disproportionate number of complaints. For example, if on a particular nursing unit a new primary care team has not yet won the trust of the families, the team will meet with the families, solicit feedback, and agree to reconvene in three months to discuss the results of changes and to chart future directions.

Finally, as part of the ongoing communications process, HRCA sends out a newsletter every three months to the families of residents. In it, the results of the last survey questionnaire and the family day feedback sessions are reviewed and any changes in policy or procedures resulting from the input of families are discussed. The newsletter need not be elaborately produced. It can be written on the institution's letterhead, photocopied, and stuffed in envelopes affixed with a computer-generated address label. What is important is the timeliness of the communication and its intent, which is to convey the impression and the reality that the families' concerns and insights are extremely important to the institution and its management and that they will always be considered in a thoughtful, systematic, and humane manner.

REGARDING DEATH AND DYING

There comes a time when there is nothing more for the LTC institution and its staff to do than to be there and to care, to try to assuage the fear of the elderly who are dying, to show them that they are not emotionally alone.[14]

Because the institution is staffed with compassionate people, there is always an incredible amount of devotion given to a dying resident. And when death is long in coming, there often occurs a bonding between staff and family that is remarkable to behold—a bonding that develops regardless of any tensions that may have marked their relationship in the past.

When the end is near, the family's religious and cultural orientation often becomes pronounced. For some, death is a passage to life everlasting, something to be accepted and perhaps even to be hoped for at the conclusion of a long and lingering illness. For others, the tradition of life after death is not well defined. What matters is existence in the present, and so there is an urgency to be a strong advocate for the dying relative now.

Whatever the family's belief system, these forces can be extremely powerful and will often dictate an extreme reaction to the event as it is unfolding. Therefore, all staff members whose job responsibilities bring them into daily contact with residents' families must be educated as to what to expect. This can be done as part of existing training or counseling sessions or in special group discussions conducted by a priest, rabbi, or minister. Whatever the format, far more is sought than the inculcation of mere tolerance. Rather, the goal is to gain understanding and respect, for if a person's religious and cultural beliefs are ignored, much of the value of his or her personhood is lost and care becomes sterile.

Families are always extremely receptive to an LTC institution's efforts in this regard, and given the opportunity, they quickly identify other, related needs. For example, it was suggested by a family member attending the HRCA family seminar some years ago that a program of memorial services for the recently deceased be instituted. At first staff resisted, saying there was no need to formalize such a thing "because the residents deal with death enough." Nevertheless, the program was begun on a trial basis, and it became quickly apparent that the staff were wrong. The participating residents (on Patterns I and II units and some Pattern III units) appreciated the services greatly, saying it was important to them to be able to grieve formally for their friends now gone. To remember. To honor.

The program as it has evolved at HRCA works this way. One or two days after a resident dies, the social worker on the unit gathers the residents together for the service. The family is asked to attend and almost always does. The social worker and rabbi share some thoughts, and other residents, staff, and family members are invited to do likewise. Prayers are sung.

The service takes no more than 30 or 40 minutes. It never gets morbid. Rather, the residents articulate their sense of loss, which is a comfort to the family of the deceased as well as to themselves. Many of them would have attended the funeral had they been able, and so they welcome the opportunity to pay respects to the departed without having to leave their home.

SOLICITING FEEDBACK FROM FAMILIES OF THE DECEASED

In many cases, after a resident's death, the family members quietly and quickly sever their ties with the LTC institution and go on about their lives. They are never heard from again, unless another elderly relative or friend is in need of long-term care services and applies for admission.

Yet sometimes family members are sufficiently touched by their association, or perhaps are sufficiently angered, to represent a useful source of insight into what the institution has done well or badly. Any prior reluctance they may have had to disclose their true thoughts and feelings—because they feared that criticism of the institution would somehow result in subtle reprisals or that praise of the caregivers might produce complacency and a consequent decline in levels of service—is removed with the death of their aged relative, and there is now no reason for them not to tell the truth.

To ensure getting feedback from family members who are willing to be open about their opinions, the LTC administrator ought to routinely write a letter of condolence (Exhibit 4-3) to the listed family contact persons of every deceased resident. To be sure, the responses received to this letter constitute an entirely unscientific sampling of opinion. Many families whose experience with the institution may have been favorable or unfavorable choose not to reply, and that decision is, of course, unimpeachable. Of those who do respond, most are positive and grateful, and some are blistering in their denunciation.

Whatever the message, all persons who take the time to respond deserve a prompt reply from the LTC administrator. To those who write kind things about the institution or its staff, a thank-you letter (Exhibit 4-4) is sent, indicating also that a copy of the respondent's letter will be forwarded to the primary care team or to whoever was singled out for special mention. A collateral purpose, beyond the simple exercise of good manners, is to take the opportunity to reiterate the institution's ongoing commitment to community service.

When a reply to the letter of condolence contains specific or unfocused complaints, they are investigated to the extent possible, just as if the resident were

Exhibit 4-3 Letter of Condolence

Hebrew Rehabilitation Center for Aged
1200 Centre Street
Boston, Massachusetts 02131

November 1, 1991

Mrs. Joan Lasky
300 Pine Street
Canton, MA 02021

Dear Mrs. Lasky:

On behalf of the Center, the residents, and our staff, I extend our sincere sympathy to you and your family on the death of your dear mother, Sylvia Grossman.

All of us share the sorrow of your loss and take comfort in knowing that we were able to contribute to her care.

We want you to know that we have appreciated the association we have had with you and that you are always welcome to visit with us. The residents of the Center with whom your mother formed friendships would also be glad to see you.

In order to bring about improvements in our programs for care of the residents, I would appreciate any recommendations you might have regarding areas in which we could effect changes. Your insight would be most helpful to me personally, to the staff, and to our present and future residents.

Please do not hesitate to call on us if we can be of any assistance.

Sincerely,

---

still alive and in the care of the institution, and a summary of findings is sent by the LTC administrator to the family member. Such an investigatory exercise can make staff very defensive, which is not an unreasonable reaction to accusations seemingly from beyond the grave. Yet when done in the proper spirit—to learn what must be known in order to make the institution a better place for present and future residents—the exercise is well worth doing. Sometimes light is shed on problems that were previously misunderstood or not fully recognized. Always, the importance of understanding and responding to the family's perspective is reinforced so that the staff recognize anew that their actions are continually open to outside and very public scrutiny.

Exhibit 4-4 Thank-You Letter

Hebrew Rehabilitation Center for Aged
1200 Centre Street
Boston, Massachusetts 02131

November 20, 1991

Mrs. Joan Lasky
300 Pine Street
Canton, MA 02021

Dear Mrs. Lasky:

Thank you for your recent note of November 12, commenting on the care received by your mother at the Hebrew Rehabilitation Center for Aged. While the task of providing the finest care that both the art and science of medicine can offer is never-ending, it is surely helped along by such encouraging words as yours. I am taking the liberty of forwarding your kind thoughts to those responsible for that care, since I know how pleased they will be to learn that their good efforts were warmly received.

Please be assured, too, that we always welcome suggestions for improvements in our programs and services. We strive continually to merit the support of our community and its individual members.

Sincerely,

cc: [Primary Care Team]
    [Nursing Unit]

EXCEPTION AND INCIDENT REPORTING

The feedback and control mechanisms that have been discussed are essentially "snapshots," that is, detailed examinations for the purpose of correcting or ameliorating situations after the fact.

LTC administrators, like all general managers, also require an ongoing flow of information—which may be characterized as exception and incident reporting—in order to avoid surprises and prevent problems or deal with them while they are happening.

Several types of daily reports, prepared by the nursing staff on each unit and, in larger institutions, summarized by the social services department for review by the LTC administrator, may be especially useful in this regard.

Activity Summary

A daily activity summary provides the LTC administrator each morning with a listing of all new admissions and all readmissions from acute care hospitals. Information given on this single sheet of paper should include

- name and resident I.D. number
- date and time of admission or readmission
- pattern-of-care assessment (PI, PII, PIIIA, PIIIB, etc.)
- pattern-of-care room assignment
- for readmissions, indication whether the family has been notified of the transfer from hospital (yes or no)

When scanning this report, the LTC administrator will focus by habit on two key indicators: Is the resident being assigned to a room out of pattern, and if so, why? Has staff been conscientious in notifying the resident's family of any change in location or in pattern-of-care status?

Summary of Residents in Temporary Locations

A daily summary of residents in temporary locations provides the LTC administrator each morning with an update of all residents who are either in hospital or quartered somewhere other than their permanent rooms. Information given on this single sheet of paper should include

- name and resident I.D. number
- pattern-of-care assessment
- pattern-of-care room assignment
- current location (acute care hospital, out-of-pattern room assignment, family home, etc.)
- date on which resident left permanent room
- number of days since resident left permanent room

When scanning this report, the LTC administrator will be especially alert to several factors: Is the list of names growing too lengthy (the administrator's instincts and experience will come into play here), and if so, why? Is any individual resident being housed too long outside of a permanent room? If this is so and the resident is being treated at an acute care hospital, what is the status? Is the social worker maintaining contact with the family? If the resident is still within the LTC institution but is residing out of pattern, why so and for how much longer?

Census Summary

A daily census summary provides the LTC administrator each morning with current data on capacity utilization. Information given on this single sheet of paper should include

- bed capacity in each nursing unit
- number of beds occupied in each nursing unit (male, female, total)
- number of temporary placements in each nursing unit
- number of beds within each nursing unit being held for residents currently at other locations (acute care hospital, family home, elsewhere in LTC institution, etc.)

This report might also include data on the average occupancy of beds month to date (MTD) and year to date (YTD), thereby providing the LTC administrator with information at a glance on bed utilization by period for the total institution.

Incident Report

A daily incident report is prepared by the head nurse of each unit from information given by attending nurses on each shift. These reports provide the LTC administrator with summary information on any resident requiring close observation for whatever reason. Information given on the report should include

- name and resident room number
- whether family has been notified (If yes, indicate initials of primary care team member who made the call; if no, explain in the notes why no action was taken.)
- notes and observations by each nursing shift
- unusual problems (This includes matters of personnel, visitors, residents, procedures, supplies and equipment, etc.; describe time, situation, disposition, or any administrative assistance required.)

Space should be provided on the incident report form for the signatures of all persons participating in its preparation, including the attending nurses on each shift and the head nurse who reviewed the document before forwarding it to the LTC administrator. Where problems or issues involve other departments in the organization, a copy of the report should also be sent to the department supervisors to encourage interdepartmental cooperation.

NOTES

1. Elaine M. Brody, "Parent Care as a Normative Family Stress," *The Gerontologist* 25 (1985): 23.

2. See, for example, Elaine M. Brody, "'Women in the Middle' and Family Help to Older People," *The Gerontologist* 21 (1981): 471–80; Ethel Shanas, "Social Myth as Hypothesis: The Case of the Family Relations of Old People," *The Gerontologist* 19 (1979): 3–9; Elaine M. Brody, Pauline T. Johnsen, Mark C. Fulcomer, and Abigail M. Lang, "Women's Changing Roles and Help to Elderly Parents: Attitudes of Three Generations of Women," *Journal of Gerontology* 38 (1983): 597–607; Elaine M. Brody, Pauline T. Johnsen, and Mark C. Fulcomer, "What Should Adult Children Do for Elderly Parents? Opinions and Preferences of Three Generations of Women," *Journal of Gerontology* 39 (1984): 736–46.

3. Steven H. Zarit, Karen E. Reever, and Julie Bach-Peterson, "Relatives of the Impaired Elderly: Correlates of Feelings of Burden," *The Gerontologist* 20 (1980): 649–55; William H. Jarrett, "Caregiving within Kinship Systems: Is Affection Really Necessary?" *The Gerontologist* 25 (1985): 5–10; Eric R. Kingson, Barbara A. Hirshorn, and John M. Cornman, *Ties That Bind* (Washington, D.C.: Seven Locks Press, 1986): 55–62.

4. Noreen M. Clark and William Rakowski, "Family Caregivers of Older Adults: Improving Helping Skills," *The Gerontologist* 23 (1983): 637–42.

5. Joan Retsinas, *It's OK, Mom: The Nursing Home from a Sociological Perspective* (New York: Tiresias Press, 1986); Sheldon S. Tobin and Morton A. Lieberman, *The Last Home of the Aged* (San Francisco: Jossey-Bass, 1976); Marian Smallegan, "Decision-making for Nursing Home Admission: A Preliminary Study," *Journal of Gerontological Nursing* 7 (May 1981): 280–85; Francois Beland, "The Decision of the Elderly to Leave Their Homes," *The Gerontologist* 24 (1984): 179–85; Elaine M. Brody, "The Aging Family," *The Gerontologist* 6 (1966): 201–06.

6. Marjorie H. Cantor, "Strain among Caregivers: A Study of Experience in the United States," *The Gerontologist* 23 (1983): 597–604; Colleen Leahy Johnson and Donald J. Catalano, "A Longitudinal Study of Family Supports to Impaired Elderly," *The Gerontologist* 23 (1983): 612–18.

7. Brody, "Parent Care," 23–24.

8. Elaine M. Brody and Burton Gummer, "Aged Applicants and Non-Applicants to a Voluntary Home: An Exploratory Comparison," *The Gerontologist* 7 (1967): 234–43; Elaine M. Brody, "Follow-up Study of Applicants and Non-Applicants to a Voluntary Home," *The Gerontologist* 9 (1969): 187–96; Linda Noelker and Zev Harel, "Predictors of Well-being and Survival among Institutionalized Aged," *The Gerontologist* 18 (1978): 562–67.

9. See, for example, Renee Solomon, "Serving Families of the Institutionalized Aged: The Four Crises," in *Gerontological Social Work Practice in Long-Term Care*, edited by George S. Getzel and M. Joanna Mellor (New York: Haworth Press, 1983), 83–96; Kristen Falde Smith and Vern L. Bengtson, "Positive Consequences of Institutionalization: Solidarity between Elderly Parents and Their Middle-aged Children," *The Gerontologist* 19 (1979): 438–44.

10. Zev Harel, "Quality of Care, Congruence, and Well-being among Institutionalized Aged," *The Gerontologist* 21 (1981): 523–31; Vernon L. Greene and Deborah J. Monahan, "The Impact of Visitation on Patient Well-being in Nursing Homes," *The Gerontologist* 22 (1982): 418–23.

11. See, for example, Rose Dobrof and Eugene Litwak, *Maintenance of Family Ties of Long-Term Care Patients: Theory and Guide to Practice*, Department of Health and Human Services Publication no. (ADM) 81-400 (Washington, D.C.: U.S. Government Printing Office, 1981), 1–79; Jonathan L. York and Robert J. Calsyn, "Family Involvement in Nursing Homes," *The Gerontologist* 17 (1977): 500–05; Rhonda J. V. Montgomery, "Impact of Institutional Care Policies on Family Integration," *The Gerontologist* 22 (1982): 54–58; Roberta R. Greene, "Families and the Nursing Home Social Worker," *Social Work in Health Care* 7 (Spring 1982): 57–67; Michael Duffy and Guy E. Shuttlesworth, "The

Resident's Family: Adversary or Advocate in Long-Term Care?" *Journal of Long-Term Care Administration* 15 (Fall 1987): 9–11; John Gross, "Update: Family Involvement in Long-Term Care," *Journal of Long-Term Care Administration* 13 (Summer 1985): 41–43.

12. Guy E. Shuttlesworth, Allen Rubin, and Michael Duffy, "Families versus Institutions: Incongruent Role Expectations in the Nursing Home," *The Gerontologist* 22 (1982): 200–08; Dobrof and Litwak, *Maintenance of Family Ties of Long-Term Care Patients,* 80–116.

13. Allen Rubin and Guy E. Shuttlesworth, "Engaging Families as Support Resources in Nursing Home Care: Ambiguity in the Subdivision of Tasks," *The Gerontologist* 23 (1983): 632–36.

14. See Elisabeth Kubler-Ross, *On Death and Dying* (New York: Macmillan, 1969); Elisabeth Gustafson, "Dying: The Career of the Nursing Home Patient," *Journal of Health and Social Behavior* 13 (September 1972): 226–35; Anne Munley, Cynthia S. Powers, and John B. Williamson, "Humanizing Nursing Home Environments: The Relevance of Hospice Principles," *International Journal of Aging and Human Development* 15 (1982): 263–84.

Chapter 5

Confronting Mental Health Issues

THE MESSY PROBLEM OF DEINSTITUTIONALIZATION

Here are two vignettes, which taken together suggest a larger reality.

Wilhelmina Franklin, 86 years old, frail, confused, and confined to a wheel-chair, froze to death in January 1985 on the grounds of the long-term care institution that was her home. Staff members reported not finding her in her room at the 9 and 10 o'clock bed checks but did not search for her until 11 o'clock. When they found her outside, she was dead. She was wearing only light clothing, and her wheelchair was tipped over next to her. About 40 years previously, Franklin was admitted to a public mental institution, from which she was trans-ferred after 24 years to the nursing facility where she died. The *Washington Post*, which reported the story, said that the circumstances of Franklin's death would be studied with special care because the LTC institution involved was an integral element in a massive court-ordered deinstitutionalization plan.[1]

In faded rooming houses and once-glorious hotels along the New Jersey shore and in decaying inner-city tenements, thousands of elderly people with physical and mental infirmities lived in conditions that some officials claimed were unsafe. In the nine months preceding, reported the *New York Times* in March 1981, 61 of these people had perished in nighttime fires. As a result of the fires, critics were calling for resettlement of the inhabitants in state institutions, from which many were moved in the name of deinstitutionalization.

Three communities on the New Jersey shore were surveyed for the article. Living in these communities were 40,000 aged, physically and mentally enfeebled people. There were no doctors available to them. There were few programs for daily recreation or rehabilitation. Medication, which was vital for many of the residents, was typically dispensed by people without medical or psychiatric training, such as a building switchboard operator.

There was general agreement among observers on two salient facts: (1) that a sizable percentage (estimates varied from 40 to 65 percent) of New Jersey's infirm elderly had at one time been treated in state psychiatric institutions, and (2) that the living conditions for these people in the community were far from splendid. But, at that point, any consensus disappeared and two polar opposite perspectives quickly emerged.

Some New Jersey state officials were adamantly opposed to putting these elderly back into state-run institutions, saying there was no guarantee they would receive better care there than they were already getting in the community. "If they're not a danger to themselves or others, they should not be incarcerated as a form of preventive custody," said the deputy commissioner of the New Jersey State Department of Human Services, which at the time operated five state psychiatric hospitals. "It's inappropriate for mental hospitals to be a catch basin of society. On balance, the community care is the better way to go, provided we put a reasonable safety net under the people."

Other public officials and private citizens were enraged at the New Jersey state deinstitutionalization program. Merchants and residents of Asbury Park, one of the communities surveyed, complained of elderly people urinating in public, exposing themselves, wandering into the ocean, and occasionally breaking into houses to find a bed. The Asbury Park health officer expressed a common sentiment: "They're releasing people who are not capable of doing anything in society. They're released with the proviso they take medication. But there's no guarantee they'll take their medication, and if they don't they slide right back into the psychosis that institutionalized them."[2]

If one assumes that social action has its roots in technological change (in this case, in significant advances in psychopharmacology), the deinstitutionalization movement may be said to have begun in the mid-1950s, when the drug chlorpromazine was first introduced to mental health institutions in various parts of the United States. In the years following, three classes of compounds were developed that became widely used in the treatment of acute and chronic schizophrenia and manic-depressive illness: the phenothiazines (such as chlorpromazine), the butyrophenones (such as haloperidol), and the thioxanthene derivatives (such as chlorprothixene).

Coincident with the introduction and widespread availability of these powerful antipsychotic drugs came a marked reduction in the number of institutionalized mentally ill patients. Until the mid-1950s, the number had steadily increased, peaking at 558,900 in 1955, but thereafter it began to decline, and there were fewer than 200,000 institutionalized patients by the late 1970s.[3] Data from the Comptroller General's five-state study (1977) confirms the precipitousness of the decline and suggests also that it was general throughout the United States (see Table 5-1).

In 1961, noting the widespread release of mentally ill persons from state-supported institutions, the Joint Commission on Mental Illness and Health, which was

Table 5-1 Decline in Mentally Ill Inpatient Population, 1963–1974

State	Population		Reduction	
	1963	1974	Number	Percent
Maryland	8,100	5,000	3,100	38
Massachusetts	17,500	6,000	11,500	66
Michigan	20,100	6,000	14,100	70
Nebraska	3,700	600	3,100	84
Oregon	4,060	1,260	2,800	69
Total	53,460	18,860	34,600	65

Source: Comptroller General of the United States, *Returning the Mentally Disabled to the Community: Government Needs to Do More* (Washington: Government Accounting Office, 1977), p. 9.

dominated by the medical profession, drew the easy conclusion: "Tranquilizing . . . drugs have revolutionized the management of psychotic patients in American mental hospitals, and probably deserve primary credit for reversal of the upward spiral of the State hospital inpatient load."[4]

But such an explanation neglects the influence of social context in determining the uses to which technological advances are put. Antipsychotic drugs, with their manifest impact on human behavior, might only have been used within the existing institutional framework to ease management problems and decrease the incidence of overt, blatant physical restraint. Instead, they became part and parcel of a public policy whose apparent objective was the mass closing of state mental institutions and the discharge of former patients to community care settings.

The availability of antipsychotic drugs may have facilitated the movement to deinstitutionalize the mentally ill, but the roots of the movement appear to lie deeper. If deinstitutionalization is to be understood as public policy—with all of the consequences, present and future, on long-term care of the infirm elderly—it must be considered from a political and economic perspective as well.

STRANGE BEDFELLOWS: SOCIAL REFORMERS AND FISCAL CONSERVATIVES

Mental health care in state hospitals had changed little from the turn of the century to the period immediately following the Second World War. However, as in many aspects of American life, the wartime experience was a watershed. The military, with its enormous manpower needs, had been astonished to find that nearly two million draftees were rejected from the services for mental disorders or deficiencies. The judgment of psychiatrists was almost always accepted in these cases, and such acknowledgment of its expertise by the military conferred new legitimacy upon the psychiatric profession and stimulated an expansion of its role and authority within the medical services.

After the war, special hospitals for veterans were created to deal with service-related and other mental problems, and a new mental health unit (which later became the National Institute for Mental Health) was developed. Thus did major federal-level involvement in mental health policy begin, and decision-making authority, which had always resided with the states, slowly removed to Washington.[5]

Because state-supported mental hospitals were the major institutional weapons in the medical profession's treatment of mental illness, they quickly fell under close scrutiny, and they did not fare well. As often happens in the history of American social reform, the reformers, in their transcendent optimism, began with the presumption that all problems were solvable if only the institutional arrangements were rendered amenable. Such a mindset almost always arrives at a predictable conclusion: Yesterday's reforms are severely flawed and must be cast aside immediately if the situation is to be improved.

Just so in the movement to reform America's mental health system. In the early 19th century, state mental hospitals had been celebrated by reformers as a great advance in the treatment of the insane. Fifty years later, the heroes were those who crusaded against easy commitment laws. In the 1920s, the heroes were those who devised community programs for mental hygiene. Now, in the late 1950s, the heroes became those who devalued the contribution of the state mental hospital system and proclaimed it was not salvageable.

Caught up in the spirit of the moment, social scientists, filmmakers, and other reformers from across the political landscape descended on the gray back wards of state-run asylums for the mentally ill, where they examined, often in mind-numbing detail, the debilitating effects of the "total institution" and, by implication, how it was paradigmatic of the larger society. The body of work they produced varies greatly in quality of investigation and presentation, but taken in its entirety the viewpoint, clearly, was that "the worst home is better than the best mental hospital" and that the mere absence of the deforming, dehumanizing pressure of life in a mental hospital would itself represent a profoundly positive social development.[6]

If one prevailing theme of American social reform is that it is unfailingly present-minded, finding in the institutional solutions of an earlier generation the roots of today's most vexing social problems, another persistent theme is that it is extremely conservative. Participants representing the very interests under attack are almost always present in force, not to resist change but to chart its course and thereby ensure that the locus of power remains essentially undisturbed. That is the story of loud and well-publicized crusades in the early 20th century against the sale of adulterated meats and drugs, against child labor, against exploitation of immigrants doing piece work in tuberculosis-infested textile lofts. It is also the story of the mid-20th century reform that focused on conditions existing in state mental hospitals.

In the context of the debate over deinstitutionalization, mainstream psychiatry had much to lose. Its root intellectual assumption was that insanity is a disease of the brain and requires medical diagnosis and treatment of the individual. Any contrary position, such as that psychosis was something systemic to American culture (or, as R. D. Laing would say loudly and often in the late 1960s, an act of heroism and a legitimate response of the alienated to a lunatic society),[7] was anathema. So, to ensure that its perspective on mental illness and its therapies might prevail, the medical establishment was entirely willing to dissociate itself from the state mental health system it had managed and to proclaim the virtues of community-based alternatives.

The president of the American Psychiatric Association, in 1958, summarized his profession's indictment of the state mental hospital system:

> After 114 years of effort, in this year 1958, rarely has a state hospital an adequate staff as measured against the minimum standards set by our Association, and these standards represent a compromise between what was thought to be adequate and what it was thought had some possibility of being realized. Only 15 states have more than 50% of the total number of physicians needed to staff the public mental hospitals according to these standards. On the national average registered nurses are calculated to be only 19.4% adequate, social workers 36.4%, and psychologists 65%. Even the least highly trained, the attendants, are only 80% adequate. I do not see how any reason-ably objective view of our mental hospitals today can fail to conclude that they are bankrupt beyond remedy.[8]

"Bankrupt beyond remedy" meant that alternative solutions must be sought. In 1961, the Joint Commission on Mental Illness and Health published its research report *Action for Mental Health.* The culmination of five years' work, the document set forth the basic goals of what were soon to become national theory, policy, and practice regarding community mental health care. "The objective of modern treatment of persons with major mental illness is to enable the patient to maintain himself in the community in a normal manner," said the Commission.

> To do so, it is necessary (1) to save the patient from the debilitating effects of institutionalization as much as possible; (2) if the patient requires hospitalization, to return him to home and community life as soon as possible; and (3) thereafter to maintain him in the community

as long as possible. Therefore, aftercare and rehabilitation are essential parts of all service to mental patients.[9]

Such recommendations, indeed the entire movement to deinstitutionalize the mentally ill, would likely have had minimal impact had it not also been for the existence of two federal programs: Medicaid, which was enacted in 1965, and Supplemental Security Income (SSI), which was enacted in 1972. These programs were never designed for the mentally disabled, but nevertheless they greatly contributed to a reduction in the size of state hospitals.

For aged, chronically ill residents—many of whom never belonged in a mental hospital but were placed there only because of organic brain syndromes, poverty, and the lack of any other societal institution to care for them—Medicaid offered a way of paying for needed medical care in more appropriate settings. SSI expanded definitions of eligibility, which guaranteed for the first time welfare payments to the mentally disabled.

The existence of these programs placed potent fiscal incentives in the hands of the mental health reformers. By 1967, it became clear that under Medicaid the federal government would subsidize from 50 to 80 percent of the cost of providing care to medically ill mental patients simply by the expedient of moving them to private nursing homes. This meant the possibility of bringing additional monies from a seemingly limitless source (the federal government) into state mental health systems, which had always been underfunded, overcrowded, and, according to some, lacking in any coherent sense of what they were about.

At first, many state budget agencies had to be convinced that there was a financial benefit to be gained by depopulating state mental institutions and transferring monies to the private sector. As usually happens, however, the hand that controls the funding directs the show. Although Medicaid and many SSI programs are state administered, the money derives from the federal government, which was committed to the transfer of funds to private SNFs and ICFs, with the states functioning as disbursing agents. So in 1972, through amendments to the Social Security Act, the federal government said it would impose financial penalties on those states that did not implement effective programs for controlling unnecessary use of mental hospitals, SNFs, and ICFs. That was the stick. The carrot was funding provided to the states (under SSI) for substantially increased cost-of-living payments to discharged mental patients. Subsequent legislation would offer additional incentives to the states for the establishment of community-based mental health services.

In baldest terms, the states had been presented with a choice. Either accept from the federal government extremely attractive funding arrangements on the condition that they depopulate state mental hospitals in favor of care provided in private institutions or incur the penalties and go it alone under the existing system. Given the multiplicity of demands on state tax dollars, as well as the reformers' cries in favor of deinstitutionalization and pressure from private interests eager to seize the opportunity and go into the nursing home business, the choice presented to the state governments was in fact no choice at all.[10]

A MORE DEBILITATED RESIDENT POPULATION

It is the LTC administrator who will, today and tomorrow, feel the daily impact of these broad social, economic, and political forces. Already, the shift of the aged from mental hospitals to nursing homes is creating a far more debilitated resident population, one with severe psychological as well as physical deficits. The promise is for more of the same, as persons who were released from state mental hospitals, having long needed but never received psychiatric treatment, or having no prior history of mental illness but now suffering from late-life dementia or other age-related organic disorders become too old to care for themselves and require the safety and support of an LTC institution.[11]

There is also a parallel trend occurring. While a more debilitated population is entering LTC institutions in greater numbers, aged people with fewer deficits are actively seeking alternatives to traditional nursing home care. Again, politics and economics are key. With the shortage of public monies affecting all levels of government, there is great concern about inflation, cost containment, and priorities regarding expenditures for the aged.[12] The health care industry, sensing that the nursing home sector may be limited in its future growth and profit potential, is responding with lower-cost alternatives directed at specific long-term care markets. These include adult day care, congregate housing, case management services, and in-home supportive services. As such "new products" become refined, widespread, and eligible for government funding, traditional nursing homes predictably will lose a significant portion of their lighter care constituency.

All of this means that, in terms of case mix, the typical LTC institution is going to attract a population with more behavioral disorders and a higher level of functional impairment than ever before.[13] As a consequence, the LTC administrator is faced with some important strategic decisions:

- Does the institution wish to restrict its resident population to those persons with less severe physical, mental, and psychosocial debilities, somehow defined?
- If so, what shall be its operative distinction between acceptable and unacceptable behavior for prospective residents?
- Are persons who are depressed, withdrawn, confused, disoriented, or hypochondriac suitable candidates for admission?
- How about persons who are assaultive, threatening, destructive, noisy, negativistic, or wandering?

- Assuming the institution has clearly drawn its distinctions, will it be able to abide by them and still compete effectively with those alternative services and other institutions now vying for a share of the same targeted market?
- If the LTC administrator is willing to accept into residence those elderly persons whose problems are severe and complex, is the institution prepared to deliver quality care not only to these but to all other of its residents and to do so economically?
- Has the institution and its staff defined, in advance, that point when a resident is understood to be too belligerent, too explosive, or too wandering to be effectively managed in a low-intensity care setting?

The changing nature of the case mix has been felt at HRCA as at other LTC institutions both large and small. Two decades ago, when the many community-based alternatives for care of the less debilitated elderly did not yet exist, the HRCA resident population was upon admission almost five years younger than today's and on average evidenced far fewer mental and physical deficits. The beds were almost equally distributed among Pattern I, II, and III residents.

Today, in sharp contrast, nearly half of HRCA residents are classified as Pattern III. The distribution of the 725 beds at HRCA looks like this:

Pattern I	116 beds	(16%)
Pattern II	279 beds	(38%)
Pattern III	330 beds	(46%)

Even more compelling evidence of the changing case mix at HRCA is the shift that is occurring within Pattern III. Through use of the functional assessment patterning system, social services staff have been able to track very closely what happens to HRCA residents over time. The data show the following tendencies:

- Subpattern IIIA residents (intellectually intact but immobile) generally remain IIIA until death.
- Subpattern IIIB residents (similar to IIIA but less communicative) generally become IIID.
- Subpattern IIIC residents (similar to IIIB but incontinent) generally become IIID.
- Subpattern IIID residents (severe intellectual loss but no major behavior problems) generally remain IIID to death.
- Subpattern IIIE residents (severe behavior problems, immobile, and vulnerable) either remain IIIE or become IIID and experience the highest death rate.
- Subpattern IIIF residents (severe behavior problems, aggressive) are variable.

So, among the Pattern III population, IIIA residents usually remain IIIA and all others tend over time to become IIID. Because this is known from internal experience, it may be inferred that, given the availability of alternatives in the community for the less debilitated elderly, an increasing percentage of new applicants to HRCA will be classified IIIA or IIID upon admission.

Indeed, the validity of that inference has already been verified. Several years ago, when HRCA was in the midst of a building renovation, it did not have enough Pattern III beds available to meet demand. People would apply for residency, and as part of the application process they would be tested using the HRCA functional assessment patterning system. Depending on the availability of beds in the indicated pattern, an applicant would either be admitted to residency as a Pattern I or II resident or would be placed on the waiting list for Pattern III.

When the building renovation was completed, HRCA staff looked at the waiting list and began reassessing those people who were still waiting for admission. They discovered, not surprisingly, that exactly the same process of deterioration had occurred in this outside sample as was occurring among current Pattern III residents. People who had earlier tested as subpattern IIIA were still IIIA (i.e., without important intellectual loss). People who had earlier tested as other than IIIA were now increasingly IIID (i.e., with limited cognitive function).

If this trend continues, and there is no reason to expect it will not, within the next several years HRCA will need to restructure its operations, reducing Pattern I facilities by at least one unit and adding at least one Pattern III unit. The nature of HRCA's resident population is changing, and the institution must adjust accordingly.

Predictably, administrators of LTC institutions elsewhere will have to engage in much the same sort of analysis and make the appropriate strategic decisions.[14]

THE REHABILITATIVE MODEL REVISITED: A BEHAVIORAL APPROACH TO CASE MANAGEMENT

Clinical diagnosis is as important in psychiatry as in general medical practice because it provides knowledge about prognosis and suggests specific treatments. However, it is also essential to identify the behavioral and emotional characteristics of the elderly resident, for, as has been previously suggested in the discussion of HRCA's pattern-of-care model (see Chapter 2), the diagnostic label is far less meaningful in a long-term care setting than a fully documented understanding of how the resident behaves and how effectively he or she is able to function. For the staff on the nursing unit floor, it is these factors, not diagnosis, that represent the crux of the case management problem.[15]

The Behavioral Management of Wandering

Wandering is characteristic of many Pattern III–type residents, who may be suffering from a neurological disorder such as senile dementia of the Alzheimer's type (SDAT) or multi-infarct dementia or from one or more psychological disorders. Yet, whatever the origins of the wandering behavior—single or multiple, organic or functional, known or unknown—its manifestations can be very troublesome to LTC staff and must be managed.[16]

One LTC institution, the Benedictine Nursing Center in Mt. Angel, Oregon, decided to try a behavioral approach to the management of residents who wandered, and the experiment proved quite successful.

The first step in the program was to identify those individuals whose cognitive impairment might cause them to wander. This was done using admissions histories and by observing the residents during their first few days at the center. Each identified resident was given a special bracelet bearing the resident's name, the designation "cognitively impaired," and a telephone number to call if he or she became lost. A photograph was placed in the front of the resident's chart, along with height, weight, eye color, and any other distinguishing characteristics. A second photograph was placed near the employees' time clock so that, when beginning a shift, staff might be reminded that the resident manifested wandering behavior.

For one or two weeks following admission, the nurses and aides on each shift who were assigned to the potential wanderers would formally introduce them to the staff of other units and departments. This was considered necessary because, as a group, these residents appeared mentally intact, were physically able, and, if lost, might otherwise be mistaken for visitors. The introductions to staff were always done with discretion and in a way that preserved the dignity of the cognitively impaired resident. For example, the staff member might say, "This is Mr. Smith. He's new here and he may need some help getting adjusted. Please offer him assistance when needed."

Another means of identification was more questionable and points to the fine line that always exists between caregiving and intrusion. Each day for about three weeks, or until all nurses and staff throughout the institution knew the resident on sight, a potential wanderer would have a red dot or small piece of red cloth affixed to the back of his or her robe between the shoulder blades. This "flag" alerted staff to the presence of a wanderer so that they might redirect the resident into the building or accompany the resident as he or she walked about. Because the intervention literally marked a class of residents in a distinguishing way, the cost (in terms of violating these residents' privacy) was weighed carefully against the perceived benefit to the residents and to the institution. In no instance, however, was the marking done without the prior knowledge and approval of the resident's family.

The second step in the program was to develop a schedule of special activities for potential wanderers. Three days a week, for one hour, there was music, exercise, and touch in a small group setting. Over time, the group was led by a variety of persons, including nurses, housekeeping staff, volunteers, and students.

The third step in the program was to assist staff in their interactions with the cognitively impaired. When communicating verbally, staff were taught to give simple instructions in unambiguous sentences. For example, rather than say, "Don't go outside," a command that requires the listener first to think of what not to do, then to unthink it, staff were taught to say precisely what they wanted done, such as "Stay in the building" or "Walk over to me." In this regard, a nurse's aide told of assisting a female resident with Alzheimer's disease to bed. The aide finished dressing her, then said, "Come hop into bed." The woman walked over to the bed, tried to hop, then looked at the aide and said, "I can't." The lesson was quickly learned. Avoid abstractions, which might be taken literally. Instead, say just what you mean.

On a nonverbal level, staff were taught that the confused elderly were acutely sensitive to the moods and attitudes of their caregivers. So nurses and aides were instructed to use a gentle, calming tone of voice and physical stroking to quiet a confused person rather than get angry and shout, which only increased agitation. For example, when attempting to dress a resident, one aide perhaps gave too many instructions too rapidly, and the elderly man grabbed her hair. If the aide had then responded in anger and attempted to pull away, the resident's distress would likely have increased and caused him to tighten his grip. Instead, the aide recognized that the man was simply responding to a bewildering situation and that her attitude would be contagious. So she calmly placed her hand on top of the resident's and said, "Open your hand." Gently stroking the resident's hand further reduced the stress and allowed him to relax and let go.

As part of the program, staff were encouraged, whenever possible, to accompany wandering residents on short walks out of the facility rather than force them to stay inside. Cognitively impaired individuals who are continually thwarted in their attempts to leave will often try again and again nonetheless and become very agitated, hostile, or combative in the process, until they sometimes must be physically or chemically restrained. It quickly became apparent to staff that more time and energy was required to deal with the consequences of such frustration than to accede to a resident's agenda and accompany him or her outside for perhaps 5 to 15 minutes.

Implementing this program step, however, required that responsibility for a wandering resident belongs not to one aide alone but to the entire staff. If and when the resident attempted to leave the building and no one on the nursing unit was free to accompany the individual, then someone from another department (dietary, administration, housekeeping, etc.) was obligated to assist.

Another aspect to improving interaction between staff and wandering residents involved identifying the feelings and needs that underlay the residents' behavior. When a woman with severe chronic dementia would say, for example, "I must go home to fix supper for my husband and children," staff were instructed to think immediately in terms of the resident's behavioral agenda. Perhaps she had a need to talk about her family or somehow recapture the warmth of that time of her life. So staff would respond by asking questions about her children, her family, or the kinds of things she liked to cook. They would repeat specific words or phrases ("fix supper," "your children") or try to articulate what they understood to be the underlying emotion ("You need to go home?" "You're worried that your family won't be fed?"). They would compliment her on what a good cook, wife, and mother she had been.

When such actions failed to distract the resident from leaving, staff would accompany him or her while continuing to repeat key phrases and articulate the underlying emotions. They would attempt to orient the resident to reality only if it seemed to have a calming effect. If it increased distress, they would immediately stop. At intervals, they would attempt to redirect the resident back to the building or nursing unit by suggesting, "Let's walk this way now." If reality orientation and redirection failed, they would continue to walk, allowing the resident to control the direction but ensuring safety.

A particularly poignant case example illustrates the effectiveness of this behavior management approach:

> This 88-year-old woman [Mrs. D.] suffered from Alzheimer's disease and Parkinson's disease but was still able to walk unaccompanied for short distances with a walker. She had been a resident for 9 months and had only attempted to leave the building on one recent previous occasion. At that time the staff attempted to and did stop her, which precipitated 3 days of agitated, restless, and angry behavior.
>
> Four days later on a sunny but cold winter day she again mistook it to be summer and felt compelled to return to her apartment to visit her sister and work in her garden. At first the staff tried to dissuade her because of the cold. Nothing that could be said would convince her, however, it was not summer. So she was accompanied outside. She was allowed to travel the direction she wished. The staff person merely followed her lead and provided safety information as needed. Several times Mrs. D. tried to convince the staff person to go inside [as if to say], "It [is] cold and no sense in two of us being lost."
>
> The staff member assured her that she had the time and was willing to be lost with her (not an easy thing for staff to do, but a critical point). She was becoming fatigued, chilled, and bewildered because she

didn't know in which direction her home lay. On noticing this the staff member asked if she wished to go inside to warm up and rest, with the assurance that if she wished to she could return to her searching. She willingly went inside but was in an unfamiliar end of the building. As the staff member and resident were greeted by name, she turned to the staff member and asked, "Do you know these people?" Skillfully the staff member replied, "Yes, and I can take you to a place where you will recognize people and things. Would you like to go?" She responded affirmatively.

At this point, a real sadness was coming over her as she began to realize her disorientation. As the two walked to the end of the building near her room, she recognized some of the staff and as she approached her room said with great surprise, "There's my room." She then turned to the staff person, and with great fatigue and sadness on her face asked, "What should I do now?" She was told to rest on her bed and that supper would be brought to her shortly. She said, "Thank you," and fell asleep. She had no agitation or restlessness following this episode and this exit seeking behavior did not recur for many months.[17]

Very soon, a taxonomy of resident "agenda behavior," the possible underlying emotions or needs, was developed, along with suggested staff responses. Some examples follow.

- When a cognitively impaired resident says, "I must write to my mother," and mother is deceased, perhaps she is longing for her mother or has a need to feel connected or to be busy. Thus, the staff member might respond by providing pencil and paper and engaging the resident in conversation about her mother.
- When a cognitively impaired resident says, "I've got to go now. My children are sick," perhaps she is fearful or is feeling sick herself. The staff member might respond by checking vital signs, asking if she feels sick, talking about what a good mother she was, asking what she thinks is wrong with her children, and walking outside with her if she insists on leaving.
- When a cognitively impaired resident says, "Get away! If you touch me, I'll hit you with my cane," perhaps he is fearful, angry, or feeling powerless. The staff member would stand away, speak softly, and gently repeat the resident's phrases and concerns. The staff member would never argue or reprimand but move closer as agitation decreases and stroke the resident's arm or rub his back if tolerated.
- When a cognitively impaired resident continually folds napkins and newspapers and collects them in her wheelchair, perhaps she has a need to be useful.

Staff members might respond by commenting that she looks very busy and is doing a good job. They would not remove the items without permission and only if necessary.

- When a cognitively impaired resident hits at a staff member who is attempting to provide care, perhaps he is fearful and unable to grasp what is expected. So the staff member might withdraw, return in 5 to 10 minutes, and explain step by step in a calming voice what she wishes to do. Or she might attempt to distract the resident by commenting how much she likes the feel of his skin, the color of his eyes, or the clothes he is wearing.

As an approach to case management, the method used by the Benedictine Nursing Center stood in stark contrast to traditional reality orientation (RO), which postulates the need to orient the cognitively impaired individual to present reality ("This is your home now," "Your husband is dead," "Your children are grown and living far away"). One of the innovators of the Benedictine Nursing Center program wrote, "With selected individuals RO may be helpful, but by and large, for the chronically cognitively impaired, it appeared [to us] that if staff members oriented themselves to the residents' agenda and needs, the outcome was more helpful and resulted in a decrease in problem behaviors."[18]

This was not to dismiss reality orientation entirely as a case management technique. The staff of the Benedictine Nursing Center agreed that "if the person has only mild-to-moderate and reversible confusion, or is asking for reality information, [reality orientation] may be valuable."   But in the severely demented, "RO seems only to deepen their anxiety and exaggerate their separation from what they trust and love. Insistently orienting persons with severe dementia often increases their emotional pain by making them 'wrong' in comparison to their perceived reality."[19]

The various program steps that have been described were primarily designed to decrease the risk and frequency of a resident getting lost within the building or wandering out of it. They were effective, but they did not eliminate the problem of wandering behavior entirely, and so there also had to be a comprehensive procedure for mobilizing staff to look for cognitively impaired individuals identified as missing. The procedure, called "Code 10," was loosely based on the institution's fire procedures. It went into effect as soon as a resident was thought to be missing from his or her unit, and it required the participation of all staff persons in the building. The steps were as follows.

1. The nurse from the missing resident's unit alerted the staff by using the overhead paging system, announcing "Code 10. Will (missing resident's name) please return to (name of unit)." Code 10 was a signal that someone was missing. The name and unit that followed told the staff who the person was. If a staff member did not recall what the resident looked like, he or she would immediately call the unit and get a description.

2. Staff on all units searched their areas thoroughly and systematically. If the resident was not located in a given area, the staff would access the overhead paging system and announce, "Unit (name) all clear." Each area reported. If the resident was found, the unit staff would announce, "Code 10. All clear." This alerted the rest of the staff that they could resume their previous activities.

3. If the resident was not found inside or directly outside the building, the LTC administrator or designate would immediately contact the local authorities (police and fire departments) and give them the resident's photograph and description. The family would be notified at a time deemed appropriate by the LTC administrator.

The Code 10 procedure was used often and it worked well. Residents were swiftly located within the building. The incidence of outside, unaccompanied wandering greatly decreased, as did staff anxiety concerning the issue. It never became necessary to contact the police and fire departments or to notify the family of a temporarily missing resident.[20]

The Behavioral Management of Late-Life Paranoia

At an LTC institution in West Virginia, a behavioral approach was used to manage a case of late-life paranoia. Ms. B. was convinced she was going to be murdered by an aide who was an employee of the nursing home in which she had previously lived. Verbalizations of these concerns had begun nine months earlier, when Ms. B. was a resident of the nursing home where the aide was employed. Five months later, fearful of being poisoned, she began to refuse food and medication for a heart problem. Two months thereafter, she suffered a myocardial infarction, was hospitalized for a short time, and then relocated to a second nursing home, where it was hoped her fears would be relieved.

Shortly after admission to the second nursing home, Ms. B. began to display extreme anxiety and hysterical crying. At first, the frequency of occurrence was minimal, with Ms. B. expressing her concerns about her impending murder only to the social worker. Over the next few weeks, however, she began to verbalize her fears to more people and display more intense anxiety, and she also began to suspect more people of wanting to harm her. Staff were concerned that her paranoid beliefs were potentially life threatening, since she might again refuse to take her cardiac medication and perhaps trigger a second heart attack.

Functionally, Ms. B. suffered from at least a moderate hearing loss, although its extent was not known. She refused to wear a hearing aid but lip-read very well. She described her hearing as "coming and going" and at times reported hearing threats from her intended murderer. She was confined to a wheelchair. Also, she had limited use of her left arm, although there was no known medical basis for this loss.

Beside her lip reading ability, Ms. B.'s behavioral assets included good conversational skills and a willingness to assist the LTC institution's staff with a monthly newsletter. In addition, she helped feed three or four other residents each day. The staff complimented Ms. B. and thanked her often, but she steadfastly refused to acknowledge the contribution she was making to the institution or its residents.

Although Ms. B.'s primary complaint was fear for her safety, she also insisted that she had lost her individuality upon entering a nursing home, and she was unwilling to request any kind of assistance from staff. She experienced occasional "blackouts" for which there was no known medical basis, although a complete neurological workup had not been done. The episodes lasted as long as 24 hours, during which time Ms. B. was incontinent and unresponsive to all outside stimuli.

The LTC institution's staff generally uncomfortable with Ms. B.'s verbalizations of her fears. Responses to her complaints included avoidance, confrontation, reassurance, and, occasionally, agreement, which staff later acknowledged probably reinforced the behavior.

The treatment program for Ms. B. consisted of 14 weekly individual sessions with two therapists, and the staff attended two in-service training sessions. In her initial meetings, Ms. B. focused almost exclusively on negative events, including paranoid thoughts and dependent staff interactions. The therapists asked Ms. B. to keep a daily record of the times she helped someone.

Following the assessment phase of Ms. B.'s treatment, the in-service training sessions for staff were held. The therapists explained Ms. B.'s condition in terms of isolation, lack of feedback, and reinforcement for verbalizations. They theorized that there may indeed have been some threat or incident of abuse or stress in the previous nursing home that provided a basis for the development of her paranoid behaviors. More reliably documented, however, were the physical losses Ms. B. had suffered, limiting her ability to move about and to hear. Given an impaired ability to receive corrective feedback, the likelihood was great, said the therapists, that Ms. B. would mistakenly interpret events and then seize upon a false belief in order to structure the misinformation and render the situation comprehensible.

Staff were asked to respond to Ms. B. in a consistent manner. Whenever Ms. B. spoke of her fears, staff were instructed to say that they understood someone was coming to talk to her about her concerns and to direct the conversation immediately to another topic. They were also asked to initiate conversations with Ms. B. at times when she was not verbalizing her fears so that every social interaction between them did not begin with an articulation of paranoid beliefs.

As the individual sessions with Ms. B continued, the therapists attempted to build a trusting relationship and to correct the misinterpretations of everyday events that presumably had led to her paranoia. For example, at one point Ms. B.

said that the person who was trying to kill her was outside the door. One of the therapists immediately opened the door and took her out into the hallway so that she was able to see that she was mistaken. The focus continued on positive events and helping behavior. Ms. B. continued to record the number of times she helped other residents, and this information was displayed graphically so that she was able to visualize the contribution she was making.

Within two weeks of the conclusion of the in-service training sessions, the staff and social worker reported that Ms. B.'s verbalizations of her fears had been almost eliminated. The blackouts, which had been noted in the records of her previous nursing home, reappeared early in treatment but quickly decreased in frequency and length and eventually disappeared. By the time therapy was terminated, Ms. B. rarely spoke of her fear of being murdered. At times she would say "he" (referring to her alleged murderer) had been at the nursing home that particular day, but these statements were made without signs of anxiety or fear. Ms. B. had also become more assertive with staff members in requesting assistance.[21]

In the case examples discussed above, the staff of the Benedictine Nursing Center and the staff of the institution in West Virginia *individualized* the residents in their charge and then responded to the specifics of the situation. In both instances, there was an interplay of clinical diagnosis, functional assessment, and common sense, which together provided the best result.

The utility of such an approach is substantiated by the experience of many LTC institutions with the phenomenon known as "excess disability."[22] Excess disability is a reversible deficit. It is said to exist when the magnitude of a person's functional incapacity is greater than warranted by the actual impairment. For example, a resident may show irreversible memory decline and language dysfunction yet have reversible excess deficits in both self-care and social interaction. The reversible deficits often constitute a greater impediment to carrying out daily activity than the disability itself.

Distinguishing between "excess" and "actual" disability is hardly an exact science. There is no one-to-one relationship between the degree of organic impairment and the overall level of an individual's functionality. The root causes of human behavior are, fortunately, a good deal more subtle than that. In the case of excess disability, they may also depend on undiagnosed physical illness or discomfort, undocumented traumatic events, a premorbid personality, historic modes of adaptation to stress, or an adverse reaction to the pace, rules, or activities of the LTC institution. All of these, plus others that may be entirely hidden from view, can predispose someone to accentuate behaviors generally associated with cognitive disorders.

One goal of nursing care in an LTC institution is (or ought to be) to prevent or reverse excess disability so that every resident functions to capacity and none becomes prematurely disabled. To accomplish this, nurses must learn to distinguish between excess and actual disability, and to do that they must know their residents as people.

Often it is the nurse's aide who understands the resident best and is able to provide needed insight to the physician, head nurse, or other caregivers. Such exchanges typically go unrecorded but nevertheless represent the essence of quality care. For example, at HRCA there was a 103-year-old man who was demented but quite strong physically. He had recently undergone abdominal surgery for a bowel obstruction and had returned to the LTC institution with a nasogastric feeding tube. The tube was uncomfortable, and after several days he yanked it out, then broke the hand restraints that had been applied. The doctor on the primary care team thought he should be medicated. A nurse's aide, who knew the resident well, thought otherwise. She said she would try to get him to sit up, because that is what he liked to do, and then she would try to give him some food. The doctor held his order for medication and returned in half an hour. The resident was sitting, dressed, and having lunch in a very happy mood. The aide said that once the resident understood what was going to be done, he stopped being combative and was his usual self again.

When a resident is individualized in this way—when the nursing staff know the resident's unique traits, personality, history, and current potential strengths—a lot of potential problems are avoided. To the observant and knowing caregiver, a resident's gestures or facial expressions or body positions or behaviors become instantly understandable, as understandable as words spoken clearly and distinctly. In responding to such subverbal communications in a compassionate and timely fashion, the caregiver is able to reduce the resident's feelings of helplessness and frustration, provide the resident with a heightened sense of competency and self-worth, and so contribute not only to immediate well-being but also, possibly, to the rehabilitation of personality.

THE USEFULNESS OF PSYCHIATRIC CONSULTANTS

Psychiatric consultants can provide several important services to LTC institutions. They can prescribe and provide pharmacologic and psychosocial interventions to help in the management of individual residents with problems. They can serve as consultants to LTC management in the design and operation of therapeutic programs and environments. They can provide in-service training and education so that LTC staff might improve their ability to assess and manage residents. They can help clarify which dysfunctional behaviors cannot be managed in an LTC setting but instead require treatment in a psychiatric hospital.

As regards all of these possible contributions, the experience of Marie-France Tourigny-Rivard, a geriatric psychiatrist and professor of psychiatry at the University of Ottawa, is instructive. For a period of 18 months, she provided consultation services to a 50-bed nursing home in a small farming town in Ontario, Canada. During her monthly visits, she evaluated new referrals, provided ongoing treatment for several residents, and presented in-service programs to staff on topics such as depression, death and dying, behavior therapy, and use of psychotropic medications.

At the end of the 18 month program, nine members of the nursing home staff—six nurses, the house physician, and two administrators—were asked to comment in writing about the consultation. From the nursing staff, the evaluations were generally positive, except for one nurse who said that sometimes the expectations of the psychiatrist were too high. Most nurses referred to ways in which the consultation had helped them, as consultees, deal with patients better. Only a few mentioned how the consultation may also have been helpful to the residents.

Of the nine staff members responding, seven said that the regular consultation had helped to decrease the nurses' level of frustration in dealing with behavioral problems and had made them more sensitive to the needs of the residents. Four nurses mentioned that they had become more active and more valued members of the assessment and treatment team. Seven of the nine staff members reported improved attitudes toward psychiatric care. Four nurses and the two administrators mentioned that they were encouraged by the experience with the consultant to try to deal with problems and that they had gained more confidence in their own capacities to handle emotionally disturbed residents.

The educational component of the consultation was especially well received. Among the comments were these: "In-services focusing on one topic were most beneficial." "We acquired a better understanding of the psychiatric problems of the elderly through in-service." "I learned to take a good history and which behaviors should be observed and recorded in nursing notes." "In-service helped me understand what is 'behind the behavior' and how it can be a manifestation of a wider problem."

The administrators' comments indicated that at first they had been reluctant to go along with a regular consultation program, fearing that problems would be identified but no solutions brought forward. A major concern was that transfers to the psychiatric hospital would remain as difficult as before. Tourigny-Rivard wrote,

> They found, however, that consultation brought them additional information and treatment recommendations which decreased the need for referral to the psychiatric hospital. They felt supported in their efforts to keep and to deal with the more difficult cases and commented that the patients with a history of mental disorders became more welcome to the nursing home. They noticed that depression was detected earlier and opportunities for treatment were offered to their elderly residents. The[y] felt the nurses' knowledge of emotional

problems increased due to "In-service" and noted an improvement in their attitudes toward elderly residents.[23]

The house physician was also a fan of the program. He commented that a number of the residents improved as a result of the consultation. He said he particularly appreciated the direct involvement of the consultant in the treatment of some cases (in the form of supportive psychotherapy) and her participation in the training of the nursing staff.

The consultant herself was pleased. She reported that after a few months nurses were providing more relevant information and observational data on the residents. The discussions began shifting from requests for her to do something that would make a behavior disappear to an attempt to understand the problematic behavior and the resident presenting it. Tourigny-Rivard wrote,

> Gradually, the nurses became more willing to assume responsibility for treatment and this was demonstrated by their active implementation of the treatment plans suggested for residents seen in consultation. Their confidence in themselves seemed to increase and they applied what they had learned from one specific situation to other similar situations. They also began implementing specific therapeutic programs for the residents in general, no longer leaving activities to irregular staff initiative.
>
> The schedule of the nursing home was enriched by a variety of regular group activities such as cooking, crafts, exercises, games, and group viewing of some educational television programs. These regular group activities were initiated by the nursing home staff. The consultant never made any judgment about the quality of life of the nursing home, nor did she make any direct suggestion that the level of activity and stimulation of the residents should increase.
>
> Morale seemed to improve as the nursing home staff gave each other support and encouragement for their therapeutic efforts. Willingness to increase their level of knowledge progressed from requests that the consultant give lectures to requests for reading materials, a step toward more active learning. The consultant found, overall, that she had started independently, but was quickly joined by an eager-to-learn, hard-working treatment team.[24]

As for the residents themselves, there were, said Tourigny-Rivard, three ways in which consultation could have had a positive impact: improvement in the pathology or behavior problem, improvement in case management, and increased tolerance toward the resident or the behavior. Of the 21 residents seen in consultation, 17 were helped in at least one of these three ways. The 4 residents who showed no improvement included a depressed man who left the nursing home to return to his family shortly after the consultation and before any significant intervention could be made, a demented woman who was known to present behavior and management problems that could not be controlled entirely while in an acute care psychogeriatric unit and who was placed in the nursing home on a trial basis to avoid long-term psychiatric hospitalization, a schizophrenic man who had to be admitted to a psychiatric facility for acute decompensation of his illness, and a depressed elderly woman who moved to another nursing home closer to her family.

The outcome study showed that for only 9 (of 21) residents, the pathology or behavioral problem improved. For 16 residents, case management improved. For 16 residents, the tolerance of staff toward the resident or behavior improved. Therefore, the consultation process did not necessarily improve or cure the pathology. It did, however, enable staff to manage and tolerate problems better, an outcome perhaps best evidenced by the fact that staff did not refer a single resident for emergency psychiatric evaluation during the 18-month consultation period.[25]

Although Tourigny-Rivard was dealing with a limited sample, her experience is quite consistent with the findings of others. Mentally disturbed residents in long-term care institutions can often benefit from individual psychiatric consultation.[26] And the teaching role of the consultant can have a substantial, wide-ranging impact. In a frequently quoted essay on the role of the consultant, Benjamin Liptzin, a geriatric psychiatrist and professor of psychiatry at Harvard Medical School, states the matter succinctly: "While the [consulting] relationship usually develops around cases, all opportunities are exploited for teaching purposes. This educational role of consultation allows the consultant to affect the care of many more people than those who receive direct case consultation."[27]

HELPING STAFF CONFRONT MENTAL HEALTH ISSUES

At HRCA, there is an ongoing series of group therapy sessions in which members of the staff whose jobs bring them into daily contact with residents meet in small groups with a psychiatrist to discuss events, behavior of residents in their care, and their own feelings.

An LTC institution need not have a psychiatrist or psychologist on its payroll in order to conduct such a program successfully. A mental health professional who has a full-time practice in the community and is interested in geriatrics and in people who work with the aged can come to the institution on a scheduled basis, and at a minimal cost, to conduct the sessions. Whatever the arrangement between the institution and the consultant (see "Finding a Psychiatric Consultant and Formalizing the Relationship" below), what is important to convey to staff members participating is that the group sessions are for *healthy* people who are engaged in a very stressful job.[28] "It is extremely frustrating to work with elderly people and not know sometimes what goes on inside them," is the way HRCA's psychiatric consultant usually begins the first meeting. "We want you to understand what is happening with those in your care, so that you can do a better job for them and, thereby, for yourself."

Each group may meet for four or five one-hour sessions, depending on the size of the gathering and the job responsibilities represented. As is made clear to all at the beginning of the first session, it is a discussion group, not a lecture series. Participants are expected to raise questions, to think actively about what their colleagues are saying, to offer the wisdom of their own experience. The group leader (the psychiatrist or psychologist) offers professional insight when appropriate and otherwise directs the discussion.

At HRCA, these sessions have been conducted continually for 20 years. In reviewing the minutes of meetings from the past two decades, two things stand out. First, the issues have remained virtually the same. Staff still struggle with the reality of residents' hallucinations, illusions, regressions, and depressions, with the reality of death and dying. The names are different, as are the details of the personal histories. But the human conditions described and the range of staff responses remain very much the same.

Second, the essential wisdom and humanity of the participants are also the same. There is not only an eagerness among staff to understand what is, or may be, happening in the minds of the residents in their care but also an instinct for the truth and a compassion that is remarkable. Following are some examples.

A common topic of conversation is residents who talk to someone who is not there. Such a resident, when asked who it is, might reply, "No one," "My boyfriend," or "Someone is beating me up." A frail woman who is blind imagines that people are gathering around her bed and having sexual relations. Another thinks she is having a love affair with Beethoven. Another hears the voice of a stranger who is teaching her how to sew.

Such stories invariably lead to fruitful discussions about hallucination and delusion, the differences between them, and the clinical relationship between them and paranoid schizophrenia. In one group, a nurse's aide suggests that people who say someone is plotting against them may feel they have done something bad in their life and are afraid of being punished for it. Another aide says that the woman who "saw" others having sex probably believes such thoughts are shameful and so reacts by thinking "It isn't me who is having these thoughts. It's other people who are doing it." To which the psychiatrist might (and did) add that ego is weakened as we grow older, and so it is more difficult to keep things out of consciousness and to repress certain feelings that are believed to be unacceptable or inappropriate, with the result that hallucinating is the way some elderly people manage their deepest wishes and anxieties.

"Are there physical conditions which might have these effects?" a nurse asks. "Yes," says the psychiatrist. "Brain tumors can cause personality changes. Also, hallucinations and delusional behavior can be caused by pernicious anemia."

Someone may introduce to the discussion the example of an elderly woman, dying of cancer, who says, "I have to have a man before I die." "Why should one assume the sex drive is absent at an advanced age?" asks the psychiatrist. "What is different for the individual is the reality of the circumstances. The fact of deterioration is difficult to accept, but fantasies and daydreams can still exist, and there is great comfort to be found in remembering when one was young."

An aide responds, "I notice that some residents always lay a hand on my arm when we meet. Maybe they need that human contact, that touching, more than we might suppose. They used to have that kind of contact in marriage and with children, and they don't have it anymore."

"When a resident says, 'I don't want to eat. Why should I eat? I want to die. Why don't you let me die?' how do you answer that?" asks an aide. The discussion that follows is the most effective sort of training, because it comes from the wisdom of the group. "'Because I love you and I want you to live' is the best answer we can give," says one. "Many of our residents feel worthless because they are so dependent on others. When an aide likes a resident and shows genuine feelings of respect, the resident acquires dignity and feels he is of value," says another.

An orderly relates that recently a resident accused him of theft, repeating the charge in the dining room in the presence of others, shouting "thief" and "robber" at him, then getting up to follow him, yelling insults. The orderly is very upset at these accusations and because of the public humiliation. The resident has, on other occasions, accused other residents and staff of stealing from him.

"What can be done to prevent this from happening in the future?" asks the psychiatrist. Discussion follows. Someone suggests a rule that only a very small amount of money be allowed in a resident's room. The group rejects the suggestion, deciding that it would be an unwarranted restriction on all residents, that the possession of money is a measure of success, and that it has a great deal of meaning in terms of security, especially to older people. "By restricting the amount of money they can have, who is being protected?" asks one group member. "The resident or the employee?"

After an hour, the group comes to see that the problem is not with the resident but with the response of the staff member who was accused. "There are several possibilities," says the psychiatrist. "The accusation may be true. The resident may be paranoid. Or the whole thing may be exaggerated. In this instance, where other residents defended the staff person, and the resident has a history of making such charges, as long as the employee knows he is honest, he should be able to handle false accusations. People who are suffering from extreme forgetfulness are very fearful they will suffer even more losses, so they lash out at others as someone to blame and to assure themselves they are not losing their minds. So, in answer to the original question 'What can be done?' there is no procedure, other than that the employee must understand the context in which he operates."

The psychiatrist asks the question, "How does the group react to a situation where a resident may be getting along fairly well and then suddenly becomes weaker physically? How do you feel about this, especially when medical intervention by the doctor has no effect?"

The discussion explores the great range of feelings about life and death and the extreme difficulty of working with patients who are suffering. One nurse says she once found it necessary to give the care of a deteriorated resident over to another because of the pain she herself was experiencing. The group agrees it was a wise move. "You have to know your own limits," says a nurse. "If you experience too much pain, perhaps a different pattern would be better for you, or perhaps you find it necessary to leave."

"I was glad when Mrs. ___ died," admits another nurse. "She had been so difficult, and it was a relief."

"Why should we think the mind should contain only the sweetest, purest thoughts?" asks the psychiatrist. "It is not unnatural for the mind at the same time to want the person to die and to live, for different reasons. Every emotion contains the seeds of its opposite."

FINDING A PSYCHIATRIC CONSULTANT AND FORMALIZING THE RELATIONSHIP

Usually, in the LTC setting, it is the nursing staff or the director of nursing who first articulates the need for a psychiatric consultation. Other times the recommendation is made by the attending physician, the medical director, the social worker who handles admissions or deals with family concerns, the activities director, or the LTC administrator him- or herself. Whatever its origin, the request for the involvement of a psychiatrist reflects an awareness on the part of the organization that important needs of residents, families, or staff are going unmet, and for this reason alone the LTC administrator should be extremely receptive to the idea.

Seeking out and forming a relationship with a psychiatric consultant also makes good sense from a legal point of view. Preadmission screening for mental illness and annual resident assessments have now been mandated as a condition of participation in Medicaid and Medicare (see Section 4211, Requirements for Nursing Facilities, Omnibus Budget Reconciliation Act of 1987, P.L. 100-203). The requirements, to date, are these:

- Effective January 1, 1989, a preadmission screening is required of all "mentally ill" and "mentally retarded" individuals to ensure that they require the level of services provided by the nursing facility and do not require "active treatment" for their condition.

- Effective April 1, 1990, each "mentally ill" or "mentally retarded" resident of a nursing facility must have an annual review to determine whether care in the nursing facility is still required or whether inpatient psychiatric services are needed. A resident is considered "mentally ill" if the individual "has a primary or secondary diagnosis of mental disorder (as defined in the *Diagnostic and Statistical Manual of Mental Disorders*, 3rd edition) and does not have a primary diagnosis of dementia (including Alzheimer's disease or a related disorder)."

- The determination as to who is mentally ill and whether a mentally ill person can be appropriately managed in a nursing home is to be made by "the State mental health authority (based on an independent physical and mental evaluation performed by a person or entity other than the State mental health authority)." The law also requires that states adjust their Medicaid rates to support these new requirements.

To be sure, some clarity is lacking in these regulations. It is uncertain from the language of P.L. 100-203, for example, whether all potential nursing home residents or only those patients admitted directly from psychiatric treatment programs require a preadmission psychiatric evaluation. Presumably, this and other questions will be addressed when the Department of Health and Human Services promulgates its final instructions relating to preadmission screening and resident review.

Nevertheless, the trend is apparent. There will be substantial changes required in the management of LTC services, and it seems certain that psychiatric issues will be receiving increased attention in the years to come. LTC administrators would be well advised, therefore, to develop a working relationship with a psychiatric consultant and begin to prepare in-house programs now.[29]

How to do so?

There are several possible places to begin the search for a psychiatric consultant. The LTC administrator might first contact the state mental health authority and ask for the name and location of the community mental health center serving the area. Or the administrator might contact the local community hospital or psychiatric hospital and inquire whether staff psychiatrists are available to consult with a neighboring LTC institution. One of the physicians at any of these places may be professionally interested in geriatric psychiatry and have time available— or know of a colleague who does.

A resident of the LTC institution may already be in treatment with a private psychiatrist, who might be willing to accept new referrals or develop a more formal relationship with the institution and its staff. The medical director of the LTC institution or other attending physicians may have a psychiatrist to whom they refer from their office practices or when hospitalized patients develop psychiatric problems.

The LTC administrator might get in touch with the local psychiatric society to obtain a listing of geriatric psychiatrists or might contact the American Association for Geriatric Psychiatry to determine whether any members practice near the institution. It is usually best to find a psychiatrist who has admitting privileges at an inpatient psychiatric unit in case more acute treatment is required.

As with any consulting relationship, there must be established from the outset a clear understanding as to what the psychiatric consultant and the LTC institution can expect from each other. Key questions for the LTC administrator to ask include these:

- How available will the consultant be for regular visits or emergencies?
- How and when can the consultant be reached by telephone?
- What will the consultant's relationship be with the nursing staff and attending physicians?
- Will the consultant be involved in staff education or program consultation as well as individual patient-centered consultation?
- Is the consultant authorized to write orders directly?
- What documentation in the residents' charts will be expected?
- Will the consultant be actively involved in residents' treatment, including the ordering of lab tests or medications for medical conditions?
- Will the consultant meet with family members or be available to them by telephone?

Probably, there should be a written contract spelling out all of the details of the consulting arrangement. Failing that, the verbal understanding between the parties must be clear and mutually agreed upon.

In addition, the consultant and the LTC institution need to have a prior understanding of possible arrangements if a resident becomes so impaired that psychiatric hospitalization is necessary. Specifically, insurance issues and their impact on treatment must be addressed.

For example, with residents who were discharged from state mental hospitals and have no hospital insurance benefits, it is often necessary to arrange for rehospitalization either with the local community mental health center or the state hospital. Will the LTC institution guarantee readmission? For private pay residents, this usually means having the individual or family continue to pay for the bed. For patients on Medicaid, there is no guarantee of payment past ten days in many states. Such a situation can leave a patient without a place to go when he or she is ready to leave the hospital. For the psychiatric consultant, it can mean a hard time at the outset trying to find a hospital willing to admit. Candid discussion of these issues by the LTC administrator and the consultant, together with careful planning, usually helps to avoid serious difficulties.

When the details are spelled out and agreed upon and the choice of candidates has been endorsed by key members of the staff (e.g., the director of nursing) the financial arrangement between the psychiatric consultant and the LTC institution can be discussed. For both the consultant and the institution, the ideal situation is for the consultant to be paid a monthly retainer covering time spent discussing cases with the staff or participating in in-service education programs. The consultant would then bill residents individually for any services provided directly to them. Without a monthly retainer, most psychiatrists will be unwilling to enter a consulting relationship with an LTC institution, because they would be entirely dependent on fees collected from third-party payers or out-of-pocket payments from residents or their families.

NOTES

1. "Woman, 86, Freezes to Death," *Washington Post*, January 17, 1985, 12; "Freezing Death Angers SE Church," *Washington Post*, January 19, 1985, D2.

2. "Jersey Aides Question Safety at Homes for Elderly," *New York Times*, March 2, 1981, 1.

3. See Andrew T. Scull, "The Decarceration of the Mentally Ill: A Critical View," *Politics and Society* 6 (1976): 173–212; Andrew Scull, "Deinstitutionalization and the Rights of the Deviant," *Journal of Social Issues* 37 (1981): 6–20; Irwin D. Rutman, ed., "Planning for Deinstitutionalization: A Review of Principles, Methods, and Applications," in *Human Services* (Project Share, Monograph Series No. 28, September 1981).

4. Joint Commission on Mental Illness and Health, *Action for Mental Health* (New York: Basic Books, 1961), 39.

5. Stephen M. Rose, "Deciphering Deinstitutionalization: Complexities in Policy and Program Analysis," *Milbank Memorial Fund Quarterly* 57 (1979): 433.

6. The literature on the mental hospital as a "total institution" is vast. The classic study is Erving Goffman, *Asylums: Essays on the Social Situation of Mental Patients and Other Inmates* (Garden City, N.Y.: Doubleday, 1961). See also Elaine Cumming and John Cumming, *Closed Ranks* (Cambridge: Harvard University Press, 1957).

7. The antipsychiatric writings of R.D. Laing were widely read and discussed in the iconoclastic sixties. See, especially, his most celebrated book, *The Politics of Experience* (New York: Pantheon Books, 1967).

8. Harry C. Solomon, "The American Psychiatric Association in Relation to American Psychiatry," *American Journal of Psychiatry* 115 (1958): 7.

9. Joint Commission on Mental Illness and Health, *Action for Mental Health*, xvii.

10. Rose, "Deciphering Deinstitutionalization," 429–60; Gary J. Clarke, "In Defense of Deinstitutionalization," *Milbank Memorial Fund Quarterly* 57 (1979): 461–79; Carol A.B. Warren, "New Forms of Social Control: The Myth of Deinstitutionalization," *American Behavioral Scientist* 24 (July-August 1981): 724–40; Carroll L. Estes and Charlene A. Harrington, "Fiscal Crisis, Deinstitutionalization, and the Elderly," *American Behavioral Scientist* 24 (July-August 1981): 811–26.

11. See National Center for Health Statistics, "Characteristics, Social Contacts and Activities of Nursing Home Residents," *Vital and Health Statistics,* Series 13, no. 27, Department of Health,

Education, and Welfare Publication No. (HRA) 77–1778 (Washington, D.C.: U.S. Government Printing Office, 1977); Fritz Redlich and Stephen R. Kellert, "Trends in American Mental Health," *American Journal of Psychiatry* 135 (1978): 22–28; Alvin Becker and Herbert C. Schulberg, "Phasing out State Hospitals—a Psychiatric Dilemma," *New England Journal of Medicine* 294 (1976): 255–61.

12. See, for example, Subrata N. Chakravarty, "Consuming Our Children?" *Forbes*, November 14, 1988, 222–32; Robert H. Binstock, "The Aged as Scapegoat," *The Gerontologist* 23 (1983): 136–43; Anne R. Somers, "Long-Term Care for the Elderly and Disabled: A New Health Priority," *New England Journal of Medicine* 307 (1982): 221–26.

13. See Thomas D. Sabin, Antonio J. Vitug, and Vernon H. Mark, "Are Nursing Home Diagnosis and Treatment Inadequate?" *JAMA* 248 (1982): 321–22; Howard H. Goldman, Judith Feder, and William Scanlon, "Chronic Mental Patients in Nursing Homes: Reexamining Data from the National Nursing Home Survey," *Hospital and Community Psychiatry* 37 (March 1986): 269–72; Barry W. Rovner, Stephanie Kafonek, Laura Filipp, Mary Jane Lucas, and Marshal F. Folstein, "Prevalence of Mental Illness in a Community Nursing Home," *American Journal of Psychiatry* 143 (1986): 1446–49; Ruth B. Teeter, Floyd K. Garetz, Winston R. Miller, and William F. Heiland, "Psychiatric Disturbances of Aged Patients in Skilled Nursing Facilities," *American Journal of Psychiatry* 133 (1976): 1430–34; Robert F. Barnes and Murray A. Raskind, "DSM-III Criteria and the Clinical Diagnosis of Dementia: A Nursing Home Study," *Journal of Gerontology* 36 (1981): 20–27.

14. For a discussion of how a Washington, D.C., long-term care institution systematically matches its applicants' needs with facility resources, see Solanges Vivens and Carole Woolfork, "Nursing Home Admissions Made More Rational," *Geriatric Nursing* 4 (November-December 1983): 361–64.

15. Barry W. Rovner and Peter V. Rabins, "Mental Illness among Nursing Home Patients," *Hospital and Community Psychiatry* 36 (February 1985): 119–20, 128; James G. Zimmer, Nancy Watson, and Anne Treat, "Behavioral Problems among Patients in Skilled Nursing Facilities," *American Journal of Public Health* 74 (1984): 1118–21; Sharon L. Bernier and Norma R. Small, "Disruptive Behaviors," *Journal of Gerontological Nursing* 14 (February 1988): 8–13.

16. It is in this context—of managing the behavior and not the illness—that the ongoing debate on whether "specialized" units should be established for Alzheimer's disease and other mental impairments can best be understood. A sampling of the literature includes Peter V. Rabins, "Establishing Alzheimer's Disease Units in Nursing Homes: Pros and Cons," *Hospital and Community Psychiatry* 37 (February 1986): 120–21; Russell J. Ohta and Brenda M. Ohta, "Special Units for Alzheimer's Disease Patients: A Critical Look," *The Gerontologist* 28 (1988): 803–08; T. Anne Cleary, Cheryll Clamon, Marjorie Price, and Gail Shullaw, "A Reduced Stimulation Unit: Effects on Patients with Alzheimer's Disease and Related Disorders," *The Gerontologist* 28 (1988): 511–14; Audrey S. Weiner and Jacob Reingold, "Special Care Unit for Dementia: Current Practice Models," *Journal of Long-Term Care Administration* 17 (Spring 1989): 14–19; Shelly B. Getzlaf, "Segregation of the Mentally Impaired Elderly: Debunking the Myths," *Journal of Long-Term Care Administration* 15 (Winter 1987): 11–14; Theodore H. Koff, "Nursing Home Management of Alzheimer's Disease: Establishing Standards of Care," *Journal of Long-Term Care Administration* 15 (Winter 1987): 15–18; Ann L. McCracken and Evelyn Fitzwater, "The Right Environment for Alzheimer's," *Geriatric Nursing* 10 (November-December 1989): 293–94; Geri Hall, M. Virginia Kirschling, and Susan Todd, "Sheltered Freedom: An Alzheimer's Unit in an ICF," *Geriatric Nursing* 7 (May-June 1986): 132–37.

17. Joanne Rader, "A Comprehensive Staff Approach to Problem Wandering," *The Gerontologist* 27 (1987): 758–59. On reality orientation as an approach to treatment, see Sylvia Sherwood and Vincent Mor, "Mental Health Institutions and the Elderly," in *Handbook of Mental Health and Aging*, edited by James E. Birren and R. Bruce Sloane (Englewood Cliffs, N.J.: Prentice-Hall, 1980): 869 and notes.

18. Rader, "Problem Wandering," 758.

19. Joanne Rader, Judy Doan, and Marilyn Schwab, "How to Decrease Wandering, a Form of Agenda Behavior," *Geriatric Nursing* 6 (July-August 1985): 199.

20. Rader, "Problem Wandering," 756–60; Rader, Doan, and Schwab, "How to Decrease Wandering," 196–99. In addition, on wandering behavior, see Lorraine Hiatt Snyder, Peter Rupprecht, Janine Pyrek, Sandra Brekhus, and Tom Moss, "Wandering," *The Gerontologist* 18 (1978): 272–80; Rachel McGrowder-Lin and Ashok Bhatt, "A Wanderer's Lounge Program for Nursing Home Residents with Alzheimer's Disease," *The Gerontologist* 28 (1988): 607–09.

21. Laura L. Carstensen and William J. Fremouw, "The Demonstration of a Behavioral Intervention for Late Life Paranoia," *The Gerontologist* 21 (1981): 329–33.

22. Elaine M. Brody, Morton H. Kleban, M. Powell Lawton, and Herbert A. Silverman, "Excess Disabilities of Mentally Impaired Aged: Impact of Individualized Treatment," *The Gerontologist* 11 (1971): 124–33; Elaine M. Brody, Morton H. Kleban, M. Powell Lawton, and Miriam Moss, "A Longitudinal Look at Excess Disabilities in the Mentally Impaired Aged," *Journal of Gerontology* 29 (1974): 79–84; Pam Dawson, Karen Kline, Donna Crinklaw Wianco, and Donna Wells, "Preventing Excess Disability in Patients with Alzheimer's Disease," *Geriatric Nursing* 7 (November-December 1986): 298–301.

23. Marie-France Tourigny-Rivard and Marilyn Drury, "The Effects of Monthly Psychiatric Consultation in a Nursing Home," *The Gerontologist* 27 (1987): 365.

24. Ibid.

25. Ibid., 363–66.

26. American Psychiatric Association, *Nursing Homes and the Mentally Ill Elderly*, Task Force Report No. 28 (Washington, D.C.: American Psychiatric Association, 1989), esp. chaps. 3 and 4, pp. 15–42. See also Joel Sadavoy and Barbara Dorian, "Treatment of the Elderly Characterologically Disturbed Patient in the Chronic Care Institution," *Journal of Geriatric Psychiatry* 16 (1983): 223–40.

27. Benjamin Liptzin, "The Geriatric Psychiatrist's Role as Consultant," *Journal of Geriatric Psychiatry* 16 (1983): 112. See also Patricia Chartock, Andrea Nevins, Harriet Rzetelny, and Pasquale Gilberto, "A Mental Health Training Program in Nursing Homes," *The Gerontologist* 28 (1988): 503–07.

28. See, for example, Christine A. Heine, "Burnout among Nursing Home Personnel," *Journal of Gerontological Nursing* 12 (March 1986): 14–18.

29. American Psychiatric Association, *Nursing Homes and the Mentally Ill Elderly*, 43–58. One of the recommendations of the APA Task Force, and of others, is that Congress amend the Medicaid law to establish a new category of nursing care facilities for the mentally ill. Current law precludes Medicaid reimbursement for specialized "psychiatric nursing homes." Regarding the management and finance of such facilities, see Bennett Gurian and Benzion Chanowitz, "Barriers to Implementation of a Public/Private Model Geropsychiatric Nursing Home," *The Gerontologist* 27 (1987): 761–65; idem, "An Empirical Evaluation of Model Geropsychiatric Nursing Home," *The Gerontologist* 27 (1987): 766–72.

Chapter 6

Money Matters

PROSPECTIVE PAYMENT SYSTEMS AND CASE MIX REIMBURSEMENT

Open the daily newspaper at almost any time during the state legislature's budget season or peruse the Sunday magazine section for yet another consideration of "the problem of aging in our society" and a discussion of nursing home economics is likely to appear. The following sequence of fact and opinion is typical.[1]

1. Rising costs and government-imposed limits on spending are combining to cause extreme distress at nursing homes nationwide.

2. The nursing homes in worst shape are those that depend on payments from the federal- and state-financed Medicaid programs for low-income people. Especially hard hit are nursing homes operating in states where Medicaid reimbursement levels are lowest or always in fluctuation.

3. Although nursing home spokespersons blame their distress on the failure of Medicaid reimbursements to keep pace with escalating health care costs, some securities analysts who follow the health care industry say that many for-profit homes are now simply paying the price of having expanded too fast. Burdensome debt, say these analysts, is taxing the ability of many operators to supervise care and manage costs.

4. Whatever its origins, the financial squeeze is causing the quality of care to deteriorate in many nursing homes.

5. One strategy adopted by nursing home operators in response to their financial situation is to restrict the access of Medicaid recipients, whose care is reimbursed by the state government at a fixed rate, and to solicit a higher percentage of residents with private means to pay the going market rate.

6. To accomplish this objective, some homes are giving first preference for available beds to private-pay patients. Others are obtaining Medicaid certification

only for some of their beds, are obliging prospective residents to sign contracts requiring them to pay their own way for months or years before accepting Medicaid benefits, or (where state law permits) are requiring residents to seek care elsewhere when they can no longer pay their own way.

Not so long ago, it was reasonably easy to make money in the nursing home business by servicing Medicaid recipients. There was, to be sure, some obligatory grousing by operators regarding the inequities of a flat-rate reimbursement system, where a single per diem amount was paid by the state for a given class of residents (SNF or ICF) regardless of the mix of needs represented by the institution's population. But the saving grace of the system, from the operators' standpoint, was that reimbursement was predicated wholly or substantially on their individual cost experience. This meant that whatever an institution spent in all of its budget categories—administrative expense per number of beds, depreciation, interest expense, and so on—that amount would eventually be reimbursed by the state, subject only to a yearly audit, varying degrees of haggling over retroactive adjustments, and (depending on the state) some limitations on nursing costs of greater than one standard deviation from the mean.

Under this system of cost-based, retrospective reimbursement, not only was there zero incentive for the nursing home operator to be cost-efficient, but precisely the opposite motivation existed. There was every incentive for the operator to spend money freely—on staff, on physical plant, on ancillary activities—with full expectation that such expenditures, regardless of their effectiveness, efficiency, or justification in terms of enhancing quality of care of the residents, would become part of the future cost basis and thereby serve to *increase* future reimbursements from Medicaid.

So operators nationwide, either by ignorance or by design, paid little attention to internal cost-control systems that might have improved the efficiency of operations in their nursing homes. The artful fiscal strategy was instead to increase costs up to the state's ceiling limits for Medicaid reimbursement. The truly adventurous would purposely exceed those limits by a judicious margin, thereby stimulating a reexamination of Medicaid rates by the state and, very often, occasioning a rate increase. Operators who did this conscientiously, year in and year out, fared very well indeed in the cost-based reimbursement game, quite apart from the level and quality of care they happened to be providing to their residents.[2]

In many states the cost-based, retrospective reimbursement system is now a thing of the past, and in other states it is under extremely close scrutiny.[3] A major change in government pricing of nursing home care has occurred. State policymakers, faced with severe budgetary constraints and a high proportion of Medicaid dollars already consumed by institutional long-term care, are actively seeking some alternative (i.e., less expensive) method for allocating payment to nursing home operators.

Specifically, they are looking at prospective payment systems, that is, methods by which payment rates to nursing homes are determined before the services are provided and any operator funds expended. The premise is that when nursing home operators know in advance the full amount of their Medicaid payment, they will have an incentive, previously lacking, to implement rigorous cost-saving measures.

Many variations on the prospective payment theme have already been instituted by the states or are now in the process of being evaluated in various pilot projects. To understand the thrust of this approach and what it means to LTC administrators and the future of institutional long-term care of the infirm elderly, it is necessary to look at the Medicare experience, first as applied to acute care hospitals, then to SNFs.

Prospective Payment under Medicare

Since 1983, Medicare has mandated a prospective payment system for acute care hospitals, renal dialysis facilities, hospices, and free-standing ambulatory surgery centers. The conceptual underpinning of the system—the basis upon which specific dollar amounts are assigned for particular services rendered—is case mix measurement through diagnosis-related groups (DRGs). Each Medicare patient is classified according to illness into one of 467 illness categories, which serve as predictors of the amount of resources required for an entire episode of care. The hospital receives a preset sum of dollars for treatment of the DRG regardless of the number of "bed days" actually used by the patient.

Without DRGs, the new system would have been formless. All earlier attempts at government-initiated cost control had focused on the individual institution's historic costs, an approach that tended to reward those institutions whose high costs were the result of years of inefficiency. DRGs discarded historical experience as a basis for a hospital's reimbursement. Also, because the system now paid off according to the patient's illness category rather than some amorphous definition of average cost, there was presumably no inherent reward garnered by hospitals caring for healthier (i.e., less costly) patients, nor any penalty suffered by hospitals caring for the very sick.

Prospective payment based on case mix measurement through DRGs was hailed by policymakers as a fair and reasonable means of controlling rising costs while allowing efficient hospitals more flexibility in managing their funds. Be efficient and reap the gain was the new message to hospital administrators. Be lax and suffer the loss was its implied corollary.

Soon after the system was imposed, however, blockages began to appear in the health care delivery pipeline. Hospitals were discharging, or were attempting to discharge, Medicare patients at the end of their DRG-appointed times with the expectation that SNFs would provide any needed continuation of care. But what was the incentive to SNFs to accept the sickest or most dependent of these people, that is, those for whom continued care would be most expensive?

Little incentive existed. Indeed, as was becoming increasingly clear, SNFs were selecting carefully among available Medicare patients, spurning those who required the most intensive nursing care and leaving them "backed up" in hospitals. While the exact size of the problem is difficult to determine, one detailed study of "backup days" in New York City suggests that such discrimination was blatant and that mental illness was an important factor in the denial of access.[4]

Thus, the problem: Limited beneficiary access under Medicare to skilled nursing facilities.

Question asked by policymakers: Can SNFs deliver adequate care to the sickest patients at the going rate?

Consensus of the industry: No, not without case mix reimbursement to make the most dependent patients more attractive to nursing homes.

Not surprisingly, Congress decided to build on the approach that seemed to be a success in acute care, and it quickly expanded the Medicare prospective payment apparatus to include SNFs. Under the terms of the Consolidated Omnibus Budget Reconciliation Act of 1985 (COBRA), an optional prospective payment rate for low-utilization SNFs (those with fewer than 1,500 Medicare patient days) was created, whereby operators might elect to be paid 105 percent of mean operating and capital costs of all Medicare facilities (both hospital-based and free-standing) rather than be paid their actual costs. Separate rates were calculated under COBRA for urban and for rural facilities. Implementation began in 1986.

On the face of it, all of this had very little to do with the financing of long-term care for the infirm elderly. For, as the data clearly show, it was Medicaid, not Medicare, that dominated the revenue flow to the nursing home industry. For example, in 1980, the average Medicare coverage of an SNF stay was 30 days, whereas the average stay for all nursing home patients, including Medicaid recipients, was 456 days. In 1983, the $529 million spent for Medicare SNF benefits represented less than 2 percent of all nursing home expenditures. By comparison, about 31 percent of Medicaid expenditures were for nursing home care (SNF and ICF), and Medicaid dollars accounted for nearly 50 percent of all monies received by nursing homes.[5] Indeed, this 50 percent figure substantially understates the role of Medicaid expenditures in the nursing home industry, because under the law Medicaid recipients had to contribute all but $25 of their monthly income (including Social Security payments) toward the cost of their care, and such contributions were counted as private, out-of-pocket payments.

Yet notwithstanding the relative insignificance of Medicare in financing long-term care for the elderly, a conceptual approach had been set, and state lawmakers began to take note. The problem, as they now understood it, was that nursing home operators, like acute care hospitals before them, lacked the proper incentives to provide needed care in a cost-efficient way. Restructure the payment system, they thought, and quality care under state-financed Medicaid might be achieved at a greatly reduced price.

THE MESSY PROBLEM OF INHERENT INCENTIVES

Cost savings is, of course, a worthy societal goal. But the formalization of a payment system embodying incentives to control costs does not, in itself, ensure humane treatment of the infirm elderly. For how will the cost savings be achieved? By improving efficiencies in all areas of the LTC institution's operation? Fine. By effecting subtle or even gross compromises in the care of the residents? Not so fine.

In any prospective payment system involving case mix measurement—whether the system be based on an individualized accounting of the specialized services provided or on a close and ongoing assessment of resident functionality—two types of inherent incentives exist: (1) incentives inherent in the data collection instrument, and (2) incentives inherent in the structural arrangements by which patient status is converted to price.[6]

Incentives Inherent in the Data Collection Instrument

If the questionnaire used to gather data on residents emphasizes (i.e., gives a "high score" to) mental illness, for example, there exists, at least preliminarily, an inherent incentive to admit and care for those who are emotionally disturbed. The logical assumption of the LTC administrator or nursing home operator, which may or may not prove to be valid, is that a high score will translate into a rate of remuneration substantial enough to warrant the additional expenditure of time, money, and effort. The reverse also holds. If the questionnaire fails to place substantial "value" on diminished mental capacity, there exists no inherent incentive for the institution to admit or care for people with this characteristic.

The reliability of the respondents, the individuals who are assigned the task of filling out the data collection instrument, is also a critical factor, since minor differences in cumulative point count may mean substantial differences in income for an institution. What are the incentives here?

Where outside caseworkers are the respondents, there is an inherent incentive to maximize initial scores in order to ensure placement, and then to maintain high point counts for those institutions that they perceive to be deserving of reward.

Where in-house nursing staff are the respondents, there is an inherent incentive to maximize the scores so that the institution, and perhaps they themselves, may benefit.

Even assuming the highest ethics and very best of intentions among respondents, the questionnaire itself rarely provides the necessary criteria for making crucial distinctions. At what point, for example, does a resident require "special monitoring" of medications? When is a resident's respiratory therapy "complex due to the nature of his or her condition"? Given the absence of uniform definitions, respondents can only apply the standards they are most familiar with, which are likely to be those of the institution for which they work.

Incentives Inherent in the Structural Arrangements by Which Resident Status Is Converted to Price

If, as in the example above, mental illness is given a high score by the data collection instrument, and this score translates directly to a high rate of remuneration, the incentive of the LTC administrator or nursing home operator to admit and care for the mentally ill is reinforced. But if the payment system fails to provide adequate funds for care of emotionally disturbed residents, the inherent incentive to admit and care for the mentally ill is removed, regardless of the scoring values incorporated into the data collection instrument.

Other inherent incentives, more perverse, involve the *changing status* of residents and the *timing* of case mix reassessments. The prospective payment system dictates that when more intensive care is required, the payment to the provider shall be higher. Assuming that the higher level of payment is more than sufficient to compensate the LTC institution for the increased cost of care being given, what happens when a resident's condition improves? Is there some provision in the payment system to reward the institution for a job well done or must it accept a revenue "hit" because the cost of caring for the resident has now decreased?

Such circumstances, as many commentators have noted, can create an inherent incentive for nursing home operators to keep residents dependent, that is, to encourage them *not* to improve. Whether this circumstance is hypothetical or real depends primarily on the speed with which the system adjusts payment downward. If the timing of case mix reassessments is such that a downward adjustment is made at virtually the instant the resident improves, there is in fact no incentive for the LTC administrator or nursing home operator to foster recovery. But if downward adjustment of payment is delayed and the price differential for the care of dependent versus independent residents is great, the inherent incentive is to admit persons who can be rehabilitated quickly so that the institution can collect the higher rate while providing care at a reduced cost.

As the foregoing discussion indicates, the permutations of self-interest in the long-term care of the infirm elderly are extremely difficult to define, much less systematize, much less regulate. Although perverse incentives exist under any case mix measurement system, they are especially malign when the basis for differentiating levels of care consists of the services provided. Such services include

- appliances
- catheterization
- decubitus care
- diets
- douche or enema
- dressings
- injections
- intravenous medication
- laboratory or specimen services
- medication monitoring
- occupational rehabilitation
- ostomy care
- physical rehabilitation
- respiratory therapy
- restorative nursing
- social rehabilitation
- special health monitoring
- suctioning or posturing
- tube feeding

The introduction of any of these services can be valuable, or irrelevant, or wasteful, or dangerous, depending on the individual circumstances of the person receiving them. But because of the way prospective payment by case mix measurement is structured (i.e., the more intensive the care required by the resident, the higher the payment collected by the provider), a perverse incentive always exists for the LTC institution to do more procedures than are necessary, or to do them badly.

Examples abound.

- A resident with major behavioral problems may be causing staff a great deal of anxiety and disrupting the lives of other residents on the unit. Heavy medication is an immediate and likely response in most LTC institutions, and it would probably result in an added payment to the provider. But a more reasonable approach from the standpoint of quality of life of the resident, as well as quality of care, is for staff to react differently to the person in some programmatic way and thereby to modify and control the excessive behavior.

- An indwelling urinary catheter is uncomfortable, creates increased risk of infection, and discourages ambulation. Installing a catheter in a resident who suffers from chronic incontinence, absent any effort by the nursing staff to implement a bladder control program or to develop other noninvasive modalities of care, is a cost-effective but inhumane solution.
- The changing of dressings takes time and therefore costs money. When done two or three times a day (or more if needed), it is the essence of good nursing by caring people. However, when done less often than necessary for the sake of economy but submitted nonetheless as a service justifying Medicaid reimbursement, it is a cynical perversion of the health care delivery system.

FUNCTIONALITY AS A CASE MIX MEASUREMENT TOOL

In the long-term care setting, lengths of stay, and therefore episode costs, are extremely variable. It is hardly unusual for an LTC institution to admit to residency on a single day two people with ostensibly the same medical condition and to find one of them deceased within a month and the other functioning well within the limitations of his or her condition five years later.

Far more important than medical diagnosis, therefore, in predicting resource consumption and related costs is limitation on activities of daily living. Resident functionality—defined by feeding, ambulation, dressing, continence, and so on— is the major determinant of the need for and cost of long-term care.[7]

To the reader who has come this far, that the authors hold this opinion should not be news. The entire HRCA functional assessment patterning system, for example, with its various classifications and subclassifications and extensive definitions of resident functionality, is predicated on the belief that how residents behave and what residents can or cannot do for themselves are key to the proper organization of long-term care services. What is important to note here, however, is that the various state Medicaid systems are coming to share this same perspective, although slowly and for their own set of reasons.

This is not to imply that any payment system based on resident dependency rather than on service characteristics will be problem-free. The greatest drawback of dependency-based pricing has already been mentioned, namely, that nursing home operators may be encouraged by the system not only to admit very dependent persons but to keep them dependent. The unhappy results would be felt throughout the health care delivery system: restricted access, inefficient use of beds, and less than optimal care.

In response to this perceived problem, a limited experiment in Medicaid reimbursement was tried some years ago in San Diego, California.[8] Thirty-six proprietary SNFs volunteered to participate, with the program to be supervised by the California Department of Health Services. There were four key elements in the program design.

1. Nursing homes would be given incentive payments for admitting severely dependent patients (i.e., those who required more than average care). Dependency would be measured by the need for nursing assistance in performing basic activities of daily living and for other unusual or costly nursing care services.

2. Nursing homes would be given incentive payments for discharging in a timely fashion those patients who were no longer in need of skilled nursing care. To discourage abuse of the incentive system and to encourage postdischarge support of each patient, the payment would be made only if the patient remained at the lower level of care or in the community for at least three months. The payment was intended to reimburse the institution for staff time expended in designing and implementing a discharge plan and for support, backup, monitoring, and other case management functions provided to the discharged patient. No payment would be given if an independent assessment showed the discharge to be inappropriate.

3. Nursing homes would be given incentive payments for achieving specified outcome goals in the case of selected patients who required special care to improve or maintain their functional or health status. If a patient required several types of special care, payments would be made for each outcome achieved.

4. No incentive payments would be given for patients expected to remain in residence less than 90 days or for those whose maintenance or rehabilitative care needs were judged routine.

Although the experimental reimbursement system incorporated some useful features, it was generally agreed that several conceptual difficulties remained.

First, there was no guarantee that the recovery bonus paid to the institution was sufficient to cover its costs, and therefore there was no certainty that an incentive to foster recovery actually existed or that it existed for all residents in all circumstances.

Second, if the recovery bonus was small compared to actual rehabilitative costs, the institution might be encouraged to expend resources only on those residents who were likely both to recover and to remain in residence for an extended period of time postrecovery. Rehabilitation of a resident who had a terminal illness or who appeared likely to have a new stroke or heart attack would be discouraged.

Third, a desire to retain bonus-paying residents might encourage the institution to defer needed hospitalization.

Even if these conceptual difficulties were resolved in an instant, the overriding problem would remain: The state would eventually perceive the open-ended bonus system as a needless extravagance and would balk at having to compensate

SNFs for services not rendered. Nursing home operators, in their turn, sensing the impermanence of the reimbursement arrangements, would opt to maximize their short-term profitability, a fiscal strategy not necessarily consistent with the best interests of the infirm elderly in their care.[9]

Yet despite the inherent conceptual difficulties, there is much to recommend case mix measurement of resident functionality as the basis for Medicaid prospective payment. It is certainly a more valid representation of the universe of long-term care than case mix measurement by service characteristics, where every service provided must be itemized. When payment is based on resident functionality, state auditors need not rely exclusively on lengthy and time-consuming examination of resident records for information but might instead observe residents (or, in larger institutions, samples of residents) directly in order to verify reports of dependence. Because the activities of daily living being audited are relatively simple to identify, a single trained observer could score a number of residents in a relatively short time.

Also, as compared with a Medicaid payment system based on service characteristics, case mix measurement of resident functionality has the virtue of being far more difficult to "game." The activities that constitute the focus of the audit cannot be readily altered by the LTC institution or its staff on short notice. It is no easy task, for example, to convince an elderly resident who usually eats independently to submit to hand feeding on the day the inspectors arrive. The use of surprise inspections for scoring purposes could ensure that institutions do not increase staff, and therefore the appearance of dependency, at the time of scoring.

FUNCTIONAL CLASSIFICATION OF RESIDENTS FOR PURPOSES OF MEDICAID PAYMENT: THE EXAMPLE OF RUG-II

Far beyond the stage of experimentation is the resident classification system for prospective payment known as resource utilization groups, version II (RUG-II). Based on a study of 3,427 nursing homes in New York State conducted some years ago, it is currently being used to set Medicaid payment rates for all nursing homes in New York.[10]

The first step in devising the RUG-II classification system was to create a measure of resident functionality that would represent all activities of daily living (ADL). Toileting, eating, and transfer were selected because these activities were clinically judged to measure both small and large motor skills as well as mental and physical functioning.

Each activity was defined according to level of functionality, and an ADL score was assigned.

RUG-II Activities of Daily Living Index

Activity	Resident Functioning Level	ADL Score
Toileting	Independent or minimal supervision and/or physical assistance.	1
	Continuous supervision and/or physical assistance, or total assistance or incontinent, does not use toilet.	2
	Incontinent, taken to toilet on a regular schedule.	3
Eating	Independent or minimal supervision and/or physical assistance.	1
	Continuous supervision and/or physical assistance.	2
	Hand fed.	3
	Tube or parenteral feeding.	4
Transfer	Independent or minimal supervision and/or physical assistance.	1
	Continuous supervision or continuous physical assistance of one person.	2
	Continuous physical assistance of two persons or bedfast.	3

Then, the level-of-functionality scores for the activities were added together to form the RUG-II ADL index number.

$$\text{ADL Index} = \text{Toileting} + \text{Eating} + \text{Transfer}$$

For example, a resident who needs total assistance in toileting, continuous supervision in eating, and the physical assistance of one person while transferring would have an ADL index of 6 (2 + 2 + 2).

The second step in devising the RUG-II classification system was to create a hierarchy of resident types representing the range of persons typically cared for in SNFs and ICFs. Five major categories were defined:

1. *Heavy rehabilitation.* Residents who receive heavy, daily physical or occupational therapy services with a treatment goal of restoration of functioning.

2. *Special care.* Very heavy care residents, often with extremely low levels of functionality, who have particular serious conditions (e.g., coma or quadriplegia) that primarily determine their care needs.

3. *Clinically complex.* Residents with particular medical or skilled nursing problems (e.g., hemiplegia, dehydration, a terminal illness) or otherwise extensive medical needs (as a group, these residents are not as functionally impaired in ADL as the special care group).

4. *Severe behavioral problems.* Residents who experience frequently and severely one or more of four behavioral problems: physical aggression, regression, verbal abuse, and hallucinations.

5. *Reduced physical function.* All residents who do not qualify for any of the above four groups (they are principally characterized by reduced ADL functioning).

These five categories were ranked, in the order shown, according to cost of care. A resident might qualify for inclusion in more than one category, but for purposes of Medicaid payment he or she would be assigned to the category that was most resource-intensive. A resident whose characteristics do not fit the definitions of any of the four highest groups would, by default, be assigned to the fifth (reduced physical function) group, which has the largest population.

The third step in devising the RUG-II classification system was to integrate the ADL index and the hierarchy of resident types. Using the ADL index range (3–10) to subclassify each hierarchic category, 16 resource utilization groups were defined.

Resource Utilization Groups	*ADL Index*
Heavy rehabilitation-A	3–4
Heavy rehabilitation-B	5–10
Special care-A	5–7
Special care-B	8–10
Clinically complex-A	3
Clinically complex-B	4–6
Clinically complex-C	7–8
Clinically complex-D	9
Severe behavioral-A	3
Severe behavioral-B	4–7
Severe behavioral-C	8–9
Reduced physical-A	3
Reduced physical-B	4
Reduced physical-C	5–7
Reduced physical-D	8
Reduced physical-E	9

The RUG-II case mix payment schedule was designed around these 16 resource utilization groups. A severe behavioral-C resident, for example, would warrant a given number of dollars per day of care; a heavy rehabilitation-B resident would be more costly; a severe behavioral-A resident, less costly.

The RUG-II classification system and similar approaches to case mix measurement used in other states attempt to create a useful taxonomy of nursing home residents so that prospective payment for services rendered can be effected on a fair and reasonable basis. Allegedly, there is also a collateral benefit, namely, that such systems provide state regulators with internal mechanisms for monitoring quality of care. According to the architects of the RUG-II system,

> A case-mix measurement system provides a powerful data system that can be used to assist in monitoring the quality of care in a nursing home. Resident assessment or billing systems contain data that can be used to track automatically outcomes for the residents. We have found that the RUG-II system and the individual items that define it provide useful measures of quality of care. A facility, while providing documentation for payment purposes, at the same time provides data usable by a quality assurance system to monitor outcome performance on both a resident-specific and an aggregate level. Such dual use puts nursing homes at risk if they over-report case-mix criteria (at the risk of indicating inappropriate care) or they under-report quality problems (at the risk of losing reimbursement). The development of a monitoring system can include many types of review: aggregate case-mix index changes at the facility level; longitudinal outcomes at the case-mix group level; longitudinal outcomes at the resident-specific level; and incidence of poor outcomes.[11]

The image of sharp-eyed auditors using system data generated by high-speed computers to corroborate the accuracy of claims and to track patient outcomes may be comforting to the regulators and terrifying to the outlaws, but it is also troubling to LTC administrators who believe deeply that rigorous quality standards, to be valid, should be internally driven, not externally imposed.[12]

As a necessary condition for continuous quality improvement, there must be a clear understanding by management of what is truly important to the various constituencies serviced by the LTC institution—the infirm elderly who are residents and those who are waiting for admission, the families, the employees, the community at large. The processes by which quality care is delivered by the institution to its residents must be rationalized down to the smallest level of detail, then monitored, then reevaluated, then restructured as necessary on a planned and ongoing basis. Every process must have a feedback loop built in so that the question "How are we doing?" can be answered quickly, accurately, and succinctly. Also, when feedback from various internal and external constituencies, including regulators, suggests the need for modifications or improvements, they should be considered, tested, and, if found worthy, integrated into the process flow as quickly as possible.

The delivery of quality long-term care to the infirm elderly is, therefore, more than a problem in regulatory politics. It is a problem in management. To the extent the regulatory system is part of the LTC institution's constituent mix, its point of view must be given full consideration. But as a force for change it is simply one among many, its wisdom is not necessarily preeminent, nor is its power absolute.

RUNNING THE LTC INSTITUTION IN A BUSINESSLIKE WAY

Prospective payment based on case mix measurement creates a whole new set of fiscal imperatives for the LTC administrator. When the case mix data indicate that an institution is entitled to a given number of Medicaid dollars under the state's prospective payment schedule, that amount is all it will receive. The Medicaid system can no longer be relied upon to indemnify the institution against the cumulative effects of ill-considered investment strategies, unwarranted expansion, or poorly managed operations. It is essential, therefore, to do the following:

- Project Medicaid revenues very carefully.
- Pay extremely close attention to the institution's operating costs.
- Install control systems and automated data processing to track the changing case mix, so as to be able to document any requests for additional Medicaid monies.

In short, it is necessary to run any LTC institution in a businesslike way. Whether the institution is chartered for-profit or nonprofit, it must function as a business or it will likely not survive.

For many LTC administrators, indeed for many nonfinancial managers in other kinds of organizations, an excursion into the seemingly mysterious world of financial planning is cause for anxiety. Perhaps it is the fear of the unknown. Perhaps it is the fear of losing control to the financial manager.

Yet the LTC administrator, who typically has little grounding in finance, can no longer avoid the fiscal imperatives of nursing home management and so must confront the relevant financial data head on. Profit statements, operating budgets, and project analyses have become an essential part of the working day, for without timely, useful, and understandable information, it would be impossible to make well-considered strategic decisions and to run the firm efficiently.[13]

There is a cart-before-the-horse problem lurking here, however. Every institution or organization has an ongoing crisis of identity. Who are we? What is our purpose? How can we accomplish that purpose while remaining true to our deepest held beliefs and most cherished self-image? Accommodating to change without becoming faceless or irrelevant is the hardest single task of management, and it requires constant strategic appraisal, of which financial analysis is an important part.

But while the institution's purpose—its statement of mission—is not necessarily etched in stone, forever immutable, neither is it scribbled on tissue. When the time comes, as it does each year, to create a financial plan for the 12 months upcoming, the individuals participating in the planning exercise are obligated to endorse the articulated values of the enterprise and not subvert them. Any institution whose reason for being is constantly compromised for the sake of what is perceived to be current fiscal reality will not long survive, or if it does, it will have become something other than what it was or what it wants to be.

For instance, if an LTC institution's reason for being is to provide quality care to extremely debilitated residents supported by Medicaid, the object of the financial planning exercise should be to find a way to validate that purpose. It may necessitate raising prices to private-pay residents, implementing cost-saving measures on the expense side of the ledger, or identifying noncritical areas of the operation that could be reduced or eliminated without impacting quality of care or the institution's future. Whatever it takes, the imperative is to find a way—or be prepared to admit that the mission of the institution is ill conceived and must be redefined.

In this context, the responsibility of the financial planners is to provide tools for monitoring, predicting, and understanding the fiscal consequences of managerial decisions and strategic options. The reports they generate—written and verbal, scheduled and impromptu—inform the LTC administrator of what is happening (e.g., receivables are soaring and vendors are worrying about payment), what has happened (e.g., cash flow has exceeded expectations and decisions must be made on where to invest the surplus), and what might happen (e.g., what will be the impact on private-pay residents of a pricing policy change from the present all-inclusive rate to a lower base rate plus additional charges for any "extra" services provided).

To take full advantage of such skills, the LTC administrator must provide the controller, accountant, or vice president of finance with a reasonable set of expectations, saying in effect, "This is what I need to know and this is when I need to know it." The mechanism that structures such inquiry and invariably leads to the asking of more and more incisive questions is the budget.

Budgets and Budgeting

A budget is a financial planning document. Its existence, indeed the very process of creating it, yields several important benefits.

A budget states goals. Without a statement of what the institution wants to achieve, written down and expressed quantitatively, there is every expectation that over time people will misconceive the institution's destination and begin to work at cross-purposes.

A budget measures progress. Without knowing the destination of the institution, it is difficult to know when, or if, that destination has been reached.

A budget stimulates thought. When staff are asked to make plans in advance, potential problems will yield to analysis more readily than they might at some later time, when the rush of events has seemingly limited the range of available options.

A budget encourages communication. Even a great plan can be put into action only if others in the institution "buy" into it. The very process of creating a budget helps to focus everyone's attention on what needs to be done and thereby builds consensus.

The "master" budget document for a long-term care institution of any size or type is generally divided into two sections: an operating budget and a capital budget. Each is discussed below.

The Operating Budget.

The operating budget provides all the information necessary to prepare a budgeted income statement. It includes (1) revenue projections, (2) operating expense projections, and (3) interest cost projections.

Revenue projections. These are estimates of income from all sources (i.e., resident room and board, reimbursed ancillary charges, other investments, etc.). The data, as presented, might look like this:

Source of Income	*Projected Revenue*
Resident room and board	$ 4,013,421
Reimbursed ancillary charges	112,392
Other	121,712
Total	$ 4,247,525

Yet when presented in this form, the data are not very useful for planning purposes. Several important questions remain unanswered: Where is the money coming from? How efficiently is capacity being utilized?

For some LTC institutions, income from room and board will derive from private payers only. For others, the sole source of revenue will be public funds in the form of Medicare or Medicaid. For still other institutions, monies will be received from both private and public sources. Therefore, in order to gauge whether the income projection of $4,247,525 (in the example above) is close to being accurate and to assess whether any strategic changes in resident case mix are warranted, it is helpful to prepare a capacity utilization estimate of "occupancy bed days" by category of payer. Using a hypothetical 145-bed institution servicing both private-pay and public-aided elderly residents as an example, the occupancy bed days estimate might look like this:

Occupancy Bed Days Projected

Private (15 beds allocated)	5,386
Public aided (130 beds allocated)	45,831
Projected occupied	51,217
Beds available yearly	52,925
Projected percent of capacity occupied	96.8%

With occupancy bed days for the upcoming year estimated, the income projection can now be expressed not only in gross dollar amounts ($4,247,525, as above) but also in per diem dollars. Doing so grounds the numbers in the reality of daily operations and facilitates comparisons with the actual performance of previous years.

Thus, for the 145-bed institution in the example, the statement of projected revenue in gross dollars and per diem dollars would look like this:

Projected Revenue

	Amount	Per Diem
Resident room and board		
Private (5,386 bed days)	$ 727,110	$135.00
Public (45,831 bed days)	3,286,311	71.70
	4,013,421	78.36
Reimbursed ancillary charges	112,392	2.19
Other	121,712	2.38
Total	$4,247,525	$82.93

With the data presented in this way, the LTC administrator can see at a glance that the projected resident mix, private versus public, will yield $78.36 per diem in room and board revenue and $82.93 per diem from all income sources. Is this sufficient revenue to operate the institution for the upcoming year? Obviously, a confident yes or no depends upon operating expense projections yet to be done. But the revenue projection formatted in this manner does encourage the asking of some important, preliminary what-if questions.

What if the number of beds allocated to private-pay residents was increased from 15 to 30? Would the institution be able to fill them or would capacity utilization decline dramatically?

What if the institution accepted heavier care residents at a higher per diem rate under the state's Medicaid prospective payment plan? Could it service that clientele economically and without compromising established quality standards?

What if the institution expanded its facilities and added 55 beds? Would local market conditions justify such an investment now or at some later date? What would be the payback assuming the current case mix and a projected 96.8 percent occupancy rate? Assuming a 75 percent occupancy rate? A 60 percent occupancy rate? Could an expanded facility be staffed adequately given the local labor market? What would be the short-term and long-term impact on quality of care?

These are incisive questions to be sure, requiring lots of thought, further statistical analysis, and input from every department in the organization. But it is precisely this sort of strategic inquiry that the budgeting exercise is designed to encourage.

Operating expense projections. There are estimates of all expenses to be incurred in the daily operation of the institution for the upcoming year. The numbers are provided by the various department heads working in conjunction with their own staff. Each department's operating budget is submitted to the financial planning person (or group), who verifies the accuracy and reliability of the data. When all departmental budgets have been submitted and checked, they are assembled into one document and delivered to the LTC administrator for review. Pointed dialogue between the LTC administrator and department heads regarding their budgets invariably follows.

To facilitate comparison with previous years' data, it is generally useful to state each projected expense item not only in gross dollars but also in dollars per diem of projected occupancy. Thus, for the institution in the example, the categories and budgeted amounts might look like this:

Projected Expenses

	Amount	Per Diem
Administrative and general		
Salary, administrative	$ 65,777	$ 1.28
Salary, officers	148,648	2.90

Salary, office staff	105,139	2.05
Management fees	261,558	5.11
Office supplies	16,574	.32
License and dues	6,733	.13
Telephone	15,022	.29
Travel and auto expense	11,394	.22
Advertising	34,184	.67
Employee benefits	91,675	1.79
Accounting	6,682	.13
Legal services	13,762	.27
Payroll taxes	139,896	2.73
Insurance	188,528	3.68
Bad debt	6,502	.13
Refunds and allowances	9,952	.20
Other taxes	22,272	.44
Total	$ 1,144,298	$ 22.34
Property expenses		
Rent	256,000	5.00
Depreciation	11,776	.23
Total	$ 267,776	$ 5.23
Plant operations		
Salaries	94,264	1.81
Utilities	99,443	1.94
Supplies	19,682	.38
Repairs	24,861	.49
Total	$ 238,250	$ 4.65
Dietary		
Salaries	285,901	5.58
Food	180,242	3.52
Supplies	26,414	.52
Total	$ 492,557	$ 9.62
Laundry and linen		
Salaries	56,455	1.10
Purchased services	28,486	.56
Linen	11,395	.22
Supplies	12,430	.24
Total	$ 108,766	$ 2.12

Housekeeping		
Salaries	178,688	3.49
Supplies	17,091	.33
Total	$ 195,779	$ 3.82
Nursing		
R.N. salaries	368,304	7.19
L.P.N. salaries	252,235	4.93
Other nursing salaries	405,629	7.92
Total	$ 1,026,168	$ 20.04
Pharmacy and medical services		
Supplies and drugs	116,016	2.27
Physicians' services	48,174	.94
Pharmacist	3,108	.06
Total	$ 167,298	$ 3.27
Recreation and rehabilitation		
Physical therapist salaries	296,644	5.79
Occupational therapist salaries	63,318	1.24
Total	$ 359,962	$ 7.03
Total operating expenses	$ 4,000,854	$ 78.12

Interest cost projections. These are estimates of all financing (interest cost) expenses to be incurred in the upcoming year. This includes all monies required to service current debt, pay interest due on resident escrow funds, and meet any other short-term financial obligations that may exist.

The revenue projections, the operating expense projections, and the interest cost projections are combined into a projected income statement, which for the 145-bed institution in the example would look like this:

Projected Income

	Amount	Per Diem
Income		
Resident room and board	$ 4,013,421	$ 78.36
Reimbursed ancillary charges	112,392	2.19
Other	121,712	2.38
Total	$ 4,247,525	$ 82.93

Operating expenses		
Administrative and general	1,144,298	22.34
Property expenses	267,776	5.23
Plant operations	238,250	4.65
Dietary	492,557	9.62
Laundry and linen	108,766	2.12
Housekeeping	195,779	3.82
Nursing	1,026,168	20.04
Pharmacy and medical services	167,298	3.27
Recreation and rehabilitation	359,962	7.03
Total	$ 4,000,854	$ 78.12
Interest		
Furniture, fixtures, and equipment	18,646	.36
Resident escrow funds	932	.02
Total	$ 19,578	$ .38
Projected income before taxes	$ 227,093	$ 4.43

The plan for the upcoming year is now taking shape. Projected income before taxes for the year is $227,093, or $4.43 per diem, at the projected occupancy of 51,217 bed days. But important questions still remain:

- Is this level of financial performance (assuming the validity of the projections) consistent with the institution's strategic objectives, its implicit trade-off between risk and reward?
- Is this level of financial performance compatible with the institution's long-term prospects? Or is short-term profitability being sought at the expense of organizational vitality, important services, or other measures of resident quality of life?
- Are the values of the organization—its reason for being as part of the community's health care delivery system—being fully supported by the financial plan?

If the answers to these questions satisfy the LTC administrator or the executive management of the institution (i.e., its parent corporation or board of trustees), the statement of projected income is done. But if problem areas are exposed, the plan must be reworked, and if necessary reworked again, until it becomes a reasonable reflection of the strategy, goals, and aspirations of the institution and the people who work there.

The Capital Budget

The capital budget is a summary of all capital projects or equipment purchases the LTC institution is considering for the upcoming year. Each department (building and maintenance, food services, nursing, social services, therapy departments, administration, etc.) must submit its own set of requests, with each line item accompanied by a cost justification or explanation of need.

A typical capital budget proposal from the nursing department might look like this:

Item Requested	Cost ($)	Justification
Recliners (8)	3,725	Replacement of 2 on Pattern II units; additional 6 on Pattern III units to increase resident comfort and improve group interaction.
Chair scale	450	Facilitate weighing of Pattern III residents.
Water mattresses (10)	2,600	Reduce incidence of bed sores on Pattern III.
Infection control cart	450	Improve efficiency in controlling infection.
Word processors (2)	2,400	For use on Patterns I and II to facilitate timely preparation of reports, etc.

The capital budget "wish list" for each department is submitted to the LTC administrator for review. Dialogue with the various department managers follows, during which the usual questions are asked: "Why do we need it?" "Does the benefit to be derived justify the cost?" The LTC administrator informs the department managers, as soon as deliberations are completed, which of their requests have been approved or denied and why.

Forecasting

Before the various budgets that make up the planning document can be finalized, a set of assumptions (or forecasts) must be articulated. This involves asking and answering various crystal-ball type questions. Typically, they include the following:

- What will the rate of inflation be in the coming year?
- Are we fully competitive in price and value with the rate being charged by the competition?
- Do we anticipate that the competition will alter its pricing structure in the coming year?
- How would such changes impact our market position?
- Will key suppliers be raising their prices in the coming year?
- Are there going to be significant shifts in elderly demographics, such as those resulting from influxes of population or changing neighborhoods, that will impact local demand for our services?
- What will be the effect on operations of any forthcoming changes in federal or state law or the regulatory structure?

The institution's best response to these questions may be simply to assume that what happened last year will happen again next year. Or the response may be grounded in complex formulae or calculations that embrace (or purport to embrace) all relevant historical trends and patterns. The nub of the problem, of course, is to discern what is going to happen that will make the future different from the past, and by how much—a task that is always difficult and often impossible.

Nevertheless, assumptions (i.e., best guesses) must be made and then communicated directly to everyone involved in the planning process. Without shared knowledge of the premises underlying the exercise, the departments will invariably impose their own perceptions of the world not yet seen, and commonality of purpose will be lost.

Ultimately, however, the LTC administrator must sit down with the various budgets that have been delivered, place projected expenses and projected revenue side by side, and ask the question, "Is this acceptable?" Perhaps the final decision will be the LTC administrator's alone. Or perhaps it will be in the hands of the board of directors.

In either instance, and regardless of whether the institution is chartered for-profit or is supported by charitable contributions, the silent imperatives of financial viability apply: There must be enough cash flow to meet *near-term* obligations (i.e., to cover all operating expenses for the coming year). There must also be enough cash generation potential to meet *long-term* obligations (i.e., to cover payments to reserves for replacement of property, plant, and equipment three, five, and ten years hence).

If the LTC institution is financially viable, good things—socially important and useful things—can happen. If it is not, it will eventually cease to exist, and any contribution to society it might have made will be lost.

Managerial Control through the Use of Variances

Variances are what happens when reality impinges upon budget projections. They are the measured differences between actual results and budgeted amounts at a fixed point in time.

Few things in life are more certain than variances, for no budget ever written has proved to be accurate in every detail. When brought to the LTC administrator's attention in a timely fashion, a variance analysis can provide important insight into how things are going.

Yet there is also a great potential danger here, depending upon how the LTC administrator chooses to regard the data. Numbers are, after all, dumb. They are ignorant of context, which must be supplied by the person looking at them. "Bad news" in the form of negative variances may not be material. "Good news" in the form of positive variances may be unworthy of celebration. But because the data are so available, spewed out by lightning-fast computers and high-speed printers, there is a tendency to become transfixed by them and, therefore, to ascribe to individual sets of numbers an importance that they do not deserve. "Paralysis by analysis" some have called it.

What, then, is important? There is no specific answer that can be given, since so much depends upon the scale of the operation. For some LTC institutions, a $2,000 variance on a budget item is cause for concern. For others, it merits only a passing glance. Nevertheless, in all instances, the Pareto 80-20 rule holds sway: The top 20 percent of items in any list (whether expenses, processes, products, or whatever) invariably yield 80 percent of the results.

For example, in any LTC institution of whatever size, three budget categories—labor (including the total benefits package), food, and utilities—usually are responsible for 80 percent of the operating costs. A first sweep through the variance report, therefore, should focus primarily on these three categories.

Then, within each category, the 80-20 rule should again be applied. Regarding food, for example, if 80 percent of costs are in meat, fish, and poultry, those areas will merit more scrutiny than payments made for condiments or carrots. Further analysis might reveal, for example, that meat expenses are growing disproportionately on a per capita or per diem basis.

At this point, some specific questions can be asked: Is the discrepancy (in meat costs, or whatever) a blip or a trend? Track the discrepant items over time, both backwards and forwards. If the discrepancy is a blip, is the situation expected to stabilize or is today's aberrant behavior likely to become tomorrow's norm? If it is a trend, what can be done to reverse it?

When the discrepant budget items are commodities, the cost control solution may lie in smarter purchasing (e.g., larger quantities, different sources, reasonable substitutes, or cooperative ventures with other institutions in the area).[14] Or perhaps the situation points to some needed capital investment (e.g., a more fuel-efficient boiler if fuel costs seem likely to soar in the foreseeable future).

Or perhaps the difficulty (e.g., a highly restrictive local labor market, which is throwing nursing costs far above budgeted expectations) is beyond the institution's control, requiring compensatory belt-tightening elsewhere, raising prices to private-pay residents, or adjusting profitability goals.

The role of the LTC administrator is not only to apply the 80-20 rule to variance analysis but, even more important, to teach staff to think in these terms. Some years ago at HRCA, for example, laundry costs had ramped sharply upward to a point where they were clearly out of control. Preliminary investigation showed that the number of pounds of laundry being produced and sent down the chutes was far greater than had ever been experienced, though the total number of residents remained the same. The response of the laundry manager was quite predictable: "I need more people and more equipment to handle the increased load."

If the increase in poundage was directly related to quality of care—the result of a more debilitated resident population needing fresh bedding or clothing more often—the added expense of laundry operations would have been acceptable. But investigation revealed the cause of the problem to be a change in nursing practice, not residents' needs. Specifically, as a result of new nursing supervisors coming onto the units, aides had begun the practice of stripping beds entirely and replacing both sheets at once rather than rotating the top sheet to the bottom as had always been done. That change in procedure nearly doubled the poundage produced by the unit and accounted for the increased burden on laundry operations.

Management quickly brought the lesson home to the nursing staff: "Think of the impact of what you are doing on others whom you do not see. When you do not properly manage your supplies, for example, the costs do not vanish. They are simply transferred to others within the organization, whose immediate solutions may be more expensive than we, as an institution, can bear."

The LTC administrator can maintain focus on key areas of the operation by receiving from fiscal services a monthly financial update. This report, which should be concise and written in simple language, ought to provide at a minimum the following information:

- Total number of occupancy bed days year to date, percentage of capacity occupied, and variances from budget projections (significant variances, either plus or minus, should be explained).
- Total revenue year to date, and variances against budget projections (significant variances, either plus or minus, should be explained).
- Detail on major expense items (salaries and wages, food, utilities, etc.) expressed in gross dollars, per diem dollars, and as variances against budget projections (significant variances, either plus or minus, should be explained).

- The institution's year-to-date position (revenues versus expenses) and the current view of year-end performance against budget.

The report should be refined over several months so that it becomes a working tool, alerting the LTC administrator, management staff, and board of directors to any situations that must be addressed.

Ratio Analysis

The question "How are we doing?" can be answered in many ways. Qualitatively speaking, if resident services are meeting the quality standards of the institution and the community, if the mortgage or rent is being paid, if working capital is adequate, if employees feel well remunerated, and if the proprietor or board of directors is pleased, then everything is all right.

The state of the institution can also be quickly assessed from a more quantitative perspective. This is often done through ratio analysis (i.e., the comparison of numbers taken from financial statements).

Ratios do not explain, they assess. By juxtaposing two unlike values, they encourage the person looking at them to make a determination as to their proper relationship. Either the comparison is felicitous and at the moment nothing more needs to be done, or a problem is signaled and the underlying causes need to be investigated.

Two ratios are discussed here: liquidity ratios and solvency ratios.

Liquidity Ratios

Liquidity ratios can be used to assess whether a firm is maintaining an appropriate level of liquidity. Too little liquidity raises the possibility of default and bankruptcy. Too much implies that long-term investments with superior profitability potential have been missed.

One liquidity ratio that is useful to controllers in the nursing home industry is the *quick ratio*, also called the *acid test*. In this ratio, current assets quickly convertible to cash are compared to current liabilities:

$$\text{Quick Ratio} = \frac{\text{Cash} + \text{Marketable Securities} + \text{Receivables}}{\text{Current Liabilities}}$$

Generally, an LTC institution's quick ratio should be 1 or more. If the ratio falls much below 1, the firm may soon experience some difficulty paying its bills. But beware of leaping to conclusions, for the drawing of a single quick ratio does not tell the whole story. Far more important is the trend revealed over time. If month after month the institution's quick ratio has ranged between 1.1 and 1.4 and suddenly it drops to 0.6, that may signal a problem. Or perhaps it is an aberration for which there is a reasonable explanation. The point is, ratio analysis is useful in pointing out areas for follow-up inquiry. It is never, in itself, conclusive.

Solvency Ratios

Solvency ratios can be used to obtain a longer-term view of financial viability. They indicate whether a firm has principal and interest payment obligations exceeding its ability to pay, not only now but into the future as well.

One solvency ratio frequently used in the nursing home industry is the *interest coverage ratio*. It compares profit before interest and taxes to the total amount of interest that has to be paid:

$$\text{Interest Coverage} = \frac{\text{Profit before Interest and Taxes}}{\text{Interest Expense}}$$

As long as the firm's profit before interest and taxes is greater than its interest expense, there will be enough money to pay the interest owed. Obviously, the higher this ratio is, the more comfortable the creditors will feel. But from the firm's perspective, once its tax and interest obligations are paid, a high interest coverage ratio may not be desirable.

It all depends upon the ownership's attitude toward risk and reward. If the intention is to be highly leveraged, a high interest coverage ratio indicates the firm could have paid out higher dividends and financed more of its expansion through increased borrowing. But such a strategy, which maximizes rate of return to the owners, also increases their exposure in the event of a downturn in the firm's profitability.

What is an acceptable level of debt relative to equity? What level of interest payments can be considered reasonably safe? In the nursing home industry, where firms typically experience minimal fluctuations in revenues and earnings, the purposeful incurring of debt is generally a safer strategy than in industries where great swings in profitability are the rule. But every firm must, at last, make this decision for itself, and what is comfortable for one set of owners or directors is not necessarily appropriate for another.

None of the foregoing discussion about the need to run the LTC institution in a businesslike way is intended to make the LTC administrator into an expert on financial management. That is why an accountant or a controller or a vice president of finance is on staff or on call. But the LTC administrator should at least have a cursory understanding of how financial managers perceive the world and, more important, how to elicit their special knowledge in order to make the institution better managed. The LTC administrator may not understand everything a financial manager does, but a common frame of reference is a good starting place for useful communication.

NOTES

1. See, for example, "Nursing Homes Face Pressures That Imperil Care for Elderly," *New York Times*, May 28, 1988, 1; Lynn Wagner, "Nursing Homes Buffeted by Troubles," *Modern Healthcare*, March 18, 1988, 33–42; "Welfare for the Middle Class?" *Boston Globe*, January 14, 1990, 73.

2. On nursing home expenditures as a target of state cost-containment efforts, see Charlene Harrington and James H. Swan, "Medicaid Nursing Home Reimbursement Policies, Rates, and Expenditures," *Health Care Financing Review* 6 (Fall 1984): 39–49.

3. Robert J. Buchanan, "Medicaid Reimbursement of Long-Term Care: A Survey of 1986 State Policies," *Journal of Long-Term Care Administration* 15 (Winter 1987): 19–27.

4. Peter W. Shaughnessy and Andrew M. Kramer, "The Increased Needs of Patients in Nursing Homes and Patients Receiving Home Health Care," *New England Journal of Medicine* 322 (1990): 21–27; New York County Health Services Review Organization, *Nursing Home Bed Shortage: Myth or Reality* (New York: New York County Health Services Review Organization, 1982).

5. George Schieber, Joshua Weiner, Korbin Liu, and Pamela Doty, "Prospective Payment for Medicare Skilled Nursing Facilities: Background and Issues," *Health Care Financing Review* 8 (Fall 1986): 79–85; Letty Carpenter, "Medicaid Eligibility for Persons in Nursing Homes," *Health Care Financing Review* 10 (Winter 1988): 67–77.

6. See Helen L. Smits, "Incentives in Case-Mix Measures for Long-Term Care," *Health Care Financing Review* 6 (Winter 1984): 53–59; E. Kathleen Adams and Robert E. Schlenker, "Case-Mix Reimbursement for Nursing Home Services: Simulation Approach," *Health Care Financing Review* 8 (Fall 1986): 35–45.

7. In addition to sources already cited, see Philip G. Cotterill, "Testing a Diagnosis-Related Group Index for Skilled Nursing Facilities," *Health Care Financing Review* 7 (Summer 1986): 75–85; Sidney Katz, Amasa B. Ford, Roland W. Moskowitz, Beverly A. Jackson, and Marjorie W. Jaffe, "Studies of Illness in the Aged. The Index of ADL: A Standardized Measure of Biological and Psychosocial Function," *JAMA* 185 (1963): 914–19; John N. Morris, Sylvia Sherwood, and Maurice I. May, *FRED: An Innovative Approach to Nursing Home Level-of-Care Assignments* (Boston: Hebrew Rehabilitation Center for Aged, Department of Social Gerontological Research, 1986).

8. William G. Weissart, William J. Scanlon, Thomas T.H. Wan, and Douglas E. Skinner, "Care for the Chronically Ill: Nursing Home Incentive Payment Experiment," *Health Care Financing Review* 5 (Winter 1983): 41–49.

9. Smits, "Incentives in Case-Mix Measures," 58.

10. Don P. Schneider, Brant E. Fries, William J. Foley, Marilyn Desmond, and William J. Gurmley, "Case Mix for Nursing Home Payment: Resource Utilization Groups, Version II," *Health Care Financing Review*, annual suppl. (1988): 39–52.

11. Ibid., 50.

12. An immediate, often symbolic, focus of concern is the vast volume of paperwork that is mandated. "Whenever government administrators prescribe unnecessary layers of busywork," wrote two physicians and a nurse representing an LTC institution in Ohio, "it adds to the cost of medical care without mending the whole problem."

We present one example in a nursing home in which "everything must be documented" or else not considered done, leading to citations and the imposition of monetary penalties by Medicaid and Medicare inspectors. We found an average of 1135 signatures and initialed boxes per month per custodial-patient chart for January 1990. The maximum was 2112, and the minimum 118. At a rate of six signatures a minute—a conservative estimate, considering that pages must be flipped through and boxes found to initial—this comes to more than 3 hours of professional time per patient, or for our 70-bed nursing home, 210 hours a month spent by staff to sign off on charts. This is the equivalent of one staff member doing nothing but signing and initialing and does not include additional hours spent double-checking for omissions by others. All this is totally unrelated to required paperwork, not to mention patient care.

We are asking ourselves at Heritage Manor, where more than 950,000 signatures and initialed boxes will be required in 1990, where we are heading and what effect the forthcoming regulations will have on us.

William D. Loeser, Emil S. Dickstein, and Margaret A. Commarata, letter to the editor, *New England Journal of Medicine* 323 (1990): 759.

13. While there are many books explaining finance to nonfinancial managers, two are especially useful: Steven A. Finkler, *The Complete Guide to Finance and Accounting for Nonfinancial Managers* (Englewood Cliffs, N.J.: Prentice-Hall, 1983); W. R. Purcell, Jr., *Understanding a Company's Finances: A Graphic Approach* (Boston: Houghton Mifflin, 1981). For a general discussion of fiscal management as it applies to long-term care institutions, see G. Wheeler, "Fiscal Administration, Organization, and Techniques," in *Nursing Home Administration*, edited by Stephen M. Schneeweiss and Stanley W. Davis (Baltimore: University Park Press), 87–104; Wesley Wiley Rogers, *General Administration in the Nursing Home* (Boston: CBI Publishing, 1980), 371–427; Keith E. Boles, "Strategic Financial Analysis for Long-Term Care Facilities," *Journal of Long-Term Care Administration* 16 (Fall 1988): 10–15.

14. See, for example, Elizabeth B. Harkins and Howard L. Smith, "Nursing Home Dietary Costs: Exploring the Determinants," *Journal of Long-Term Care Administration* 14 (Winter 1986): 17–21.

Chapter 7

Legal, Medical, and Ethical Issues

How to begin to discuss the bundle of legal relationships that impact the professional life of the LTC administrator? Perhaps by articulating the purpose of this chapter. It is not to teach the LTC administrator how to be a lawyer, any more than the purpose of the preceding chapter was to teach him or her how to be a financial manager. The oft-repeated maxim is entirely apt: When one has a specific legal problem, one should seek the advice of competent legal counsel.

Rather, the purpose here is to alert or sensitize the LTC administrator to an important reality. Virtually every action, procedural or substantive, taken in the course of one's daily professional activity has legal implications and possibly legal consequences and therefore must be considered under the general heading of "risk management." Statutes and regulations govern the LTC institution's every interaction with its employees, its residents and their families, and the state. Though the interests of each of these constituencies, as expressed in law and custom, are often dissimilar and sometimes contradictory, the consequences of ignoring the possibility of legal repercussions may be severe.

In one sense, this imperative is already too well understood. Many LTC administrators, fearful of violating or misinterpreting some unseen standard or norm, have repressed any inclination they may once have possessed toward the new, the untried, and the innovative and have become entirely risk averse. Such an excess of caution is quite understandable given the growing public awareness of the ethical and legal issues involved in LTC administration—among them, the appropriateness of decisions to treat, to transfer to a hospital, not to resuscitate, to hydrate, and to feed—and the concomitant willingness of the courts to be active participants in the decision-making process. But the cost to LTC institutions and, it might reasonably be argued, to society at large has been considerable in terms of good minds shut down, new ideas lost, and improvements in services gone unimplemented.

165

As a corrective, this chapter encourages the LTC administrator to adopt a proactive management style with regard to legal and ethical issues. The message is this: Understand the legal context, to be sure, but also recognize that the law is dynamic and the regulatory apparatus is, or can be made, malleable. So, assess your position with a clear eye and, where circumstances warrant, have the courage to do the right thing, to shape events rather than be buffeted by them.

Below, there is first an examination of the regulatory apparatus, including a discussion of how to respond effectively to the rules and authority of the state and to the people who are charged with interpreting them. This is followed by an examination of various legal liabilities implicit in the LTC administrator's daily contact with employees, residents, and families, including a discussion of how to maintain the highest ethical standards while minimizing the risk of legal action.

SEARCHING FOR STANDARDS: THE REGULATORY STRUCTURE AND HOW IT HAS CHANGED

As often happens when looking for the historical roots of present circumstances, the precipitating event seems not only far removed but also rather trivial.

On July 3, 1957, Clifford M. Davis fractured a leg while at work. He was a yard conductor for the Virginian Railway Company and had been instructed by his supervisor to spot railway cars at a loading platform on a spur track of the Ford Motor Company plant at Norfolk. Forty-three cars were involved in the switching. Some were already empty and standing idle at the platform. Others, those needing to be unloaded, were waiting outside the plant in the shifting yard. The entire operation, Davis was told, had to be completed during the lunch period at the Ford plant, which was 30 minutes.

Two brakemen were assigned to assist him, neither of whom were experienced in the task at hand. The senior brakeman had never before functioned in the senior role, nor had he ever spotted cars at this plant. The other brakeman had only limited familiarity with the logistics of the job.

A switching operation involving this many cars might easily take an hour or more, so Davis knew he had to work at an accelerated speed. Ordinarily, as a yard conductor, he would have directed activities from the ground. But because of the time constraints, and because the senior brakeman had informed him of his own inexperience, Davis decided to take a position on top of the cars so that he might be better able to provide quick assistance.

Several minutes into the operation, one of the brakemen called for help. Davis raced along the top of the boxcars toward him. Upon coming to a gondola car, he was obliged to climb down a ladder. He slipped, fell to the ground, and fractured his leg. He was brought immediately to a doctor furnished by his employer, the railroad. The doctor treated the fracture.

Davis sued the Virginian Railway Company under the terms of the Federal Employers' Liability Act. He claimed the railroad's instruction to complete the switching operation within 30 minutes, plus the inexperience of the brakemen assigned to the job, had precipitated his injury. He also claimed that the doctor to whom he had been taken was guilty of malpractice, having failed to immobilize the fracture properly.

At the trial the judge sustained the motion of the defendant, the Virginian Railway Company, to strike the plaintiff's evidence and so discharged the jury. The Virginia Supreme Court of Appeals rejected Davis's petition for writ of error, in effect affirming the judgment of the trial court. Davis appealed to the U.S. Supreme Court, which agreed to review the findings. The question posed by the case, said Mr. Justice Clark in explaining the Court's grant of certiorari, was important to the uniform administration of the federal statute.

In its decision, *Davis v. Virginian Railway Company* (1960), the Supreme Court reversed the judgment of the appeals court and remanded the case to the trial court for further consideration.[1] It should have been the responsibility of the jury in the trial court, said Justice Clark in the majority opinion, to decide whether the 30-minute time constraint and the inexperience of the brakemen precipitated Davis's injury. By withdrawing the question from the jury, the trial judge had usurped its proper function.

All of this would appear to be unimportant to the professional interests of LTC administrators, except for one further consideration—Davis's malpractice claim. The trial court had held that the railroad was not liable for any negligence on the part of the physician it had furnished to the injured employee. The Supreme Court let that stand, saying it found no evidence sufficient to support a malpractice recovery. Justice Clark stated,

> Proof of malpractice requires two evidentiary steps: evidence as to the recognized standard of the medical community in the particular kind of case, and showing that the physician in question negligently departed from this standard in his treatment of plaintiff. . . . The evidence shows that the physician was of unquestioned qualification and treated petitioner in accordance with his best medical judgment and long practice. The only evaluation concerning his treatment was that of Dr. T——, another physician who had treated petitioner, who testified that he did not 'think that [the treatment] is proper.' . . . This offer of proof was fatally deficient. No foundation was laid as to the recognized medical standard for the treatment of such a fracture. No standard having been established, it follows that the offer of proof was not sufficient.[2]

With those few sentences the Supreme Court validated review of medical decisions and practices according to community standards. Defining what constitutes "recognized medical standards" was left open to public question, and in the years since the *Davis* decision every interested party—medical providers, experts testifying in medical malpractice litigation, and especially regulators evaluating health care delivery systems—has expressed an opinion on how things ought to be done.

The impact of this ongoing search for standards has been especially noticeable in the nursing home industry. When the federal government became directly involved in nursing home regulation after 1965, few nursing homes could meet existing federal requirements. Strict enforcement of these would have barred most nursing homes from participating in the Medicare program and therefore would have prevented many Medicare patients from receiving needed services. So, in what was originally intended to be an interim measure, the U.S. Department of Health, Education and Welfare decided to certify nursing homes that were only in "substantial compliance" with Medicare standards. Thus, the thrust of federal and state regulatory efforts was to encourage, assist, or coerce substandard institutions to achieve compliance after they had been admitted to the Medicare and Medicaid programs rather than to insist that standards be met as a condition of approval.

Compliance, even when achieved, had little to do with quality of care. The central concern of the federal regulators and the state regulatory agencies acting as their agents was that institutions be fire safe and clean and that staff not be abusive to residents. The implicit assumption was that if the institution was structurally adequate for its intended purpose and the operator affirmed in writing his or her intent to deliver appropriate care, this constituted assurance, for regulatory purposes, that care of adequate quality was being provided.[3]

"Bricks and mortar" requirements and "paper compliance" were relatively easy to translate into federal regulations. But over the next decade of enforcement, these criteria came increasingly to be regarded as insufficient by many nursing home operators, residents' families, consumer advocates, and state and federal regulators. The new public welfare goals that were being articulated called for assurance of good outcomes or, at the least, no adverse outcomes. The debate on how best to accomplish this was joined on many fronts, and predictably the major impetus for change came via the courts.

In 1975, a class action was brought on behalf of Medicaid recipients residing in nursing homes in Colorado against Colorado nursing home operators, state government agencies and officials, and the U.S. Secretary of Health and Human Services. The suit alleged that the secretary, along with the other defendants, had violated the Medicaid Act by failing to implement a system of nursing home enforcement that guaranteed that Medicaid recipients actually received high-quality care. Over the next several years, the suit was redefined. Claims against the Colorado government defendants were dropped, a separate trial for the nursing home operators was ordered, and the plaintiffs were joined by the People of the

State of Colorado in the complaint against the federal defendant, the Secretary of Health and Human Services.

After traveling through the lower courts, *Estate of Smith v. Heckler* (1984) was heard by the U.S. Court of Appeals for the Tenth Circuit, which found for the plaintiffs. The judge held that (1) the Secretary of Health and Human Services has "a duty to promulgate regulations which will enable her to be informed as to whether the nursing facilities receiving federal Medicaid funds are actually providing high quality medical care," and (2) by promulgating a "facility oriented" enforcement system rather than a "patient oriented" system, the secretary had failed to follow the focus of the act, and such failure was "arbitrary and capricious."

Whereupon the Court ordered the secretary to set up a proper system of regulatory scrutiny. "The court is not a 'super agency' and cannot control the specifics of how the Secretary satisfies the duty," said the judge in rendering the verdict. "This is not a question of controlling the Secretary's discretion because the Secretary has failed to discharge her statutory duty altogether. Thus, the court should 'compel performance and thus effectuate the congressional purpose,' behind the statutory scheme."[4]

There followed a stylized dance between the plaintiffs and the Department of Health and Human Services that lasted for another five years. At issue was how to define the proper role, if any, of the regulators. In October 1985, a newly appointed Secretary of Health and Human Services announced a new long-term care survey process called PaCS (Patient Care and Services Survey). "By bringing surveyors face to face with a representative sample of patients or residents," he said, "[PaCS] would enable surveyors to identify their needs and problems more accurately and, subsequently, to determine how well care is being provided to meet those needs." Surveyors would be required to follow specific procedures and to review according to structured worksheets.[5]

Neither the plaintiffs nor the court were impressed. In *Estate of Smith v. Bowen* (1987), the United States District Court for the district of Colorado found that no survey forms or guidelines had been published in the secretary's rule and no details were given concerning the criteria for assessing the physical condition of patients or the standards for determining deficiencies. "The need for a definitive and certain methodology is . . . readily apparent from the variations in the operations of state agencies and levels of state funding for those agencies," said the court.

> State survey agencies play the critical role in determining whether facilities participating in Medicaid are providing high quality medical care. Several witnesses testified that the PaCS methodology gives surveyors considerable discretion in deciding whether a facility is in compliance. The Secretary needs to adequately define and guide the

state surveyors' functions to ensure that there is uniformity in evaluating the delivery of health care. Uniform guidelines are imperative for achieving that goal.[6]

The court also found merit in the plaintiffs' argument that the failure of the secretary to include sufficient detail in the regulation might preclude effective enforcement. An institution cited for deficiency could claim it did not have adequate notice of what was required or expected, the court said, and that position might well be upheld "under commonly accepted principles of fundamental fairness."

There followed another round of proposed rulemaking by the secretary. This time the document included extremely detailed guidelines for the surveyors on how to observe, what to ask in interviews, what records to review, and what evaluation factors to apply.[7] Once more the plaintiffs objected, saying that the procedures, guidelines, and forms proposed by the secretary had been published only for comment by interested parties and had not been included within the text of the final rule, thereby rendering their usage unenforceable. The secretary responded that to include such a level of detail in the body of the rule would make any necessary modifications exceedingly slow and difficult.

The Colorado district court, in *Estate of Smith v. Bowen* (1987), agreed with the plaintiffs and found the secretary in contempt. "To become and remain informed," it said, "the Secretary must establish uniform standards for facility performance and a uniform methodology for evaluating that performance to ensure the delivery of high quality health care. Thus, the regulations required for these purposes must be prescriptive and legislative."[8] In order to purge himself of contempt, the secretary was ordered to promulgate a new rule establishing standards of care and the methodology, forms, and directions for the states' certification process.

At this point Congress and the president effectively removed the conflict to another arena. On December 22, 1987, the Omnibus Budget Reconciliation Act of 1987 (OBRA '87) was enacted. The new law included extensive revisions to the Medicare and Medicaid statutory requirements for nursing facilities and signaled at least a temporary cease-fire in the nearly decade-long debate between the legislative and executive branches on the proper place of regulation in the governance of the nursing home industry.

Among the newly mandated requirements were the following:

Quality. Nursing homes must maintain or enhance "the quality of life of each resident."

Evaluation. At least once a year a nursing home must conduct a comprehensive assessment of each resident's ability to perform such everyday activities as bathing, dressing, eating, and walking. Results of such assessments will be used to prepare a written plan of care describing how the individual's medical, psychological, and social needs will be met.

Screening. A nursing home must not admit into residency any person who is mentally ill or mentally retarded unless a state agency first certifies that the individual requires the type of care provided in a nursing home. The state agency must also determine whether the individual needs "active treatment" for the mental illness or retardation.

Nurses. A nursing home must have licensed nurses on duty around the clock and must have a registered nurse on duty for at least eight hours a day, seven days a week. State officials may grant an exemption if the nursing home can show that it was unable to recruit the necessary personnel and that the exemption would not endanger the health or safety of residents.

Training. Every nurse's aide must receive at least 75 hours of training in nursing skills and residents' rights. Nursing homes are responsible for ensuring that nurse's aides are competent to perform the tasks they are assigned.

Registry. Each state must maintain a registry of people who have completed the training course for nurse's aides. If an aide is accused of neglecting or abusing residents or stealing their property, the state must investigate. If the charge is verified, the finding will be recorded in the registry. Nursing homes must check the registry before hiring nurse's aides.

Staff. Any nursing home with more than 120 beds must have at least one full-time social worker with at least a bachelor's degree in social work or similar qualifications.

Transfers. Nursing homes must ordinarily give 30 days' notice before discharging or transferring a resident. The resident may challenge such decisions by filing an appeal under procedures to be established by each state.

Access. Nursing homes must permit "immediate access" to any resident by relatives and by federal and state officials, including specially designated ombudspersons. Every state will have an ombudsperson to investigate complaints about long-term care institutions. Residents, relatives, and their attorneys may file complaints.

Penalties. If a nursing home fails to meet federal standards, the government may deny payment under Medicaid and Medicare and may appoint new managers to operate the institution. Payment must be withheld if the home is found to be substandard in three consecutive annual surveys.

The costs of compliance to the new law were to be shared by nursing homes, the federal government, and some residents. The Congressional Budget Office estimated the federal government's portion of this expense for five years to be $832 million, mainly for additional payments to nursing homes under Medicaid. In addition, states were expected to incur added costs of at least $572 million over the five-year period. It was also expected that nursing home residents not covered by Medicare or Medicaid would experience substantial increases in charges as nursing homes tried to recover the costs of hiring and training the additional employees required by the statute.[9]

Several weeks later, on February 2, 1989, the Secretary of Health and Human Services published a new set of requirements for LTC institutions participating in Medicare and Medicaid programs. The document embodied the regulatory revisions set forth in OBRA '87 as well as many suggestions received in response to the October 1987 notice of proposed rulemaking that had been found procedurally inadequate by the Colorado district court.[10]

As this brief historical excursion suggests, the interaction of involved parties, interest groups, government agencies, courts, legislative bodies, and executive authorities—in sum, the entire regulatory process   has taken on a life of its own. Each new requirement, when codified, suggests to advocates on the local, state, or national level the need for additional levels of explanatory detail, which in turn leads to further regulation, which in turn occasions more inquiry, which in turn results in the imposition of new standards. Long since accepted without challenge is the prevailing world view of the regulators: Inspection is adversarial; measurement is for purposes of punishment, not learning; the imposition of minimal thresholds of structure, process, or outcome represents a positive force for change; and the gathering and publication of performance data will somehow induce otherwise indolent providers to improve their care and their efficiency.

BEING SURVEYED: HOW TO DEAL WITH THE REGULATORY SYSTEM

Everyone has heard this story, or some variation thereof. An elderly man parks his car, gets out, and prepares to put some money in the parking meter, which has expired. Before he is able to do so, he suffers a massive coronary attack and collapses on the sidewalk. A local shopkeeper sees what has happened and calls the emergency medical squad, which arrives quickly and begins to administer cardiopulmonary resuscitation. A crowd gathers, drawn to the flashing lights of the EMS van, and the sight of the crowd attracts still more onlookers. Into the midst of this scene, just as the medical squad is preparing to load the victim into the van for the race to the hospital, arrives a meter maid on her scooter. She sees the red flag of expiration on the parking meter, writes a ticket, places it under the windshield wiper of the offending vehicle, and putters off, oblivious or indifferent to all that is going on.

This sequence of events may never have actually happened. Yet because it resonates in our collective experience as city dwellers, it has become part of our modern folklore, told and retold as if true. Everyone recognizes the "meter maid mentality," that mindless, bureaucratic application of rules no matter what the mitigating circumstances of the given instance.

Most LTC administrators, in calm and reflective moments, would probably acknowledge that regulators have a valid place in the world, that they may indeed be providing a valuable service to the nursing home industry when they scrutinize and report fairly on an institution's management, its financial viability, and the quality of care being given. Most administrators would probably also agree that the regulators' statistical sampling and inspection of typical survey items such as menu plans, the temperature of autoclaves, the temperature of food when it arrives at the resident's room, the presence of odors and presence of decubiti, provide a reasonable, if limited, depiction of the larger reality of long-term care.

What enrages LTC administrators and causes some to adopt an obstreperous, passively aggressive, or otherwise confrontational posture when the state arrives to conduct a survey is the "see red flag, issue ticket" mindset that many regulators have regarding matters having nothing whatever to do with the institution's management, financial viability, or quality of care. The following example, from the files of a large LTC institution, is illustrative.

There was a major, multiyear renovation underway in one of the facility's residence buildings. All building systems—electrical, plumbing, and air exchange—were to be renewed or upgraded, and extensive remodeling of residents' rooms and common areas was to be done. The plans included installation of central air conditioning, with separate controls in each room; bedside telephone hookup for each resident; redesigned bathrooms; large closets and built-in dressers and shelves for increased storage of residents' personal items; new bathing facilities; freshly painted and stenciled decor; and new dining areas, sitting rooms, and nurses stations on each floor.

In all, six residence floors were involved in the renovation. The schedule called for completing work on floor 6, which was already vacant, then moving residents from the floor below into the renovated rooms, and repeating the process for floors 5, 4, 3, 2, and 1. A great deal of planning and effort by almost every department in the institution was devoted to ensuring that the construction and the relocation of residents to their new rooms be done with a minimum of disruption.

State law required that a separate occupancy permit be issued for each floor before moving residents into the newly renovated rooms. From management's perspective, however, the more time required to complete the entire project, the greater the potential for disruption to all the people living in the building. There was no doubt about the value of the project, for the architectural plan, the quality of the workmanship, and the amenities provided to residents far exceeded any existing standard for nursing home construction. So, notwithstanding the language of the state regulation regarding the occupancy permit, when the renovation of floor 6 was completed, LTC staff immediately moved the residents into their new rooms and then called the regulator.

When the regulator arrived, she looked at the fresh surroundings and at the residents in their new rooms. She commented that the bedrooms, bathrooms, and common areas were indeed nicely done. She reminded the staff that the regulation called for an inspection before, not after, occupancy. She duly issued the permit.

LTC staff followed the same procedure when floor 5 was completed. Same favorable comments from the regulator. Same reminder about the letter of the law. Same result. The permit was issued.

One member of the management team, however, found the approach troubling. "We ought to obey the state regulation," she said. "Clearly, the regulators are impressed by the renovations we are making to the institution. We have always had an excellent reputation for quality of care. I'm sure the regulators will be prompt and cooperative."

So, when floor 4 was completed and ready for occupancy, but before moving any residents into their new rooms, LTC staff called the state department of public health and requested an inspection for purposes of issuing an occupancy permit. The regulator came, looked at the freshly painted walls, the new closets, the new bathrooms, the central air conditioning with individual controls, the new nurses stations, the new dining room and sitting areas, and refused to issue the permit.

"Why?"

"Because there are no beds in the rooms," the regulator answered. "I can't issue a permit unless there are beds in the rooms."

Staff reviewed the procedure as it had been previously followed in occupying floors 6 and 5. "We have found it least disruptive to move small groups of residents at a time," they said. "We bring the residents' personal belongings to their new rooms, along with their beds. We make sure that each person is comfortably settled. Then we move the next group."

"Sorry," said the regulator. "The regulation is quite specific in this regard. No beds in the rooms, no permit."

"We don't have extra beds for all the residents on the floor," staff said. "If we move all the residents' beds up here first, they will be living on the floor below without any beds. Is that what you want? You want them downstairs while their beds sit up here in empty rooms?"

Same reply. No permit.

So management announced its intention to move the residents onto the newly renovated floor anyway, with or without an occupancy permit. It informed the regulator that the institution's first responsibility was to its residents and that staff had no intention of allowing even a single person in their care to be inconvenienced or endangered by bureaucratic intransigence.

The residents were moved onto floor 4.

The state responded angrily. Telephone calls flew back and forth between the LTC institution and the commissioner of public health, who said she fully supported the regulator's position. She said her department intended to commence decertification proceedings immediately.

Decertification is one of the biggest guns in the state's regulatory arsenal. When it is finalized, the LTC institution is no longer eligible to participate in Medicare or Medicaid programs, with all of the attendant adverse consequences for its public reputation and economic well-being. The process begins with the state placing the institution on either a 90- or 23-day decertification track (the longer time frame is accorded to places with a favorable history of substantial compliance). At the end of the period, decertification is automatic unless the institution has submitted to the regulators in writing (usually within 45 days in the case of the 90-day track) a plan of correction promising to remedy the problems or otherwise address the state's concerns. A follow-up survey by the state is then conducted to verify that the plan is actually being implemented as written. Even if an institution is subsequently removed from the decertification track and a positive recommendation for participation in Medicare and Medicaid programs is made, continued monitoring by the regulators, sometimes on a weekly basis, can be expected.

Threat of decertification because of willful disregard of a state regulation requiring an occupancy permit brought into sharp relief the question that underlies the entire regulatory structure: Who is in charge? More immediately, it presented the management of the institution with a choice. Should it shrink before the authority of the state, tug at its forelock and promise henceforth to play by the rules as written or interpreted by others, in which case the institution would probably escape with a slap on the wrist and a minor blemish on its written record? Or should it reassert the validity of the decision to occupy the renovated floor and therefore respond to the state's threatened sanction as if the LTC institution's management, not the state, was the best judge of how to care for the elderly?

As in any of life's purely existential situations, it is best to assess one's position with a clear eye before acting. The administrators of the LTC institution knew that in the past their relationship with the regulators had been generally good. They knew the institution had a public reputation for providing quality care to its residents, as proved by the length of its waiting list. They knew from survey questionnaires and other in-house feedback programs that they had the support of a sizable majority of residents' families.

So, with some confidence, the management of the LTC institution replied to the commissioner, "Look closely at your statute. If you decertify, the state will be immediately obligated to make alternative living arrangements for every resident receiving public assistance, which is over 400 people. Are you sure you want to do that? Are you sure you want to listen to the complaints of the families when they hear their infirm elderly relatives are being forced by your office to move to someplace they don't want to be?"

"Is that really what the statute says?"

"Read it."

So the threat of decertification was quietly dropped, and the occupancy permit for floor 4 was subsequently issued.

Although the sequence of events just described may be unusual, the intensity of feelings underlying it is not. LTC administrators must make choices all the time regarding their posture vis-a-vis the regulatory system. Some administrators choose to be confrontational; others opt to be submissive. Many are inconsistent in their response, fighting too hard over minor issues, while permitting larger, more questionable matters of interpretation to slide by uncontested. Most feel victimized to some extent by the regulatory process. More than a few become cynical and resigned.

There is, of course, no denying the power that the regulatory system can bring to bear on an LTC institution's viability. One option, as noted, is decertification. Another, which is usually chosen when an institution has been placed on a decertification track several times in the span of one or two years, is delicensing. Indeed, delicensing may be the only course of action available to a state regulatory authority when confronting an institution that has a history of repeated deficiencies, is not receiving any public monies, and is servicing only private-pay residents.

When the regulatory system wishes to act in the most immediate and visible fashion, it can impose an admissions ban. Such action usually occurs when an LTC institution is found to have placed its residents in life-threatening situations or is otherwise considered to be guilty of gross, continual mismanagement. In many jurisdictions, an admissions ban may also be implemented temporarily in the event of medical emergencies such as flu outbreaks.

In several states, the most decisive action that can be taken by regulators faced with a seriously deficient institution is receivership. Once imposed, the government authority assumes full managerial control of the facility and, in effect, spends the institution's money in an attempt to bring it into compliance with state and federal regulations. Receivership is very difficult to have lifted, and it usually results in the sale of the institution at a price significantly lower than the market might otherwise have set.

In contrast to such extreme courses of action, there are also many intermediate forms of sanction available to the regulators. These typically involve some sort of consent agreement, such as restricting levels of care, setting staffing patterns, placing targeted expenditures in an escrowed account, establishing a management plan or set of priorities, or contracting for substitute management for a specified period. Many of these actions are now formalized within the federal regulatory structure. For example, new Medicare and Medicaid provisions sanction denial of payment for new admissions, the imposition of monetary penalties on a daily basis, and the appointment of temporary management.

As an LTC administrator, how should you respond when a regulator threatens to impose any of the above-mentioned punishments? Regardless of your personal or managerial style, assuming you have a true commitment to providing the highest quality care at a fair price, the advice offered here is this: *Do not do anything, no matter who says to do it and under what authority, that is not in the absolute best interest of the residents for whom you are responsible.*

Such a stance vis-a-vis the regulators may strike some LTC administrators as excessively confrontational, but it is nevertheless a highly pragmatic (and conservative) position. The fact of the matter is, the rules and regulations that constitute the regulatory system are the creation of well-meaning but fallible people trying to apply unambiguous language to a world of potentially mitigating circumstances. When the words do not quite fit the reality, as often happens, the words are subject to interpretation. Sometimes, a previous interpretation is understood to be policy even though the policy was never formalized.

As a practical matter, therefore, if in the conduct of a survey you are cited for a situation that you believe has been misunderstood or unfairly perceived by the regulator, request a copy of the written rule or ask that the regulator put the interpretation in writing. The burden of providing documentation belongs to the regulatory agency. The burden of providing care to your residents belongs to you. If you or your institution caused harm to a resident because you dutifully obeyed a foolish or ill-advised interpretation of regulatory policy, you would not be absolved of responsibility by a court of law because you assumed the regulator was right or that his or her opinion somehow took precedence.

Although you should never allow a written record of deficiency you disagree with to go unchallenged, the tenor of your response ought to depend entirely on the context of the discussion. For example, you may not wish to overdramatize the regulator's mistakes in conducting a survey if he or she notes the deficiencies on an observation sheet only (rather than in the formal record) and indicates a willingness to work with you as a consultant rather than as an adversary. Good relations with regulators are much to be preferred and should be strived for unless or until it becomes apparent that the regulators are interested in punishment, not process.

If a problem between your institution and the regulatory system persists, the following recommendations may be helpful.[11]

1. State your objections to the citation in writing. If the language of the regulation that has allegedly been violated differs from what you consider to be the regulation's intent, spotlight this discrepancy. Provide an alternative explanation or description of the circumstances or situation in dispute. Attach all relevant documentation in support of your position, including, where appropriate, testimony of satisfied residents or their families.

2. Review the assembled document with your attorney. In situations where some form of regulatory sanction appears to be imminent, assess your situation objectively and plan your approach. How does each level of government that is involved view the dispute? How strong (or weak) is your institution's record of compliance? What are the strengths and weaknesses of your case, the government's case, the witnesses for both sides, and any alternative courses of action that have been suggested? Can the problem be resolved by a successful appeal and hearing leading to a settlement? Or is the problem endemic and a sale of the institution the only realistic solution?

3. Unless a staff member has been guilty of resident abuse and terminating his or her employment will satisfy the regulators and resolve the problem, try to maintain continuity of key personnel until the dispute is settled. Otherwise, changes in the management team will hinder development of your defense and weaken the impact of your testimony.

4. Alert your local professional association to the existence of your problem. Solicit their advice and support. Ask if any other members have recently faced a like situation. If some members have, contact them for their perspective.

Meanwhile, keep on acting in the best interests of your residents as you understand their best interests to be—regardless of who says to do things differently—until a revised interpretation of the regulation in dispute is forthcoming or the matter is otherwise adjudicated.

MANAGING RISK THROUGH THE BUILDING OF RELATIONSHIPS

Modern philosophers who are ethicists concentrate chiefly on moral dilemmas. They like to identify quandaries that the decision maker faces and then search for moral rules and principles that will help to solve or resolve these moral binds. It is a perspective that adjusts nicely to the task of criticizing professional decision makers (lawyers, doctors, LTC administrators, and the like). But it does not offer much help to elderly individuals or their families facing the ordeals of sickness, legal crisis, infirmity, and fading powers. People in such situations need guidelines for action, to be sure. But more than that, they need strength of character.[12]

The LTC administrator cannot, of course, provide strength of character where, in the unusual instance, no character exists. But he or she can almost always help others understand the context of current circumstances more fully and so enable them to chart their own path through events using the insight and intuition of a lifetime as a compass. To help constituencies change the focus of their inquiry from "What are you planning to do about it?" to "How shall I, and we, behave toward it?" is not only the essence of compassion, it is also the crux of risk management.

In the long-term care setting, examples of such compassionate and prudent activity abound. If a resident is delusional and sees the physician who prescribes medication as an agent of the devil, or if the resident is violent and presents a danger to others, the institution will generally go to the family (if one exists) and seek consent for some alternative form of treatment. Assuming there has already been a lot of intervention with the resident and accompanying communication with the family, by the time the resident has come to this degree of delusion or violence the situation is well understood by all parties. The primary care team is thus able to say freely to the family members, "Given the reality of circumstances, here are what appear to be our options and here is the course we recommend." The exchange that follows may be difficult emotionally, but because the interests of the institution have been personalized and the resident and the family have been given as much input into decision making as possible, the discussion is almost always congenial, hardly ever confrontational.

When an LTC administrator truly communicates with residents and their families, when communication has been continuous over time, when an atmosphere of openness has been nurtured and developed, the institution is not likely to be sued. A lawsuit, when it occurs, almost always represents a failure—a breakdown—of trust between parties who feel they can no longer deal with one another openly and honestly. People sue LTC administrators and LTC institutions when they feel that they themselves, or their aged relatives, have been hurt, or when they perceive an institutional arrogance or lack of caring and see no recourse other than to try to inflict pain in return.

Below are three case examples that testify to the crucial importance of communication in building relationships and indicate the problems that may arise when communication is absent or faulty.

Case Example 1: Scrambling to Rebuild Confidence

Almost always a lawsuit is preceded by warning signals, usually in the form of a letter written by a family member acting on a resident's behalf. Language is a key to gauging the depth of the anger present.

For example, when the person writing or speaking chooses to describe at great length the scale of the hurt received, he or she is probably signaling that the door is open for further discussion and that time remains to resolve the situation without third-party involvement. But when the communication, either written or verbal, is terse and impersonal, the likelihood is that the dispute will soon be removed to a legal arena.

An example of this sort of letter—polite, disclosing little, and portending legal consequences—is taken from the files of an LTC institution.

December 2, 1989

Dear_____,

When we visited my Mother, Louise M., on Sunday, November 19, she had a large red bruise, approximately three inches in diameter, on her right arm. On her left arm, she had several small bruises the size of a nickel (5 cent piece).

We would appreciate your investigation into this matter, giving us a written report of your findings.

Sincerely,

The person writing this letter was the resident's son, who lived about twelve hundred miles distant. He and his wife were in the area in mid-November to be with a daughter when she gave birth, and they stopped in at the LTC institution to visit his mother. The woman lived on a Pattern III–type unit, severely debilitated and unable to speak. The son and his wife noticed bruises on her arms. They said nothing to staff, fearful that if they registered a complaint, something even more dreadful might happen to mother. They returned home and for several weeks worried about what they had seen. Finally, in early December (perhaps at the recommendation of their attorney), they wrote asking for additional information.

Investigation of the matter by LTC management revealed the existence of several sets of problems. When the nurse in charge of the unit where the woman resided was first approached, she dismissed the son's complaint, saying that the bruises were probably caused by contact with the bedrailing. This was not, however, a satisfactory explanation, since the description of the bruises in the letter was not consistent with bedrail injuries. Further inquiry revealed that similar injuries on that unit had been reported to the head nurse as early as October, and the evidence strongly suggested that they were being caused by a particular nurse's aide pushing residents into their wheelchairs. Why did the head nurse not immediately respond to the report of injuries? Was the nurse's aide still being employed?

The second problem area involved the son's fear of adverse consequences to his mother if he dared to say anything about what he had seen. In a subsequent discussion, he said he felt particularly helpless because he and his wife lived at such a distance. But that explanation sidestepped the underlying issue, which was that his immediate instinct had been to treat the LTC institution as an adversary. What had management done, or not done, to create such a high level of mistrust?

The first set of problems was corrected by personnel changes and staff reeducation. All nursing unit staff were included in the review of the case, and primary care team members were reminded of their individual responsibilities to act as first-line monitors of colleagues' performance and to be alert to any unusual circumstances.

The task of rebuilding the family's confidence in the institution was accomplished less satisfactorily. It became apparent in management's discussions with the son that various feedback programs (e.g., an annual family survey questionnaire) were having little impact. When newsletters from the institution, nursing unit updates, or solicitations of opinion arrived in the mail at the son's residence, he would read them, then, for whatever reason, toss them aside.

Nor was his daughter, who lived locally, much involved in the care of her grandmother. Recently pregnant, she was busy with the needs of her own family and had little time to spare. As a consequence, when the son visited his mother and found the bruises on her arms, he had no recent history of positive experience, no reservoir of trust, to counterbalance the possible implications of what he saw, and it was easy to presume an ongoing and willful disregard of his mother by all LTC staff.

A great deal of time and effort went into reestablishing communication between the institution and the family. The person primarily responsible for the rapprochement, after initial telephone contact was made by the LTC administrator, was the social worker, who acted as the family liaison member of the primary care team. All parties agreed that a series of direct reports from the social worker to the son regarding his mother's condition would be useful, and family members were invited to write or call anyone in the organization at any time if questions or problems arose. The LTC administrator called the son periodically thereafter to be sure he remained comfortable with the care his mother was receiving and the steps being taken to keep him informed.

These various communications were successful inasmuch as no legal action by the family was forthcoming. However, the family remained wary of the LTC institution and generally suspicious of its motives. When trust slips away, it can never be fully recaptured.

Case Example 2: Widening Participation in Decision Making

A 107-year-old man, weighing perhaps 75 pounds, lay in a Pattern III–type unit totally contracted. He had decubitus ulcers, and when the nurses irrigated the decubiti, he would wince. Otherwise, he was not communicative.

The nursing staff felt that pain medication should be administered before removing the dressing and irrigating, and they pressed the physician to prescribe it. The family, one of whose members was a medical student who was acting as an unofficial adviser, wanted no medication given that could conceivably shorten life.

Because the man had lived on the unit for seven years, the family and the primary care team shared a long history. In retrospect, it was clear that frustration and exhaustion had taken its toll on both sides, though at the time no one recognized the signs of burnout. So the relationship between the family and the primary care team grew increasingly tenuous until one day, in one exchange, it disintegrated entirely.

During the meeting, the physician gave his recommendation that a narcotic should be administered for pain. The family asked, "Could the medication possibly shorten life?" The physician should have replied, "Of course, any pain medication can suppress respiration, and so there is always some risk. But this is such a tiny amount of morphine we are talking about, I think the chances are very small." Except, in this instance, the physician said only, "Yes." That is, it could possibly shorten life.

The family immediately refused to give its consent, and the lines were drawn.

The physician, enraged at the challenge, went directly to the LTC administrator. "It is an issue of proper treatment," he said. "I think the institution should seek a court order removing decision-making authority from the family."

Instead, the LTC administrator immediately convened an ad hoc advisory group consisting of himself, the physician-in-chief, two doctors who lived and worked in the community, and a psychiatrist. The primary care team delivered its report and reasserted its opinion that medication for pain was warranted. The medical members of the advisory group then went to look at the resident. Each returned with the same conclusion: There was no clear evidence that the elderly man either was or was not in pain and that what the doctor and nursing staff were seeing and interpreting as pain may have been only reflex action. The unanimous recommendation of the group was to treat the resident as the family wished.

More important, the advisory group recognized that the substantive issue before them was staff burnout. Specifically, they recognized that a fine physician and a dedicated nursing team simply could not deal with this particular resident and family any longer. One of the doctors in the advisory group said he would accept a transfer of the resident to his unit if the family gave their consent. The psychiatrist met with the family, who were unaware of the deliberations, and explained that as a result of many years on the case the current primary care team was exhausted. The psychiatrist asked for and received the family's permission to transfer their relative to the other unit.

Soon thereafter, the resident died in his sleep. The family were comforted by the ending. The LTC staff generally felt that they had done the best they could. And by convening a special group to review the treatment decision, the LTC administrator had managed to keep the primary care physician from seeking redress through the courts and to assuage any litigious feelings that may have existed on the part of the family.

Case Example 3: Compounding a Mistake in Judgment with Insensitivity to Feelings

An 81-year-old widow, Zelda Z., had lived on a Pattern I unit for four years. Like all Pattern I residents, she was reasonably alert and mobile. Her main physical infirmity was an arteriosclerotic heart, for which she took daily medication.

She was not happy living at the LTC institution. She spent most of her time in a rocking chair, often refusing to participate in recreational activities, and she made few friends. She did, however, seem to enjoy taking herself downtown once in a while via public transportation for a day of shopping.

Zelda Z. was beginning to experience some occasional memory lapses and failure in judgment. But because nothing had transpired to indicate she could not continue to leave the institution on her own, the primary care team was reluctant to impose any restrictions on her freedom of movement, as would have occurred if transfer were made to a Pattern II unit. So, despite her borderline status, they decided to keep her on Pattern I.

One summer day, Zelda Z. got on a bus and did not return. After waiting a time, the administration called the police and notified her daughter, an only surviving child, who immediately hired a private detective to commence a search. For several days, LTC staff believed that Zelda Z. might have gone to live with some unknown relative without informing anyone, because her relationship with her daughter was known to be stormy and her general dissatisfaction with life at the institution was hardly a secret. But as more days passed and there was still no word from her, many began to fear the worst.

The daughter was frantic and questioned the staff incessantly. The staff, upset by the disappearance, responded by instituting changes in policy on Pattern I units. They posted signs everywhere that read, "No residents can leave the building without first getting permission at the desk."

Twenty-two days after she disappeared, Zelda Z.'s body was found by security personnel of the public library downtown during a routine check of a firebreak corridor. She had apparently stopped to use the library restroom, and on leaving it, had proceeded through two emergency exit doors and into a passageway. The second door shut and locked behind her. At the other end of the corridor was a vaultlike fire door fortified with three-inch granite and weighing an estimated 800 pounds. She could not budge this door either and was trapped.

There was a central-alarm console at the library security station that might have signalled with a flashing light that an emergency exit door had been opened. But the console had long since been disconnected because many library doors once intended to be emergency exits were now used as regular passageways. A battery-powered audible alarm on the door opening into the corridor where Zelda Z. died was found later to be inoperative. Even had it functioned properly, the bell could not be heard outside the corridor.

Zelda Z.'s body had been discovered on the 10th day of the month, the 22nd day of her disappearance. The maintenance schedule called for library security personnel to check the corridor where she was found on the first day of the month. But the schedule had not been followed, and investigators wondered if Zelda Z. might still be alive if the lapse in procedure had not occurred.

The autopsy performed by the county medical examiner failed to establish time of death conclusively, but did confirm that Zelda Z. had died of heart failure brought on by lack of food and water. She had written a letter, found beside her body, in which she said she did not know how long she had been trapped in the corridor.

The story got sizable play in the metropolitan daily newspapers. It focused mostly on the horror of an elderly woman being trapped in a crypt and on the laxity of library maintenance and security procedures. Zelda Z.'s personal history, including her place of residence, was also mentioned prominently.[13]

The daughter sued the LTC institution for complicity in her mother's death. Though the formal charge was malpractice, the real reason for the lawsuit, in the opinion of the LTC administrator, was that he had mishandled their relationship. The administrator believed strongly in the rehabilitation concept, an integral part of which is the fostering of each resident's independence to the limits of his or her functionality. During the period of Zelda Z.'s disappearance, he was sure that she would soon be found safe. His primary concern, therefore, was the effect her disappearance was having on the concept of the institution—the signs being posted, the diminution of confidence among residents and staff, the subtle and not so subtle changes in policy and attitude that were threatening to make the place less of a "home" and more of an "institution."

His mistake was to voice these concerns to the daughter while her mother's whereabouts were still unknown. In retrospect, he realized he should have been far more kind, far more understanding of her feelings, and a good deal more circumspect in his remarks.

With a personal tragedy now exacerbated into a legal conflict, the question was how to proceed. The LTC institution's attorneys urged it to settle the claim without the publicity of a trial. The LTC administrator thought otherwise. Notwithstanding his botching of the discussion with Zelda Z.'s daughter, he felt that the principle of maximum independence was worth upholding. If a settlement were made, it would signal to staff that they had done something terribly wrong, that they should not have allowed Zelda Z. to leave the grounds alone. Once staff got that message, they would become excessively cautious in their evaluations of residents and slowly the character of the institution would begin to change.

So the case went to court, where, as often happens, the verdict fully satisfied no one. The court ruled that the LTC institution shared some of the blame for Zelda Z.'s death and that the elderly woman herself was also in part responsible. It awarded a minimal financial settlement to the daughter, presumably for her pain and suffering.

Zelda Z.'s death was a tragic outcome, made worse by the mishandling of the relationship with the daughter. Along the way, many decisions by LTC management and staff could justifiably be called into question, and there was ample opportunity for those involved to learn from their mistakes.

LESSONS TO BE LEARNED

Each of the three case examples above raises, directly or indirectly, some important management issues. The remainder of this chapter is devoted to a discussion of these issues and their implications.

Employee Dismissals and the Risk of Wrongful Discharge

In case example 1, a resident was found to have bruises of suspicious origin on her arms. Follow-up investigation by staff revealed that the injuries were probably caused by an extremely careless, perhaps abusive, nurse's aide. What are the possible legal consequences of terminating this employee?[14]

Until about ten years ago, unless the workplace was ruled by a collective bargaining agreement, the employee could be dismissed immediately and without much fanfare. The common law doctrine known as employment-at-will prevailed. It held that an employer is free to terminate any employee for any cause, or for no cause, so long as the employee had been hired without a specific contractual term of service.

Over the last decade, however, courts have so frequently found exceptions to the employment-at-will doctrine that some attorneys now believe the exceptions have swallowed the rule. This is not to say there has been a general abrogation of employment-at-will in most jurisdictions. It does mean, however, that the power of the employer in a nonunion workplace has become far more restricted.

An at-will employer's freedom to terminate an employee may be limited by the courts in three ways. First, courts may find that the reason for terminating an employee violates public policy (e.g., an employer fires a "whistleblower" who has reported health or safety violations to the proper authorities).

Second, if the company's employee guidebook promises that procedural or substantive safeguards attach to the employer's decision to terminate, courts may find that these provisions constitute terms of an employment contract, since employees presumably weigh the promised protections in their decision to stay on the job rather than to seek another position elsewhere.

Third, courts may rely on the covenant of good faith and fair dealing implied in all contracts and so hold that employers must give good reason and provide a fair process when dismissing an employee.

When courts or arbitrators adjudicate cases involving employee termination, the standard usually applied is *just cause*. This is the operative principle, whether the terminated employee is at-will, is under a personal services contract, or is governed by the terms of a collective bargaining agreement. If just cause is found by the reviewing authority to exist, the termination will almost always be upheld. If it is found not to exist or if procedural or substantive errors on the part of management are discovered, the termination stands a good chance of being disallowed.

For the LTC administrator, therefore, the key to minimizing the risk of reversal is, as always, careful prior planning. Specifically, every LTC institution should write and regularly update an employee guidebook that addresses the broad range of circumstances likely to confront the institution and its staff. The purpose of this guidebook—or, in its stead, the institution's policy manual—is *not* to anticipate every eventuality that might occur in the course of performing every job within the organization. Such a document would be hopelessly unwieldy, would inevitably be incomplete, and would invariably do more damage by stifling creativity than it might ever prevent.

Instead, the guidebook should convey clearly to all employees, in broad yet explicit terms, the expectations of management regarding their behavior on the job, and it should indicate the disciplinary response to be expected in the event of serious infraction. If the sole penalty for resident abuse (either physical, verbal, or emotional) will be termination of employment, say so. If willful disregard of safety or security regulations may result in immediate dismissal, say so. If insubordination, gross incompetence, and recurring tardiness are grounds for discharge, say so. If theft, fraud, or dishonesty will not be tolerated, say so.

The employee guidebook represents the first level of written communication between management and employees regarding acceptable and unacceptable behavior. A second level of written communication, a more formal and specific statement of management's expectations, is the job description. These two documents, the employee guidebook and the job description, should be reviewed with each new employee on the first day of hire. The new employee should be required, as a condition of employment, to sign an agreement acknowledging that he or she has received copies of these documents and fully understands what they say. The signed agreement then becomes part of the employee's permanent file.

If all of this written documentation is in place and the hiring procedures are duly followed, any subsequent termination of an employee because of substandard performance becomes a relatively simple matter. If a reviewing authority such as a court or an arbitrator becomes involved, it will want to know whether due process has been observed and so typically will ask the following questions.

Did the employee have adequate warning that his or her conduct was in violation of the company's rules? Expect the reviewing authority to ask for a written statement of policy—whether it be found in the employment contract, in the employee guidebook, or in the job description—as a counterweight to any claim of ignorance of the rules on the part of the employee being terminated. The purpose is to confirm that (1) management is serious in its attempt to create an environment of high-quality care for its residents, and (2) all employees are bound by this set of expectations because they have been explicitly informed of the rules that apply.

Did management have sufficient evidence in hand at the time of the disciplinary action to establish just cause? When an employee is charged with a serious offense, such as resident abuse, there is always a tendency on the part of management to want to terminate the offender immediately (so as to prevent any recurrence) and to gather the incriminating evidence thereafter. The downside risk of such an approach is that information gathered after disciplinary action is completed may be ruled inadmissible by the arbitrator or court, thereby exposing the institution to the possibility of reversal and forced reinstatement of the employee.

A more prudent course, from both the employer's and the resident's perspective, is (1) to immediately issue a written warning to the employee suspected of resident abuse, and (2) to suspend the employee pending the outcome of a full investigation. This approach will prevent further abuse to any resident and will indicate to the arbitrator the seriousness of the incident as well as the institution's intent to investigate it thoroughly.

Did management meet the requisite standard of proof? In the absence of any superseding standard of proof written into an individual contract or collective bargaining agreement, the test most frequently applied by an arbitrator in termination cases is *preponderance of the evidence.* By this standard, it is not required that the employer prove its case beyond a reasonable doubt in order to terminate an unworthy employee.

Were the rules of the institution applied fairly and without discrimination? In deciding on a course of disciplinary action, the employer must be sure that it is reasonably related to the offense and that it takes into account the employee's past conduct. Thus, if an employee has no prior record of difficulties, he or she should receive a lighter punishment than an employee with a long history of disciplinary problems—unless, of course, the offense is so egregious (such as resident abuse) that it warrants immediate termination regardless of circumstances.

The employer must also be sure that the rules have been applied evenly to all employees over time. Thus, if enforcement of a particular rule has been lax in the past, management cannot suddenly institute a policy of strict enforcement without giving adequate prior notice to those who are impacted.

Assessing the Risks of Wrongful Acts

In each of the case examples, members of LTC staff either did or did not take certain actions and the result may have been injury to a resident. What are the legal consequences of "wrongful" acts, both to the supervisors of the responsible individuals and to the LTC institution itself? How can the LTC administrator effectively manage the risk? To answer these questions, here is a brief overview of liability law.

People are responsible individually for what they do and what they do not do, and they can be held personally liable for wrongful acts that directly result in injury. In addition, the supervisors of the responsible individual, and the institution itself, may face *vicarious liability* for the wrongdoing. Under the principles of "agency," which is a part of contract law that embodies the concepts of "master" (employer, supervisor, principal) and "agent" (employee, supervisee, contractee), a master is civilly liable for injuries to the person or property of third parties as a result of the negligence of an agent so long as the negligent act occurred within the scope of the agent's employment or job responsibilities. This doctrine is called *respondeat superior*, which translates from the Latin as "let the master answer." It applies to intentional as well as negligent wrongdoing by the agent, but only in those situations where the master should reasonably have foreseen the intentional misdeed.

Three elements are necessary for the creation of an "agency" relationship on which vicarious liability may be imposed. First, the parties must voluntarily consent to enter into an arrangement whereby the agent will act for the benefit, and under the direction and control, of the principal. Second, the agent must be acting on behalf of the principal. Third, and most important, the principal must retain the general power to control and the right to direct the means and methods of the agent's work.

Each of these elements is clearly present in the case of employees of LTC institutions, assuming they are acting within the scope of their job descriptions. Administrators, physicians (in a closed, salaried medical staff), nurses, nurse's aides, therapists, dieticians, pharmacists, all other full- and part-time staff, volunteers, agencies (such as laboratories) whose performance is supervised by or generally under the control of the facility—for the acts and omissions of all of these individuals and groups the LTC institution may be held vicariously liable.

In addition to personal and vicarious liability, the institution may also have *corporate liability*. This is a relatively recent development in civil law. Until the mid-1960s, health care facilities, including LTC institutions, had some measure of protection against lawsuits for negligence on the part of their employees and the independent professionals with whom they contracted. Most were owned and operated by local governments or by private, nonprofit, charitable organizations. Publicly owned facilities were generally protected from lawsuits under the theory of *sovereign immunity*, which holds that government agencies should be immune from legal liability because permitting an individual to drain the public treasury would penalize other potential recipients of public services. Private, voluntary facilities were ordinarily protected by the similar legal theory of *charitable immunity*, which holds that permitting one injured individual to deplete the funds of a charitable institution would possibly deprive too many other needy persons of that institution's charitable services.

Health care institutions were also shielded from negligence suits by the *empty shell theory*. Under this construct, facilities such as nursing homes were considered merely physical structures providing a workplace for physicians and other health professionals to practice and bed and board for the patients upon whom the professionals were practicing. The institution itself was seen to have no independent relationship with the patients or residents, and consequently it had no direct responsibility to them that could be legally enforced.

Changes in health care delivery patterns, especially in the long-term care of the infirm elderly, and accompanying shifts in public policy values have substantially weakened the rationales underlying these longstanding protections to the point that today they are virtually nonexistent. The preponderance of nursing homes are now owned and operated by proprietary (private, for-profit) corporations, and only a relatively small percentage remain under the control of local governments and charitable organizations. As regards for-profit institutions, the charitable and sovereign immunity doctrines clearly do not apply. In addition, most local governments have enacted statutes that voluntarily waive some of their sovereign immunity status, reflecting the public consensus that innocent individuals who are injured by a government agency deserve access to redress for suffering. Also, charitable immunity has become severely weakened because the courts have come to recognize that nonprofit institutions, including nursing homes, manage to the "bottom line" and otherwise act managerially much like their proprietary counterparts. Since nonprofit facilities tend to behave like proprietary entities, they should be treated in the same way for negligence purposes.[15]

The empty shell doctrine has also been abandoned in most jurisdictions. Since *Darling v. Charleston Community Memorial Hospital* (1965), the courts have come to view health care facilities as more than mere physical structures providing a workplace for health care professionals and housing for patients or residents.[16] Institutions such as nursing homes form independent, direct relationships with each of their residents, and they therefore have certain independent, direct, and legally enforceable obligations and are subject to the forms of legal exposure that exist under the respondeat superior doctrine.

Because an LTC institution is legally answerable for any civil wrongs committed by one of its employees while functioning within the scope of the job, and because it has an institutional relationship with each resident and, therefore, an independent obligation to see that care of an acceptable level of quality is delivered, the LTC administrator must accept certain risk management responsibilities explicitly. Some of these are already well understood and have already been discussed in this book in other contexts. The LTC administrator has a duty to

- maintain buildings and grounds properly and in a safe condition
- purchase and maintain equipment, supplies, medication, and food properly
- develop and implement appropriate written instructions and policies regarding resident safety
- screen, train, monitor, and supervise facility employees carefully, including volunteers and students

Finally, and most important for purposes of the present discussion, the administrator has a duty to screen, monitor, and supervise independent contractors with whom the LTC institution has a business relationship, most notably private physicians enjoying medical staff privileges.

Negligence in performing any of these duties that results in harm to a resident may expose the LTC institution and its management to liability. Where the person responsible for the harm is a physician, the LTC institution may be found negligent for having granted or failing to limit staff privileges if (1) the criteria used to evaluate the applicant were insufficient to determine competence and character, (2) the institution had reason to know the physician was incompetent or of poor character, or (3) the institution should have discovered by due diligence that the physician was incompetent or of poor character.[17]

The managerial implication of the liability law follows directly from this brief overview and may be simply stated: As in every other aspect of building an organization, one must begin by hiring or contracting with the right people and by defining the processes within which they work in a way that ensures the highest quality care and, thereby, a minimum of risk.

Building the Medical Staff

Not every physician is well suited to work with the infirm elderly in an institutional long-term care setting. Many refuse to make visits to nursing homes, and those that do often do so reluctantly. Why? Though much of the evidence tends to be anecdotal, a survey of Michigan physicians begun in 1981 and concluded in 1986 provides some useful insights.[18]

Over one-half (58.6 percent) of the 930 surveyed physicians reported that they had made no nursing home visits during the previous month. Of those that did, most made five or fewer visits per month. A small number of physicians were responsible for treating a disproportionate number of patients: Two-thirds of all reported nursing home visits were made by only 5 percent of the surveyed physicians. Internists and cardiologists were less likely to visit nursing home patients than general practitioner osteopaths. Older physicians were more likely to visit than their younger counterparts.

The survey questionnaire included a list of six possible reasons for not visiting nursing homes. Respondents were asked to rate the importance of each in their decision not to visit, assigning the value "very important," "somewhat important," or "not important." They were also asked to specify any additional reasons they might have for not visiting, and over one-fifth of the physicians responding did so.

More than half (52.5 percent) of nonvisiting physicians stated that low reimbursement was a significant (very important or somewhat important) factor, but only 22 percent said it was very important. Many respondents indicated that high travel costs effectively reduced their payments. Others pointed to the "red tape" associated with collection. This was a typical comment: "When I go to the nursing home I usually only have one or two patients to see—and usually only once a month—the fee is too low and the hassle to collect is discouraging. To make it worthwhile, [I] should have 10–15 patients to see, so the time and effort would justify the fee for that many at one time."

Most physicians denied that a dislike for nursing home patients kept them away, but a substantial minority (19.3 percent) said this reason was very important or somewhat important in their decision. Comments from this group of respondents suggested that their aversion was to the nursing home environment at least as much as to the clientele. One respondent stated, "Nursing homes are an unforgivable sin of our present day society. Population consists of human rejects, awaiting death." Another said, "Nursing homes are inadequately staffed. Patients go from hospital in stable condition to the nursing home where they are neglected, not fed properly, not given their medications when needed, and generally are 'warehoused' like criminals. In general they are inhumane, depressing, besides offering virtually nonexistent reimbursement to an ethical physician."

Almost one-fifth (18.5 percent) of respondents reported the lack of a nursing home close to their office as a very important reason for not making nursing home visits. This group tended to view nursing home care as something "extra" that took away from leisure time, and they rarely cited any other reasons, such as low fees, for not visiting. One physician made this typical comment: "Not enough hours in the day. I formerly gave up my Wednesday and Saturday afternoons to visit nursing homes. This is premium time and I believe too many patients fail to realize this."

Forty percent of respondents cited the low number of nursing home patients in their practice as a very important factor in their decision not to make any visits. Said one physician, "The majority of my patients believe in the family's responsibility in care for [the] elderly."

A few respondents (4.6 percent) reported that the nursing home in their community had its own staff physicians and hence they were not needed. In some instances, the decision to stop making nursing home visits was not voluntary but the result of pressure from the nursing home administrator or the patient's family. Commented one physician:

> I have seen the hard sell technique used by nursing homes: i.e., within one week of admission, families who have been satisfied with care in my office and hospital ask to have the physician at the nursing home assume care without explanation.
>
> I [was] asked if I minded another physician checking my patients monthly. My response was either I would care for them or the "Company Doc" would. They [the nursing home] made the decision for me.

About one-tenth (9.4 percent) of respondents objected to federal nursing home regulations, particularly those regarding frequency of visits, and the way skilled care and custodial care were defined. Many also questioned the motivation of facility operators. These physicians were typically much older than others in the sample and were trained in an era when the federal government played virtually no role in the financing of health care services. The following comment is representative of this group:

> I resent being told I must be in the nursing home at certain times. Approximately 5–6 years ago I cared for 50–60 patients in several area nursing homes. Governmental regulations became intrusive to patient care, requiring me to see patients on a monthly basis who may have required weekly or only every 3–4 month visits for specific problems. Patients were being forced into classification by the nursing home to increase their reimbursement. I disagreed with all the above.

That such perceptions exist among some physicians ought not to come as a surprise. For the LTC administrator it constitutes a reaffirmation of what he or she probably already knows: The challenges of caring for the infirm elderly in institutional settings are not *lesser* challenges than caring for patients in the acute care hospital setting, they are *different* challenges. Perhaps the biggest challenge—and for physicians new to institutionalized long-term care, the biggest adjustment—is dealing with sometimes difficult families. Other challenges include working as a coequal member of a primary care team; caring for chronic, irremediable conditions; dealing with demented residents and thus having to find sources of job satisfaction where there is little or no personal contact; confronting new ethical issues and treatment decisions; meeting responsibilities not only to patients but to other persons within the LTC organization and to the institution itself; coping with the stresses of multiyear relationships with patients, families, and colleagues.

It is a special sort of person who can accept, indeed relish, this unique set of challenges. A doctor from the staff of a major medical center in Chicago, writing in the *New England Journal of Medicine*, pointed to the most important qualification of a "good nursing home physician," that he or she must, above all, genuinely like old people. From this premise, the writer sketched an occupational profile:

> He is foremost a gerontophile—a term that, if hitherto uninvented, is long overdue. He is not put off by the infirmities of the aged. He realizes that there is much to learn about gerontology, and he is permanently educable. He is also medically mature; he does not require immediate satisfactions and strives willingly for distant and uncertain goals. He does not suffer from the common misperception that the turnover of patients in nursing homes is rapid; he is aware that the average stay of a resident is measured in years. The important corollary, of course, is that he looks forward to establishing close, warm long-term relationships with patients. He knows that his stance may be necessarily paternalistic, but he rejects the role of hard lawgiver.[19]

As the preceding discussion suggests, the recruiting and supervising of a medical staff is a major managerial challenge for the LTC administrator. It exists whether the staff consists of private physicians who have been granted admitting and treating privileges, salaried physicians who are full- or part-time employees of the institution, or some combination thereof.

The task of recruitment and supervision necessarily begins with the hiring of a medical director. Medicare regulations require that every SNF facility employ, at least on a consultant basis, a licensed physician in this role. The medical director is responsible for coordinating medical services in the facility and for ensuring the adequacy and appropriateness of the medical care provided to residents. Among other things, the medical director must delineate the responsibilities of attending physicians, though in smaller LTC institutions the medical director will likely be the de facto primary care physician for most of the residents.

The first priority of the LTC administrator, therefore, is to select as medical director a licensed physician who (1) has sufficient expertise to perform competently in a long-term care setting; (2) is understanding of the obligations of the position, as delineated in the job description; and (3) is willing to devote the requisite number of hours per week in order to fulfill the obligations of the position. The medical director must be adequately compensated so that turnover in the position will not be a recurring problem.

When screening candidates for medical director and for medical staff membership, the following items are key.

The physician must enjoy working with the elderly. As already noted, this is the primary requirement, for the medical staff as for every other position in the LTC organization. Persons who have a special affection for the elderly seem, very often, to have had as children a strong attachment to a grandparent, perhaps even stronger than to the parents. Family history might, therefore, provide a clue—perhaps the mother died early and the child was raised by his or her grandparents. Whatever the source of the attachment to the elderly, it must exist or the candidate will ultimately prove unsatisfactory.

The physician must be competent. All applicants for medical staff privileges should be thoroughly investigated. This includes verification of academic degrees, professional licenses, specialty board certifications, other institutional affiliations past and present, and personal references. As a precondition to employment or association with the LTC institution, the candidate should already enjoy staff privileges at a Joint Commission–accredited hospital.

The physician must be caring. It is arguable whether this personal quality is essential in an acute care hospital setting. But in an LTC institution, where relationships are forged and maintained over a long period of time, it is crucial. If the candidate does not project a caring demeanor, it is likely he or she will not be well suited to the LTC environment regardless of medical competence.

The physician must enjoy working as a team member. Medicine, more than the more collaborative professions, tends to attract independent personalities to its ranks. There is, therefore, a relative scarcity of doctors who enjoy, much less have experience in, working as a member of a primary care team. The successful candidate must be willing, by instinct, to accept nurses and social workers as equal partners in caregiving. Many otherwise fine physicians, attuned to the protocols of the acute care hospital, find themselves unable to do so.

The physician should ideally have some background in geriatrics. Geriatric medicine has certain unique features. Experience is useful, but if an otherwise qualified physician does not yet have it, he or she will soon acquire it.[20]

Restricting the Medical Staff

For an LTC institution to have its medical staff function smoothly within a primary care team construct, staff privileges should be limited to those physicians who are willing to accept the requirements of participation.

The decision to restrict, or closely delimit, the medical staff may require considerable courage on the part of the LTC administrator. There may be an outcry from some local physicians or from the institution's board of directors or corporate parent, who may see a vast network of referring doctors as something well worth retaining. So the LTC administrator must have a firm conviction that restricting the medical staff will enhance quality of care and thereby help to ensure the long-term financial viability of the institution.

A preliminary consideration is the facility's current reputation. A good place, one known in the community as having high standards of care, need not rely on scores of doctors for referrals. Unlike acute care hospitals, where the recommendation of the physician with staff privileges almost always is accepted by the patient or family without question, families of the infirm elderly usually take an active role in evaluating and selecting a long-term care institution. If the perception of the marketplace is favorable, there is probably already a substantial waiting list for admission.

In such instances, the LTC administrator might make it a condition of acceptance that any new resident become a patient of the in-house medical staff. Or, as an alternative, the LTC administrator might opt to actively "sell" the applicant and family on the quality of medical services available at the institution. This would involve carefully explaining the many virtues of the primary care team concept and perhaps noting the frequent failure of outside doctors, however well-intentioned, to conduct regular rounds. The residents might be given the option of redesignating their primary care physician every two months following admission so that any decision to sever a longstanding relationship with a family doctor will not be seen as irrevocable.

Another possible approach to restricting medical staff is to build it slowly through recruitment, periodically accepting doctors from the community onto staff as part-timers. Typically, in making these evaluations, the LTC administrator would look first at those individuals who already have a sizable number of patients in residence.

Outside physicians who are unwilling to participate as members of a primary care team but who have a sincere interest in maintaining contact with a former patient may be accorded consulting privileges. Very often, such physicians, as they become more familiar (and comfortable) with the organization of medical services at the institution, opt to become more actively involved and accept invitations to join the staff as part-time members.

Improvements in the quality of care delivered by primary care teams is one virtue of a restricted medical staff. Another is that doctors on staff will gradually develop a loyalty to the LTC institution and to the in-house rules, regulations, procedures, and peer review activities that are part of life within a structured health care organization. One likely collateral benefit: The medical staff will more willingly perform the various tasks required of the institution by the state as a condition of its licensure, including participation on quality assurance committees, credentialing committees, medical records committees, pharmacy and therapeutics committees, and the like.

Overseeing the Medical Staff

The LTC administrator can hardly be expected to stand at the shoulders of members of the medical staff, commenting on their decisions and demeanor as they make their rounds and otherwise interact with residents. Nevertheless, the administrator must take an active role in overseeing the medical affairs of the institution. Not to do so would be an abdication of responsibility as a health care professional and as the manager immediately accountable for the institution's long-term financial viability.

How can the LTC administrator assure him- or herself and others that the quality of medical care being delivered at the institution is superior? Answer: By applying the same principles of internal and external review that are used throughout the organization. The following policies may be useful:

1. Any physician enjoying treatment privileges at the institution must allow a "house doctor" assigned by the LTC administrator or the medical director to see residents any time the physician is away.

2. The reviewing physician will issue a written report on the quality of care observed, with copies sent to (1) the LTC administrator, (2) the physician being evaluated, and (3) the medical director (where appropriate).

If the LTC administrator is reluctant to evaluate the credentials of a candidate for house doctor, he or she can request the local community hospital or nursing home association to do the evaluation.

In addition to such in-process control checks, the LTC administrator can also rely on the various feedback mechanisms that have already been instituted throughout the organization. Family survey questionnaires are a valuable source of insight into the quality of medical care being delivered. Likewise, employee opinion and attitude surveys and input from staff meetings, especially the remarks of nurses and social workers (the other partners in the primary care teams), can direct management's attention to possible areas of concern.

The problems revealed in the feedback data are usually unrelated to issues of medical competence. Rather, they almost always involve interpersonal skills or suitability of placement, as in these examples:

- A doctor assigned to a unit most of whose residents had advanced Alzheimer's disease might become depressed, a painful way of discovering that he or she needed substantive contact with patients in order to flourish professionally. Discussion with LTC management would perhaps result in a transfer to a unit with a less debilitated population.

- A doctor might have difficulties establishing long-term relations with demanding families. Discussion with LTC management would perhaps lead all parties to conclude that the doctor could best serve the institution as a consultant rather than as a primary care physician.

- A doctor might be wonderful in one-on-one relationships with families and patients but be unable to give the necessary time to the other members of the primary care team. Discussion with LTC management would perhaps affirm that the doctor would be happiest and most productive in a more independent setting.

In all such instances, the LTC administrator must function as a general manager, making decisions that best serve the interests of the residents, their families, the institution, and the public at large. The object of scrutiny here may be physicians, but the process of finding and evaluating information and balancing the needs of various constituencies is the same process used with all other departments of the organization.

Withdrawing or Withholding Treatment

In one of the case examples, the doctor and the family found themselves in dispute over the proper course of treatment for a 107-year-old resident who was totally contracted. An ad hoc advisory panel of medical staff, convened by the LTC administrator, reviewed the case and recommended that the wishes of the family be followed.

The case raises, explicitly or implicitly, many of the issues that currently bedevil our society in its quest for the "right rule of behavior" regarding withdrawing or withholding of treatment. Among the underlying questions are the following.[21]

- Is the resident's own expression of his or her desires regarding the continuation of care determinative—must we necessarily follow them—or are there limits to such autonomy? For example, must we honor a resident's decision to refuse some life-sustaining treatment in the face of laws that prohibit assisting another to commit suicide?

- Assuming we wish to honor the resident's decision, what evidence do we need to establish what it is? Are advance directives, such as a living will or the naming of a surrogate decision maker, deserving of the same deference as the resident's contemporaneous instructions?

- What of the resident who leaves no advance directive and is, or becomes, decisionally incapacitated? Who speaks on behalf of this resident, and what is the appropriate standard to use? Can a family member speak for the resident simply on the basis of their relationship, or must a court appoint the spokesperson as guardian in order to establish formal authority?
- Where a surrogate decision maker is appointed by a court, does that person have the same range of authority that the resident him- or herself would have if competent, or are there substantive or procedural limits?
- Are there legal or ethical implications to the means by which treatment is terminated? That is, should a distinction be drawn between acting (i.e., withdrawing a treatment that has been ongoing, such as disconnecting a respirator) and not acting (i.e., withholding a new therapy, such as not administering the next course of medication)? Does disconnecting a piece of technological apparatus, such as a respirator, have the same moral import as disconnecting a passive device, such as a feeding tube? In this context, is it useful to debate whether a treatment is "ordinary" or "extraordinary"?

As a result of detached examination by many attorneys, judges, and medical ethicists, some answers to these vexing questions are gradually emerging. The answers may be contradictory, depending on which state or court has issued the decision. They may resolve a given question only for the moment, with rapid changes in technology or social mores rendering last year's best judgment moot. Nevertheless, they do provide the LTC administrator with a framework from which to examine the legal issues.

At the heart of the matter is the doctrine that the ability of all persons to make their own treatment decisions must be considered unimpaired until proved otherwise. Residents become incompetent to make medical decisions when they are unable to understand information about their medical condition and its implications or are unable to communicate their decisions even though they may understand. Arriving at a determination that a "decision-making capacity" exists or does not exist is, at bottom, an exercise in common sense. This claim is supported by the 1983 report of the President's Commission for the Study of Ethical Problems in Medicine and Biomedical and Behavioral Research, where it is stated that the determination is a "judgment an informed lay person can make."[22]

However, when the long-term care resident is clearly unable to make medical decisions, then his or her previously expressed wishes become extremely significant in dictating the treatment plan. For example, in the case of *In re Peter* (1987), a 65-year-old nursing home resident lay in an irreversible coma, a condition in which she could live "indefinitely." But she had made clear her intentions regarding termination of treatment and had appointed a friend to speak for her in a power of attorney executed before she lost decision-making capacity. The court, acting on the friend's instructions, allowed the removal of the nasogastric tube that sustained the woman with essential nutrients and fluids. In doing so, the court held that the question in such cases is whether there exists "clear and convincing evidence" that the patient would have declined the treatment. When there is, the patient's views provide the basis to proceed and the treatment may be withdrawn without regard to impact on the patient's life expectancy and without any objective balancing of the burdens and benefits of the questioned treatment.[23]

Often, however, there is no clear and convincing evidence of the patient's desire to forgo treatment. In such instances, the court may choose to validate some "substituted judgment" of what those wishes might have been. For example, in the case of *In re Jobes* (1987), a 31-year-old woman lay in a coma for seven years as a result of an automobile accident. She was sustained by a jejunostomy tube (j-tube) inserted in her abdomen that provided her with essential nutrients. She had left no evidence of her desires regarding termination of treatment. Her husband sought removal of the j-tube, but the court concluded that he was expressing his views as to her interests rather than her own. Nevertheless, the court held that the doctors could follow his instructions, saying that in the absence of the patient's own directions,

> family members are best suited to make substituted judgments for incompetent patients not only because of their peculiar grasp of the patient's approach to life, but also because of their special bonds with him or her. Our common human experience informs us that family members are generally most concerned with the welfare of the patient. . . .
>
> Mrs. Jobes is blessed with warm, close, and loving family members. It is entirely proper to assume that they are best qualified to determine the medical decisions that she would make.[24]

Though the court in *Jobes* assured itself that the patient's "warm, close, and loving family" would be most concerned with her welfare in making the decision, it was quite aware of the obvious problem, namely, that in the absence of formal instruction or other hard evidence, the patient's own views must remain unknown, and therefore it is never entirely certain that the family's views are consistent with what the patient would have said.

As a result, the court in *Jobes* limited its rule to cases in which the patient is in an irreversible coma. Further, it specified formal review procedures whereby the prognosis of irreversible coma must be confirmed by independent medical judgment. For hospitalized patients, this meant review by a hospital prognosis committee; for nonhospitalized patients, like Jobes herself (she was in a nursing home), review by two independent physicians was required. Also, said the court, if the doctors have doubts about the instructions given them by family members, they can seek appointment of a guardian to review the termination decision.

Thus, the decision-making authority in cases like *Jobes* becomes considerably circumscribed when compared to that of the friend who held the patient's power of attorney in *Peter*. In effect, *Jobes* allows family members to withdraw life-sustaining measures only in limited instances (irreversible coma) and where the court would probably have reached the same result applying a more objective standard.

When the patient is not in a coma (so that *Jobes* does not apply) and has not left clear instructions (so that *Peter* does not apply) anticipated life expectancy becomes the critical, if not determining, factor. For example, in the case of *In re Conroy* (1985), the patient was an elderly woman who lived in a nursing home. She was not in a coma but did suffer from severe, permanent mental and physical impairments. Doctors agreed that her life expectancy was less than one year regardless of what was done for her. She left no clear instructions.

By the time the state supreme court decided the appeal in her case, she had died. Two years later, the *Peter* court, reviewing the decision in *Conroy*, affirmed that the patient's life expectancy is extremely important in determining whether treatment can be terminated. Where a patient has a life expectancy of more than one year if treatment is provided, said the court, treatment cannot be withheld.

Important conditions, however, may be imposed by the court on the family's authority to authorize the withdrawing or withholding of life-sustaining treatment, even when life expectancy is less than one year. Once again, it depends on the court's knowledge of the patient's probable preferences. Where there is some "trustworthy" evidence that the patient would have refused further treatment but the evidence falls short of meeting *Peter*'s "clear and convincing" test, treatment may still be terminated if the burdens of continued life "markedly outweigh" the benefits to be derived from that life. But where there is no trustworthy evidence of the patient's preference, it is not enough that the pain and suffering of continued life "markedly outweigh" the benefits. In such instances, there must also be a finding that the patient will suffer so much pain that prolonging his or her life "would be inhumane."[25]

All three of these cases—*Peter*, *Jobes*, and *Conroy*—were decided by the New Jersey Supreme Court. Because it has addressed these questions more often and more comprehensively than any other American court, the opinions of the New Jersey court are influential. But they are not universally binding. Under the New Jersey approach, it is extremely difficult to withdraw or withhold care from a person who has never expressed views in support of that course. If such a patient is not in an irreversible coma and might live for more than one year with full support, treatment must continue. Even if the noncomatose patient's life expectancy is less than one year, treatment cannot be terminated in the absence of "inhumane" levels of pain, unless there is trustworthy evidence that the patient would want the care withdrawn. So, although New Jersey has accepted the possibility of terminating life-sustaining care on the basis of an objective determination of the patient's best interests rather than the patient's own judgments, it has carefully limited that possibility.

Other courts may depart from the New Jersey approach in both directions. For example, New York allows withdrawal of life-sustaining care only on the patient's own authorization, leaving little if any room for employment of more objective factors in cases where the patient's views are inaccessible. Massachusetts, on the other hand, is more willing than New Jersey to end a patient's life on the basis of a third party's objective assessment.

New York's views are set down in *In re Mary O'Connor* (1988), which involved a 77-year-old woman who had been institutionalized after suffering a stroke three years earlier. The doctors agreed she had sustained significant brain damage, rendering her permanently incapable of participating in her medical care decisions. She was, however, not comatose. She could respond to simple commands, such as "turn over," and was at times able to sit up in a chair.

O'Connor's case came to court because she had lost her gag reflex, making it impossible for her to swallow food. As a result, her doctors wanted to insert a nasogastric tube. This was opposed by her two daughters, who understood that without it she would die of thirst or starvation. There was conflicting evidence regarding whether she had the capacity to experience suffering if the daughters' instructions were followed. The physician testifying for them noted that O'Connor could be given pain killers if this was a concern.

The New York Court of Appeals rejected the daughters' claim under a standard allowing care to be terminated only when "it was established by clear and convincing evidence that the patient would have so directed if he were competent and able to communicate." O'Connor had left no clear instructions on such matters when competent. The daughters could only report on a few casual conversations in which she suggested that she would not want to be sustained artificially. But she had never discussed the withdrawal of food and water, nor had she said whether she would want care withdrawn even "if that would produce a painful death." This kind of evidence fell far short of the New York standard. O'Connor's statements that "nature should be permitted to take its course" and that she would not want to be "a burden to anyone" are the kinds of statements that older people "invariably make," said the court. "Few nursing home patients would ever receive life-sustaining medical treatment" if such statements were sufficient.

So, in its decision, the New York Court of Appeals emphasized that "the right to decline treatment is personal," that "the inquiry must always be narrowed to the patient's expressed intent," and that "the clear and convincing evidence standard requires proof sufficient to persuade the trier of fact that the patient held a firm and settled commitment to the termination of life supports under the circumstances like those presented." Since O'Connor's own views were inaccessible, the opinions of her daughters on what she might have wished or what constituted her best interests were considered irrelevant.[26]

If this represents one substantial deviation from the New Jersey approach, the Massachusetts approach deviates in the opposite direction. In *Brophy v. New England Sinai Hospital* (1986), a once healthy, active man suffered a ruptured aneurysm at the base of his basilar artery, leaving him permanently comatose. Being unable to swallow, he was sustained by a gastrostomy tube (g-tube), which supplied hydration and nutrients directly to his digestive system. His family wanted the g-tube disconnected, but the hospital refused. Brophy suffered no complications from the use of the g-tube in the 18 months it had sustained him, and there was no reason to believe that he would not survive at least several more years in his current condition.

New Jersey would have applied *Jobes* to the *Brophy* facts; given Brophy's comatose state, the family's request would have been honored. Massachusetts, however, did not take the New Jersey approach of adopting more relaxed rules under specific circumstances like permanent coma or short life expectancy. Rather, it chose to adopt a relaxed version of the "substituted judgment" standard for general application to all cases. Brophy's family testified to conversations of years earlier in which he made the kinds of comments that New York, in *O'Connor*, found insufficient. They also reported a comment made at the hospital after the rupture of his aneurysm, in which he said to one of his daughters, "If I can't sit up to kiss one of my beautiful daughters, I may as well be six feet under."

This record might not be adequate, under New Jersey's *Conroy* test, to provide "trustworthy" evidence that Brophy would want to end his life. Nevertheless, the New Jersey court would apply *Jobes*, not *Conroy*, and the family could authorize removal of the g-tube because of the irreversible coma. Massachusetts, however, was willing to rely on the family's representations in *Brophy* without limiting its holding to comatose patients. In fact, the court in *Brophy* hardly addressed the question of whether it had adequate evidence of the patient's desires, even though it grounded its decision on each individual's right to make such decisions. Instead, the Massachusetts court chose to treat the family's expressions as if they were the patient's own wishes.[27]

In Missouri, the evidentiary requirements for a family to have treatment ended are among the strictest of all states. In a landmark case, *Cruzan by Cruzan v. Harmon* (1988), a young woman, Nancy Cruzan, had lost all upper brain function as a result of an automobile accident and remained in a permanent coma six years later. She had sufficient brainstem function to breathe on her own, but her nutrition and hydration were maintained by a g-tube. Her parents, having given up all hope for her recovery, sought to have the hospital remove the tube. The hospital refused to do so without judicial authorization. A trial judge issued the necessary order but was reversed by the Missouri Supreme Court.

The court concluded that the state's interest in preserving life was not offset by any clear or convincing evidence of Nancy Cruzan's own wishes or by any demonstration that the feeding tube was "heroically invasive" or burdensome. In its decision, the court also drew a distinction between "letting die" and "making die." Emphasizing that Nancy Cruzan was not terminally ill but could live indefinitely in a coma if care was continued, it said, "This is not a case where we are asked to let someone die. . . . This is a case in which we are asked to allow the medical profession to make Nancy die by starvation and dehydration."[28]

Some difficult ethical considerations were thus brought into sharp focus for national review: Whose rights were being fought for, Nancy Cruzan's rights or her parents' rights? Whose preferences were being advanced? As regards the involvement of the physicians, is there a valid distinction to be drawn between assisting to breathe and assisting to take food and water? What are the proper limits of technology? Whenever physicians have the capacity to extend life but do not employ it (e.g., opting under some circumstances not to resuscitate), one can say they are "making the patient die." How, then, can one classify the withholding of a respirator, an antibiotic, or essential surgery as reasonable acquiescence to a natural course of events but the withdrawing of a g-tube as an action subject to judicial review and perhaps blame?

The United States Supreme Court agreed to review the Missouri court's ruling in the *Cruzan* decision, and in June 1990 it delivered its opinion. Eight of the nine justices agreed that a person whose wishes are clearly known has a constitutional right to the discontinuance of life-sustaining treatment. But the justices differed over how specific a person must be in making his or her wishes known. By a vote of 5 to 4, they ruled that the state of Missouri could sustain Nancy Cruzan's life because her family had not shown by "clear and convincing evidence" that she would have wanted the treatment stopped.[29]

Justice Scalia, while concurring with the majority in both instances, argued for judicial restraint:

> What I have said . . . is not meant to suggest that I would think it desirable, if we were sure that Nancy Cruzan wanted to die, to keep her alive by the means at issue here. I assert only that the Constitution has nothing to say about it. . . . Our salvation is the Equal Protection Clause, which requires the democratic majority to accept for themselves and their loved ones what they impose on you and me. This Court need not, and has no authority to, inject itself into every field of human activity where irrationality and oppression may theoretically occur, and if it tries to do so it will destroy itself.[30]

Perhaps Justice Scalia's insight was the crucial lesson of the *Cruzan* decision—that partly by volition, partly by default, the courts have become the institutions to which many people immediately turn for guidance on problems of conscience and morality and that, by implication, the institutions that used to provide a coherent framework within which an individual could form moral and ethical opinions and reach conclusions seem no longer to be trusted, at least not entirely.[31]

Establishing Limited Treatment Protocols

If the foregoing discussion about the path of judicial opinion suggests anything, it is that there are no magic tricks, no legal secrets, that will make administrative and clinical decision making easy and reduce the probability of legal entanglement to zero. Rather, as is true in all other contexts, the best protection from lawsuits arising out of termination of care disputes lies in providing residents with high-quality care and humane, respectful treatment. Conduct by the LTC administrator and the staff that is ethically, socially, and clinically appropriate and that represents the institution's good faith and wisest judgment is the surest form of legal risk management.

As always, the key is to pay attention to interpersonal relations, which in turn means careful planning and open communication. Planning begins with a candid self-scrutiny of the LTC institution's values and beliefs regarding withholding or withdrawing of care. The LTC administrator, along with the medical director, must ask, What treatment procedures does this institution intend to perform and what does it consider to be beyond its purview?

The need to formalize decision making regarding medical treatment for the terminally ill in LTC institutions was stressed in the 1983 report of the President's Commission for the Study of Ethical Problems in Medicine and Biomedical and Behavioral Research and was documented by the findings of a 1984 survey of licensed nursing homes in Minnesota. In the Minnesota study, researchers found that although there was widespread acceptance of orders limiting treatment (65.9 percent of the facilities surveyed accepted DNR orders and 73.3 percent accepted other orders to limit treatment), only 23 percent of LTC institutions had formalized their procedures for arriving at and documenting the residents' care plan decisions.[32]

Formalizing the process of decision making requires the writing of a limited treatment protocol. Such a protocol, which is basically a statement of the steps to be followed in creating treatment plans for individual residents, typically includes the following components:

- a statement of the objectives of limited treatment
- a delineation of prescribed and prohibited care
- a description of the decision-making process
- a review of documentation procedures
- an assurance that any orders limiting treatment will be subject to periodic review

Orders to limit medical intervention may be of two types: those prohibiting resuscitation only (DNR) and those concerned with a broad range of other limitations of treatment (e.g., "Do Not Hospitalize" orders). In its protocol statement, the LTC institution must make the distinction between DNR and other prohibited or prescribed modalities of care extremely clear. The objective of a DNR order is highly specific: It is to limit cardiopulmonary resuscitation only. A DNR decision does not mean that other aspects of care are to be limited. For example, a resident may wish to have a DNR order but may also want aggressive medical treatment, including antibiotics and hospitalization, if he or she becomes ill.

For residents who request limitations of treatment beyond DNR, their treatment plans must be individualized to reflect their wishes. One resident may want no life-extending treatment whatsoever. Another may be willing to accept life extension only if current quality of life can be maintained. A resident with a cardiac problem, for example, may choose to be treated with a drug regimen but decline cardiac surgery.

In addition to ensuring that the limited treatment objectives of each resident's care plan are clearly defined, the protocol statement should also identify those treatments that are suggested, required, or prohibited by the LTC institution consistent with its mission. Most LTC institutions identify emotional support, religious support, skin care, turning, positioning, grooming, bowel-bladder rehabilitation, maintenance of sensory functioning, and oral feeding as obligatory. Protocols that address the problematic area of feeding often suggest that a conscientious effort be made to orally feed terminally ill residents but that, when this fails, tube feeding need not be started.

When a resident's care plan has been written according to the procedures in the protocol statement, decision making is facilitated. The decision as to whether a transfer to an acute care hospital is appropriate for an individual who has already decided against life-extending treatment is based on the objectives given in the care plan. For example, a resident with severe shortness of breath from pulmonary edema may have declined invasive life-prolonging treatments but also indicated that comfort is a primary care plan objective. In this case, hospitalization would be appropriate if a vigorous diuresis is the only means of relieving suffering.

Ethical decision making must always, of course, balance risk against reward. The decision to hospitalize or not to hospitalize, for example, must take into account that in an infirm elderly population the occurrence of falls, nosocomial infections, confusional states, and adverse drug reactions during hospitalization are more common and more severe than in other patient populations. Are the potential risks and discomforts of hospitalization outweighed in the given instance by the diagnostic and therapeutic benefits that are anticipated?

In the protocol statement, the resident's right of self-determination must always be affirmed. Any competent individual has the final authority on what are to be the limits of his or her care and has the right to restate his or her wishes regarding treatment at any time. In cases where the resident is, or is believed to be, cognitively impaired, the protocol must insist on documentation of the resident's longstanding views on limiting care as a means of providing substituted consent. Family members, doctors, nurses, social workers, and clergy who have loved, treated, cared for, and assisted the resident over time may all be helpful in this process. When a substitute decision maker has already been designated, the person's name and relationship to the resident, along with any supporting documentation, should be included in the medical record.

Finally, the administrative process must include continuing education of the LTC institution's employees so that they fully understand the rationale behind the limited treatment protocol, the spirit with which the residents' care plans are formulated, and the manner in which the residents' decisions should be carried out. The nursing staff, especially, deserves consideration in this regard. A nurse might easily view an order to withhold or withdraw nasogastric feeding, for example, as a deprivation of care. When it is explained that the order is consonant with the resident's desire to receive spoon feeding for as long as possible, with all the nurturing and caring implications of such feeding, the nurse may be more comfortable with the task of carrying out the resident's previously expressed wishes.[33]

How successful the implementation of the institution's limited treatment protocol will be depends entirely, and predictably, on the ability of its staff, especially its medical staff, to communicate. Where interpersonal skills are highly developed, the interaction between institution and resident or family generally flows smoothly and the risk of legal entanglement becomes virtually nil.

Certainly, the best time to raise the issue of limitations on treatment is as soon as possible after the individual has been admitted to residence, both for legal reasons (see "Advance Directives, Limited Treatment Protocols, and the Law" below) and in the interests of open communication. Delay serves no good purpose. Indeed, contrary to what is sometimes their expectation, doctors new to geriatrics often find that their patients have already given the matter considerable thought.

The subject should be broached in normal conversation, as if between new friends who are just beginning a long-term relationship. The discussion might begin like this:

> I need some guidance from you. I want you to help me in planning your care.
>
> I'm sure you know there are occasions when people just collapse and die suddenly. Their breathing stops. We know that in younger people it is possible to bring them back to life by administering artificial respiration and trying to get their heart to beat again. That

usually means having a tube put down your throat so that a machine can breath for you.

I have to tell you that in our experience, and in the experience of other long-term care institutions, this procedure is not usually successful. It was designed to save healthy young hearts, not people with many chronic illnesses. So, because of our experience, we have stopped doing it here. But I want your directives—what do you want me to do?—in case you stop breathing and have to be hospitalized where they have full facilities.

Some residents will respond, "I'm glad you asked me, because I've thought a lot about it," and begin to express treatment wishes in detail. Others will be uncomfortable and will reply, "I'll talk about it in a few weeks." In the latter instance, raise the issue again at the requested or an otherwise appropriate time.

The worst possible occasion to commence discussion about treatment directives is when a resident becomes acutely ill and must be transferred to a hospital without the subject ever having been raised. To ask such questions of a person who is in the midst of severe distress is not only unnecessary, it is unconscionably cruel.

The eliciting of information cannot always be done in a straightforward manner. Considerations such as cognitive impairment and the dynamics of family relationships often intervene, as occurred in the following case example.

An LTC institution admitted into residence a woman who appeared to be very sharp mentally. She knew the date; she knew where she was; she knew many details about where she had lived. But the primary care physician suspected that she was in an early stage of dementia, because her medical record showed she had always been something of a hypochondriac, running to doctors constantly for every ache and pain. Now when he asked, "How are you feeling?" she replied, "No problems. My blood pressure is fine."

The primary care team was having difficulty getting the discussion about advance directives to connect. Whenever the question was raised, the woman would say in a matter-of-fact tone, "Of course I want you to bring me back to life." Was this truly her wish? Or was she simply not understanding the thrust of the conversation?

The physician called the woman's son and informed him of the situation. The son replied, "I am sure my mother would not want to be resuscitated. We had a terrible experience with my father. He had Parkinson's disease and was resuscitated, and it was all downhill after that. I'm sure my mother would agree she wouldn't want that to happen to her."

But when the physician mentioned her late husband's experience to the woman, the memory did not register. So he called the son's wife. He said, "Your mother-in-law is not as intact as you think." The wife agreed immediately and said her husband was not able to see it.

The physician called the son again. "I think your mother's judgment is failing," he said. "She didn't remember that her husband had had severe Parkinson's disease. Frankly, I feel uncomfortable about relying on her judgment to resuscitate. I want you to make a decision." The son remained reluctant until the physician informed him that the decision could be changed at any time. He then readily agreed to have the DNR order entered in his mother's chart.

"We are trying to do what is best for your mother and for you," said the physician. "I know how difficult the situation must be for you."

The variations on this theme of how to confront the consequences of the inexorable passage of time are endless, as many variations as there are infirm elderly people and families and family histories. Yet there is a common thread. It is that in those LTC institutions that are truly aware of their legal and ethical responsibilities and are devoted to delivering care of the highest quality, the staff quickly come to understand that their obligation to each resident ultimately requires them to evaluate the benefits and burdens of treatment from the resident's perspective alone. Accepting the validity of another's perspective and helping that person bear the consequences of decisions that flow from it is one of life's supremely difficult challenges.

Advance Directives, Limited Treatment Protocols, and the Law

Among the possible kinds of advance directives, *living wills* have received the greatest attention. In many states, the enactment of living will statutes has been a direct response to popular pressure.

Notwithstanding the intensity of the debate, these statutes usually contain provisions sufficiently restrictive to rob them of most of their usefulness. For example, the statutes typically limit living wills to the withdrawal of "life-sustaining treatment" from individuals who are "terminally" ill. Situations in which patients are in a coma and may live for months or years without ever regaining consciousness so long as treatment is provided are effectively removed from consideration by the law. Likewise beyond the pale are progressive debilities such as Alzheimer's disease.

Also, living will statutes often contain restrictions on when or how the documents may be executed. The California act, for example, allows the execution of living wills only by individuals who have been diagnosed as terminally ill, and then only after a waiting period of at least 14 days. Many patients in such a condition are unable to maintain decision-making capacity for another two weeks. Even without the required waiting period, these provisions effectively exclude anyone who suffers a stroke or accident that suddenly leaves him or her without decision-making capacity.

Finally, living will statutes that authorize the withdrawal of life-sustaining treatment cannot provide a basis for affirmative acts such as the humane administration of morphine to a terminally ill cancer patient in great pain when the injection will shorten or end life. State legislatures, like courts, have great difficulty confronting and explicitly endorsing the deliberate hastening of death, and they are justifiably fearful of potential abuse.

In some respects, the debate in many states over the language of living will statutes is superfluous. Any adult with a friend or relative who he or she is confident will act in his or her best interests can simply appoint that person to act for him or her in the event of incapacitation. Such an appointment can be made in a document called a *durable power of attorney*.

Durable powers of attorney avoid many of the difficulties present with living wills and are recognized in the majority of states. They are not without ambiguities, however. First, the maker of a power of attorney cannot grant his or her agent more authority than has the maker. To the extent the competent patient's right to resist medical treatment is in doubt, the same doubts will apply to the agent as well. Indeed, the doubts may be greater if state law does not explicitly authorize use of powers of attorney for medical decision making. In such cases, health care professionals may refuse to accept the agent's authority to make decisions with which they disagree, despite the broad language usually contained in statutes authorizing the use of durable powers.

Second, there is some feeling that the relative informality with which powers of attorney can be executed casts doubt upon the appropriateness of their use in exceptionally important (i.e., "life or death") decisions. For that reason, and in response to the great public discussion preceding and following the U.S. Supreme Court's decision in the *Cruzan* case, many state legislatures are reviewing the laws authorizing durable powers with medical applications in mind.[34] Massachusetts, for example, enacted a health care proxy law in December 1990. Under this law, any person aged 18 and older can designate a "health care agent" to make decisions about treatment in the event the attending physician decides the patient is unable to make decisions for him- or herself.

For the LTC administrator, the issue of advance directives and limited treatment protocols is linked directly to the institution's eligibility for Medicare and Medicaid funding. The specific legal requirements are as follows.

Beginning December 1, 1991, as stated in the Omnibus Budget Reconciliation Act of 1990 (P.L. 101-508), all hospitals, skilled nursing facilities, home health agencies, and hospice programs receiving Medicare or Medicaid funding must provide written information to all adult care recipients regarding the state's laws on advance directives. Such information must include

1. a statement of the individual's rights under state law (whether statutory or as recognized by the courts of the state) to make decisions concerning his or her medical care, including the right to accept or refuse medical or surgical treatment and the right to formulate advance directives (e.g., a living will or durable power of attorney for health care, as provided by state law)
2. a statement of the written policies of the health care institution regarding the implementation of the individual's rights under state law

In addition, as a further requirement of participation in Medicare and Medicaid programs, the health care provider must agree

- to document in the medical record of each patient or resident whether or not the individual has executed an advance directive
- not to condition the provision of care or otherwise discriminate against a patient or resident based on whether or not the individual has executed an advance directive
- to ensure the institution's compliance with requirements of state law, whether statutory or as recognized by the courts of the state, respecting advance directives
- to provide, individually or with others, education for the staff and the community on issues concerning advance directives

Where the institution receiving Medicare or Medicaid funding is a skilled nursing facility, the federal law explicitly states that the mandated information must be provided to the individual at the time of admission to residence.

NOTES

1. Davis v. Virginian Railway Company, 80 S.Ct. 387 (1960).

2. Ibid.

3. See, for example, Bruce C. Vladeck, *Unloving Care: The Nursing Home Tragedy* (New York: Basic Books, 1980), 52–57; Institute of Medicine, *Improving the Quality of Care in Nursing Homes*, 146–70; Thomas G. Morford, "Nursing Home Regulation: History and Expectations," *Health Care Financing Review*, annual suppl. (1988): 129–32.

4. Estate of Smith v. Heckler, 747 F.2d 583 (1984).

5. Department of Health and Human Services, Health Care Financing Administration, "Medicare and Medicaid Programs; Long-Term Care Survey; Proposed Rule," *Federal Register* (October 31, 1985) vol. 50, no. 211, pp. 45584–87; Department of Health and Human Services, Health Care Financing Administration, "Medicare and Medicaid Programs; Long-Term Care Survey; Final Rule," *Federal Register* (June 13, 1986) vol. 51, no. 114, pp. 21550–58. See also Stephen J. Balcerzak, "Update: The New Long-Term Care Survey Process," *Journal of Long-Term Care Administration* 13 (Winter 1985): 106–8.

6. Estate of Smith v. Bowen, 656 F.Supp. 1093 (D. Colo. 1987).

7. Department of Health and Human Services, Health Care Financing Administration, "Medicare and Medicaid Programs; Long-Term Care Survey; Proposed Rule," *Federal Register* (July 1, 1987) vol. 52, no. 126, pp. 24752–88.

8. Estate of Smith v. Bowen, 675 F.Supp. 586 (D. Colo. 1987). See also Department of Health and Human Services, Health Care Financing Administration, "Medicare and Medicaid Programs; Long-Term Care Survey; Proposed Rule," *Federal Register* (October 16, 1987) vol. 52, no. 200, pp. 38582–606.

9. "New Law Protects Rights of Patients in Nursing Homes," *New York Times*, January 17, 1988, 1. See also Institute of Medicine, *Improving the Quality of Care in Nursing Homes*, esp. pp. v–x, 1–44; William L. Roper, "Pursuit of Objectives Can Be Fairly Measured," *Provider* 14 (December 1988): 14–17.

10. Department of Health and Human Services, Health Care Financing Administration, "Medicare and Medicaid Programs; Requirements for Long-Term Care Facilities; Final Rule with Request for Comments," *Federal Register* (February 2, 1989) vol. 54, no. 21, pp. 5316–73.

11. See Charles F. Chester, "Standards of Care and Sanctions for Breaches: The Survey Process in Long-Term Care," *Journal of Long-Term Care Administration* 17 (Fall 1989): 21–24.

12. See William F. May, "The Virtue and Vices of the Elderly," in *What Does It Mean to Grow Old? Reflections from the Humanities*, edited by Thomas R. Cole and Sally A. Gadow (Durham, N.C.: Duke University Press, 1986), 41–61.

13. "Police Investigate Library Death of Woman, 81," *Boston Globe*, August 11, 1977, 44; "Dead Woman in Library Was Missing 22 Days," *Boston Globe*, August 12, 1977, 3; "Library Safety Systems Fail—and a Trapped Woman Dies," *Boston Globe*, September 6, 1977, 1.

14. Mark A. Hall and Ira Mark Ellman, *Health Care Law and Ethics* (St. Paul, Minn.: West Publishing, 1990), 179–83; Charles Frederick Chester, "Union Strikes, Patient Abuse, and Legal Protection for the Nursing Home," *Journal of Long-Term Care Administration* 13 (Summer 1985): 50–54; David T. Marks, "Legal Implications of Increased Autonomy," *Journal of Gerontological Nursing* 13 (March 1987): 26–31.

15. Marshall B. Kapp, *Preventing Malpractice in Long-Term Care: Strategies for Risk Management* (New York: Springer, 1987), 57–67.

16. Darling v. Charleston Community Memorial Hospital, 33 Ill.2d 326, 211 N.E.2d 253 (1965).

17. Kapp, *Preventing Malpractice in Long-Term Care*, 65–66.

18. Janet B. Mitchell and Helene T. Hewes, "Why Won't Physicians Make Nursing Home Visits?" *The Gerontologist* 26 (1986): 650–54; Janet B. Mitchell, "Physician Visits to Nursing Homes," *The Gerontologist* 22 (1982): 45–48. In addition, see Dulcy B. Miller, Regina Lowenstein, and Ricky Winston, "Physicians' Attitudes toward the Ill Aged and Nursing Homes," *Journal of the American Geriatrics Society* 24 (1976): 498–505.

19. Theodore B. Schwartz, "For Fun and Profit: How to Install a First-Rate Doctor in a Third-Rate Nursing Home," *New England Journal of Medicine* 306 (1982): 743–44. In addition, see Leslie S. Libow and Perry Starer, "Care of the Nursing Home Patient," *New England Journal of Medicine* 321 (1989): 93–96; Leslie S. Libow, "Geriatric Medicine and the Nursing Home: A Mechanism for Mutual Excellence," *The Gerontologist* 22 (1982): 134–41.

20. For some nursing homes, the employment of geriatric nurse practitioners has proved to be a cost-effective way to improve quality of care. See, for example, Joan L. Buchanan, Robert M. Bell, Sharon B. Arnold, Christina Witsberger, Robert L. Kane, and Judith Garrard, "Assessing Cost Effects of Nursing-Home-Based Geriatric Nurse Practitioners," *Health Care Financing Review* 11 (Spring 1990): 67–78; Robert L. Kane, Judith Garrard, Carol L. Skay, David M. Radosevich, Joan L. Buchanan, Susan M. McDermott, Sharon B. Arnold, and Lloyd Kepferle, "Effects of a Geriatric Nurse Practitioner

on Process and Outcome of Nursing Home Care," *American Journal of Public Health* 79 (1989): 1271–77; Rosalie A. Kane, "Geriatric Nurse Practitioners as Nursing Home Employees: Implementing the Role," *The Gerontologist* 28 (1988): 469–77; Robert L. Kane, Lou Ann Jorgensen, Barbara Teteberg, and Jean Kuwahara, "Is Good Nursing-Home Care Feasible?" *JAMA* 235 (1976): 516–19.

21. See Hall and Ellman, *Health Care Law and Ethics* 236–340; also Kapp, *Preventing Malpractice in Long-Term Care*, esp. 77–187.

22. President's Commission for the Study of Ethical Problems in Medicine and Biomedical and Behavioral Research, *Deciding to Forego Life-Sustaining Treatment* (Washington, D.C.: U.S. Government Printing Office, 1983).

23. In re Peter, 108 N.J. 365, 529 A.2d 419 (1987).

24. In re Jobes, 108 N.J. 394, 529 A.2d 434 (1987).

25. In re Conroy, 98 N.J. 321, 486 A.2d 1209 (1985).

26. In re Mary O'Connor, 534 N.Y.S.2d 886, 531 N.E.2d 607 (1988).

27. Brophy v. New England Sinai Hospital, Inc., 398 Mass. 417, 497 N.E.2d 626 (1986).

28. Cruzan by Cruzan v. Harmon, 760 S.W.2d 408 (1988), cert. granted, Cruzan v. Director, Missouri Dept. of Health, 110 S.Ct. 2841 (1990).

29. "Justices Find a Right To Die, But the Majority Sees Need for Clear Proof of Intent," *New York Times*, June 26, 1990, 1.

30. "Excerpts from Court Opinions on Missouri Right-To-Die Case," *New York Times,* June 26, 1990, A18.

31. See especially "The Court's Angels," *Wall Street Journal*, June 27, 1990, A12. On December 26, 1990, Nancy Cruzan died of dehydration at the Missouri Rehabilitation Center, Mt. Vernon, Missouri, 12 days after a feeding tube was removed at her parent's request. A state judge found sufficient evidence to remove the tube when Cruzan's coworkers testified she said she never wanted to "live like a vegetable."

32. Steven H. Miles and Muriel B. Ryden, "Limited Treatment Policies in Long-Term Care Facilities," *Journal of the American Geriatrics Society* 33 (1985): 707–11.

33. Muriel B. Ryden and Steven H. Miles, "Limiting Treatment in Long-Term Care Facilities: The Need for Policies and Guidelines," *Journal of Long-Term Care Administration* 15 (Spring 1987): 23–26; Richard W. Besdine, "Decisions to Withhold Treatment from Nursing Home Residents," *Journal of the American Geriatrics Society* 31 (1983): 602–606. See also Dallas M. High, "Standards for Surrogate Decision Making: What the Elderly Want," *Journal of Long-Term Care Administration* 17 (Summer 1989): 8–13; Fenella Rouse, "Living Wills in the Long-Term Care Facility," *Journal of Long-Term Care Administration* 16 (Summer 1988): 14–19; Dennis A. Robbins, "Update: The Removal of Life Supports in Long-Term Care Facilities," *Journal of Long-Term Care Administration* 13 (Spring 1985): 3–5; Justine Thompson, Kathleen K. Pender, and Justine Hoffman-Schmitt, "Retaining Rights of the Impaired Elderly," *Journal of Gerontological Nursing* 13 (March 1987): 20–25; Marisue Cody, "Withholding Treatment: Is It Ethical?" *Journal of Gerontological Nursing* 12 (March 1986): 24–26. On "Do Not Resuscitate" orders for the elderly, see Daniel R. Longo, Robert Burmeister, and Matthew Warren, "'Do Not Resuscitate': Policy and Practice in the Long-Term Care Setting," *Journal of Long-Term Care Administration* 16 (Spring 1988): 5–11; Donald J. Murphy, Anne M. Murray, Bruce E. Robinson, and Edward W. Campion, "Outcomes of Cardiopulmonary Resuscitation in the Elderly," *Annals of Internal Medicine* 111 (1989): 199–205; Donald J. Murphy, "Do-Not-Resuscitate Orders: Time for Reappraisal in Long-Term-Care Institutions," *JAMA* 260 (1988): 2098–101; Stuart J. Youngner, "Who Defines Futility?" *JAMA* 260 (1988): 2094–95; David L. Schiedermayer, "The Decision to Forego CPR in the Elderly Patient," *JAMA* 260 (1988): 2096–97; Tom Tomlinson and

Howard Brody, "Ethics and Communication in Do-Not-Resuscitate Orders," *New England Journal of Medicine* 318 (1988): 43–46; Arnold Wagner, "Cardiopulmonary Resuscitation in the Aged: A Prospective Survey," *New England Journal of Medicine* 310 (1984): 1129–30.

34. See Hall and Ellman, *Health Care Law and Ethics* 283–88.

Chapter **8**

Marketing, Public Relations, and Community Involvements

In the preceding chapters, many issues relating to the delivery of quality long-term care services to the infirm elderly have been addressed: How to organize and administer operations efficiently. How to balance fiscal considerations against other institutional demands and imperatives. How to promote harmony and cooperation among employees and managerial staff. How to interact with the state and federal regulatory apparatus. How to minimize risk through greater understanding of the changing legal environment.

These are, generally speaking, "hard" issues of management. That is, the introduction of significant change in any of these areas will have a substantive, probably measurable effect on the lives of the people who are directly involved in the daily activities of the LTC institution—its staff, its residents, and the families of residents. Reorganize the management structure, redirect the flow of money, rearrange the pace or timing of resident services, reformulate the state regulations, or rewrite case or statutory law and a profound change in the workings of the institution will immediately be seen, heard, felt, smelled, or tasted.

By virtue of their immediate impact, hard issues are necessarily given precedence on any agenda of managerial activity. Far more difficult to define, less measurable in their impact, and therefore easier to dismiss or ignore are the soft issues that relate to marketing, public relations, and community involvements. It is these aspects of LTC administration that are the focus of this final chapter.

PERCEPTION IS REALITY

Think about the last time you entered a place of business or called on the telephone and instantaneously formulated a judgment about the nature of the establishment—its expertise, its trustworthiness, its eagerness to have you as a customer—based on nothing more than the tone of voice or manner of presentation of the person who greeted you. If the firm's representative was cheerful, natural, concerned, and sympathetic, you probably responded positively. This did not, in and of itself, clinch the sale or guarantee that the cordial relationship would continue. But it did carry you willingly to the next stage of the interaction. By contrast, if the representative was apathetic, cold, condescending, or robotic—the four deadly sins of customer service—you either opted to terminate the relationship immediately or proceeded to the next stage of the interaction with heightened caution and one eye on the door.

Such events, and countless other verbal and nonverbal exchanges between business establishments and those who would be customers, confirm what common sense tells us to be true: People use appearances to make judgments about realities. They rely on instinct and intuition, taking bits and pieces of information and using them to infer characteristics of the whole (fairly or unfairly). In the typical customer service exchange, it is not what is said that matters, but what is heard. It is not what is shown, but what is seen. It is not what is meant, but what is understood.

That "perception is reality" is an article of faith among marketing experts and their kin, political consultants and communications gurus. "A product is more than a tangible thing," wrote Theodore Levitt in *The Marketing Imagination*. "From the buyer's viewpoint, the product is a promise, a cluster of value expectations of which its nontangible parts are as integral as its tangible parts."[1] Dispassionate logic may impose a distinction between substance and metaphor, between reality and the symbol of reality, but for the buyer caught up in the rush of the marketplace—for example, an infirm elderly person, spouse, or child desperately seeking a comfortable and caring institutional setting—the distinction between tangible and intangible, real and imagined, can and often does become blurred.

Recognizing this, shrewd vendors of any product invest heavily in symbolic values. Politicians pose before the flag, bankers transact their affairs in granite temples, and attorneys receive their clients in hushed, paneled sanctuaries. Automobile manufacturers make motor cars but market class sensibility, cosmetics manufacturers mix chemicals but advertise hope, and computer hardware and software manufacturers seduce even the most technically literate buyers with appeals to sight, touch, and the promise of power.

All of this may seem to the LTC administrator to be far removed from the problems of providing quality care to the infirm elderly, but it is not. Every LTC institution, whatever its size or organizational structure or type of ownership, has a set of marketing challenges. First, the institution must resolve its crisis of identity, that is, it must know and be able to articulate its reason for being, its special capabilities and talents, its short-term goals and long-term aspirations.

Next, it must learn as much as possible about the various public constituencies it serves and the "cluster of value expectations" that energizes each of them.

Finally, it must marry institutional capabilities to public needs in an attractive or innovative way so that when tomorrow arrives, or a year from tomorrow, or a decade from tomorrow, a steady stream of residents, employees, volunteers, or donors (or whatever group has been targeted) will have been ensured.

Put another way, the strategic marketing exercise involves the asking of some basic and (to readers of the present volume) by now quite familiar questions about constituencies, resources, and mission. Taken as a whole, these lines of inquiry—and the thoughtful responses they elicit—create a framework for self-scrutiny and a means by which the LTC administrator and his or her staff can chart the direction of the institution into the short- and long-term future.

THINKING ABOUT STRATEGIC MARKETING

In small LTC institutions, the strategic marketing function may be the sole responsibility of the LTC administrator, one of the many "hats" of general management he or she routinely wears. In somewhat larger institutions, the task may be assigned to several members of the management team functioning as an ad hoc group. In still bigger institutions, the position (variously called marketing director, marketing planner, or planning director) may be clearly defined within the table of organization.

However it is structured, and whether the LTC institution is chartered for-profit or nonprofit, the persons conducting the strategic marketing exercise must be comfortable thinking in the following terms.[2]

Profit Planning. The planner's aim here is to devise a "product mix" (i.e., a menu of long-term care services) that will generate sales and profits (or funds for future development) at levels of risk that are acceptable to the owners or board of directors.

Long-Run Trends, Threats, and Opportunities. The planner's aim here is to identify the major problems and challenges that will impact the institution five or ten years hence, then to translate these into opportunities in the form of new products, new markets, and new marketing strategies that will ensure the long-term viability of the institution.

Customer Types and Market Segments. The planner's aim here is to discern how each customer defines "value" and "quality" and, from that analysis, to determine how to maximize the institution's appeal to its most profitable market segments.

Systems for Market Analysis, Planning, and Control. The planner or the members of the planning group should feel at ease with numbers and enjoy thinking through the financial implications of a marketing plan. The goal here is to devise a financial reporting system that can pinpoint strategic problems and opportunities as they emerge.

The questions that are asked by the persons conducting the planning exercise logically follow from this strategic view of the world, and they relate specifically to the LTC institution's markets, resources, and mission. The information derived enables management to design both short-term plans (e.g., an annual budget) and long-term plans that are clear, innovative, data-based, and, above all, true to the organization's sense of self and purpose.

The three main kinds of inquiry are market analysis, resource analysis, and mission analysis.[3]

Market Analysis

Market analysis focuses on three questions: What is the business environment? What is the market definition? What is the market need?

The Business Environment

The questions relating to the business environment are essentially the same as asked during the forecasting phase of the budget preparation exercise (see "Forecasting" in Chapter 4). They include the following:

- What important social, political, and economic trends are affecting the long-term care industry in the state? In the nation?
- Are there any significant shifts in elderly demographics, such as those resulting from influxes of population or changing neighborhoods, that are affecting local demand for long-term care services?
- Are there any economic or demographic changes that are impacting the structure of the local labor force or family income?
- For LTC institutions involved in the care of Medicaid recipients, are state reimbursement levels keeping pace with the changing needs of the resident population?
- For LTC institutions involved in the care of private-pay residents, are prices and values fully competitive with the rates being charged by the competition? How would the institution be affected if its primary competition suddenly adjusted its prices upward? Downward? If it switched from an all-inclusive pricing policy to a low base rate, with any additional services provided billed as extras?

Market Definition

The questions relating to market definition are intended to help define the primary market served by the LTC institution. The basic question is, Of a world full of infirm elderly people, who are the intended customers? The market may be defined according to one or several of the following categories:

- *Geography.* This category groups potential residents or their families according to where they live, work, or regularly visit. Except for very unusual circumstances, such as an LTC institution that endeavors to service a regional or national clientele, people will generally reject any location that is not familiar, convenient, and accessible.
- *Level of Care Required.* This category groups potential residents according to level of care required. Does the institution intend to service a market of infirm elderly individuals manifesting the broadest possible range of physical, psychological, and psychosocial impairments? Or does it intend to define parameters for admission more strictly? If the latter is the case, how does the institution intend to deal with current residents whose functionality suddenly or gradually falls below "acceptable" limits?[4]
- *Ability to Pay.* This category groups potential residents or their families according to income. Some LTC institutions choose to service the private-pay market exclusively. Others, the Medicaid market only. Others, both markets in some fixed or fluctuating proportion.

An LTC institution that defines its market by means of this last category faces a unique strategic marketing problem: Should the services available to private-pay residents be differentiated in some respect from those offered to residents whose care is subsidized by some form of public assistance? If so, how and to what extent? The problem is messy for several reasons. On the one hand, elderly individuals (or their families) paying perhaps $150 to $200 per day for long-term care might reasonably insist on some special benefit that is not generally available (or is not perceived to be generally available) to the entire resident population. On the other hand, transfers from private-pay status to Medicaid are hardly uncommon, and an institution eager to bestow special treatment (private rooms, special menus, etc.) on the well-to-do might be resented greatly by those same individuals or their families when their preeminent status is no longer affordable.

The imposition of class distinctions is always a dangerous policy for an LTC institution, which is not to say that for some institutions it may not be an entirely appropriate, indeed valuable, marketing tool. For example, how better to persuade prospective residents receiving public subsidies that the quality of care provided by the institution is exemplary than to point to individuals in residence who are willing to pay their own money to be there? Whatever the decision reached by the planner in the individual instance, it must be based on full knowledge of the needs, perceptions, and expectations of the market segments being served. The classic admonition to "know your customers" is applicable here, and everywhere else, in the strategic planning exercise.

Once the market for long-term care services has been defined, the parameters must be tested and validated. Specifically, the question must be asked, Is the market as defined of sufficient size—that is, are there enough potential customers in it—to justify the institution's existence? If the answer given is yes, how is this known to be true? On the basis of historical experience? On the evidence of surveys of comparable demographic or geographic regions?[5] In all cases, the evidence must support the conclusion or some redefinition of the primary market is likely warranted.

Market Segmentation

Once the primary market has been defined, it is necessary to identify the major market segments to be served. Probably the category of segmentation that is most useful for marketing long-term care services is *demographics*. Infirm elderly individuals who have already experienced substantial losses and their families usually place great value on being where people and things are familiar. For many, this makes commonalities of ethnicity, language, cuisine, education, income, or religion extremely powerful and attractive. Frequently, demographic character-istics are closely linked to geography, reflecting the tendency of like groups to form homogeneous clusters in neighborhoods. In such cases, targeting (through newspaper advertising, direct mailing, guest lectures, invitations to guided tours or institutional functions, etc.) is relatively simple and can be very effective.

A closely related category of segmentation is *psychographics*, which refers to lifestyle attitudes and behavior patterns of individuals. People within the same demographic group may nevertheless exhibit vast psychographic differences. Lifestyles, eating and drinking habits, awareness of and attitudes toward health issues, self-image, personal beliefs, fears, and emotions can be potent bonding agents or, where commonality does not exist, cause for extreme distrust and estrangement. Because psychographic similarities may counterbalance, even ne-gate, dissimilarities in ethnicity, religion, and so on, appeals to them can be an extremely useful marketing technique.

While these considerations may seem to the LTC administrator to be quite otherworldly, the issue of market segmentation invariably comes down to a simple set of questions: What subgroups within the primary market would seem to have a favorable disposition toward the institution and its services and thus be consid-ered worthy of active pursuit as customers? Are these segments of sufficient size to justify targeting? Is the competition already actively soliciting them? If so, are they doing so successfully? Unsuccessfully? Why?

Needs Assessment

Once again, the questions to be asked by the planner are quite simple: What are the special needs of each market segment identified? What are the expecta-tions of each segment? How does each define value?

The difficulty, of course, lies in trying to arrive at valid answers, since every bit of conventional wisdom must be questioned. For example, in a recent study of 150 mentally intact nursing home residents and 150 nurse's aides in 45 LTC institutions located in five states, researchers found that what residents viewed as important often differed markedly from what the nurse's aides thought the residents would consider important. For instance, when asked to rank items on a list in order of importance, residents rated as most important being able to leave the home for a short period of time to go for a walk or to run errands. Second in importance was being able to use a telephone. Aides, in comparison, thought that residents would be most concerned with choosing recreational activities and entertainment, a choice that the residents rated fifth of ten. The aides placed leaving the home third on their list and using the telephone tenth.

"None of the people in the nursing home said anything about living wills and durable power of attorney," remarked the director of the Center for Bioethics at a flagship state university, somewhat in amazement. "Almost no one said anything about feeding tubes or resuscitation or almost anything having to do with medicine. There was no high drama, no machines buzzing.

"Instead, a whole new world unfolded. There were ethical problems that I had never given any thought to."[6]

So presuppositions must be challenged and hard data relied upon wherever possible.

The most useful information on what the market expects of the institution may already be in the institution's possession or be obtainable within several months. One good source of information (if the files exist) consists of the completed preapplication inquiry sheets, preapplication questionnaires, and intake interview sheets generated by the admissions office over the last several years. (For a discussion of "Managing the Admissions Process," see Chapter 4; also see Appendixes K, M, and O for sample formats.) These historical documents, taken together, can yield an impressive array of data on vital strategic issues such as the following:

- Who has been soliciting information about the institution?
- What are the current living arrangements of those making inquiries?
- What are the presenting problems (i.e., the reasons application for residence is being made or considered)?
- What are the family situations and relationships?
- What are the projected levels of care?
- Is the mix of applicants changing noticeably over time?
- Is the ratio between initial inquiries and applications received changing over time?

Perhaps a significant number of referrals are originating with the social services departments of local acute care hospitals or with the trust divisions of large metropolitan banks on behalf of their confined trustors.[7] If so, do these connections warrant further exploration? Can they be more fully cultivated?

Perhaps callers to the LTC institution are continually asking for specific information about physician referrals, medical services, local and state government programs, and so on. If so, should the institution advertise itself as a central repository of such information and make it available to anyone interested via a toll-free telephone number? Would the cost of the service be justified by improved goodwill in the community and an increase in the number of applications for admission?

In any case, such questions, with the inevitable follow-up of "Why?" or "What does that tell us?" or "How do we know for sure?" will lead to even more focused inquiry and will go a long way toward identifying for the planner the specific needs of the market segments being served.

"Value" is a subset of need. It is a thing firmly fixed in the eye of the beholder, encompassing not only the tangible aspects of long-term care but also its aura— that "cluster of expectations" that can be as much symbolic as real. The reality, of course, comes first. No family, especially one having the financial wherewithal to go elsewhere, is about to place an elderly relative in an institution that reeks of urine or disinfectant, keeps residents in bed all day, restrains residents unnecessarily, serves cold and unappetizing food, and commingles alert residents with those who constantly scream or are incontinent. All of which is to say that any LTC institution must first cross a minimum threshold of competency.

That expectation met, the planner's task is to appeal to perception. Relevant questions abound. Is the staff's interpersonal manner—the way they speak with families, the way they answer the telephone—off-putting or inviting? Do the institution's written communications to its public constituencies appear to be carefully conceived or are they slapdash? Do the families perceive opportunities for their aged relatives to make choices about daily life and care? Is the atmosphere of the place homelike and caring? Does the structure appear to be safe and clean? Is the decor appropriate to the taste of the clientele? Is the cuisine appropriate to the taste of the clientele? Is the presence (or absence) of a particular religious orientation comforting to the clientele or disturbing?

If feedback from the family constituency has been institutionalized (as suggested in Chapter 4), useful answers to such questions about perceptions and feelings are immediately at hand. Notes taken by social services staff on the insights and opinions of families of new residents in gatherings such as the HRCA family seminar program, analyses of previous years' family day questionnaires, reports of the primary care teams on the family day feedback sessions held on the various nursing units—all of these, taken together, can provide a wealth of information to the planner on how satisfied current residents and their families are with the institution, how trustworthy and caring they think the institution is, and what they consider to constitute value in the long-term care of the infirm elderly. From this data, plans can be laid to build an attractive image and maximize appeal.

Resource Analysis

Given that opportunities and problems exist in the market, the question remains whether the LTC institution will be able to take advantage of the former and correct the latter. Accordingly, the strategic planners must next make a dispassionate assessment of the resources available to the institution.

Every LTC institution, whatever its mission or its markets, consists ultimately of two things:

1. Inanimate materials—the facilities and equipment and furnishings and money that are necessary for the delivery of the long-term care product but, by themselves, are passionless and guarantee the customer nothing.
2. People—the individuals throughout the organization whose talent and energy and commitment, properly managed, transform the building and all the things it contains into a caring and socially useful institution.

So the planner must ask, What are the major strengths and weaknesses of the organization? Of the facilities and equipment? How might improvements in either (or both) enable the institution to develop existing markets more fully or target new markets with a greater chance of success? Such questions are the stuff of general management, and the answers are derived, at least in part, from the instruments of feedback and control that have been recommended in previous chapters and perhaps have been set in place by the LTC administrator over the preceding months and years.

For nonprofit institutions, there is an additional focus to the resource analysis: What opportunities exist to strengthen the financial base of the institution? How might new sources of funding be targeted? There are several approaches the LTC administrator may find useful.

One tried-and-true method is to develop membership groups consisting of family members of current or past residents, their friends and acquaintances, or anyone with a genuine interest in the good work being done by the institution. The people who join are usually highly visible and active members of the community, which has the effect of broadening the institution's base of support over time. Typically, these associate groups sponsor activities (such as breakfast meetings with guest speakers, outings, bazaars, etc.) and use the monies collected to make purchases of special equipment, establish innovative programs for residents, or fund scholarships for present or future nursing staff. Individual members of the associates groups can also be solicited directly by the institution during annual fund-raising drives, and those who are especially active and enthusiastic on the institution's behalf may ultimately step up to the board of trustees.

Another useful fund-raising method is to encourage members of the community, especially the children of current or past residents, to consider the institution as part of their own estate planning. For example, a gift of a life insurance policy to a charitable institution will generally result in an immediate tax deduction for the cash surrender value of the policy (if any) at the time of the gift. The premiums paid by the donor each year thereafter would be a charitable tax deduction for the year paid. On the death of the donor, the proceeds of the policy would pass to the institution tax free, and the funds would not be taxable to the donor's estate.

Mission Analysis

With the market analysis and the resource analysis satisfactorily completed, the strategic planners can now articulate the mission of the institution with clarity and precision. The questions to be asked and their answers flow directly from the discussion that has preceded.

- *Mission.* Does the LTC institution have an updated statement that clearly defines the business it is in, the clientele it is serving, the services it is providing, and the direction in which it is heading?
- *Customer Definition.* Who does the institution intend its customers to be?
- *Needs Targeting.* What specific customer needs does the institution intend to satisfy?
- *Market Targeting.* On which market segments does the institution intend to focus?
- *Competitor Identification.* Who will be the major competitors in these market segments?
- *Market Positioning.* What competitive benefits, both tangible and symbolic, does the institution intend to offer its target markets?

In one sense, the strategic planners' task is a difficult one, for they must decide how many "attributes" to build into the long-term care menu of services (i.e., the product line) and how to package these attributes for maximum appeal. In another sense, however, the task is made less forbidding by the fact that all LTC organizations do marketing already, wittingly or unwittingly. They search for prospective customers. They develop a product line. They price the products, although often (depending on clientele) within limits set by one or more government agencies. They advertise the existence of the institution and the availability of its products. They distribute the products. The main issue for the LTC administrator and the management team, therefore, is whether they wish to improve their marketing effectiveness or continue to perform the function as they have always done.

Several alternative approaches exist for introducing a formal marketing mechanism into an LTC organization.

For larger institutions, one possibility is for the LTC administrator to appoint a marketing committee, whose charter would be to identify (1) the marketing problems and opportunities facing the institution and (2) the major marketing needs of various administrative units. The committee might also be given the task of determining whether the institution has a need for a full-time director of marketing.

For smaller institutions, another possibility is for the LTC administrator to appoint one or several task forces to carry out the various phases of the institutional audit. The reports generated would stimulate development of a consensus on institutional goals, positioning, and strategy. Even if the task forces fail to find dramatic solutions, the participants usually gain a fuller appreciation and understanding of the institution's problems and the need to work together to solve them.

In any size institution, especially one where the LTC administrator and the head of marketing are the same person, the LTC administrator might opt to engage the services of specialized marketing firms, such as a marketing research group, an advertising agency, or a direct mail consultant. A marketing research group might be hired to survey the needs, perceptions, preferences, and satisfaction of the targeted market segments. An advertising agency might be hired to develop a corporate identification program or an advertising campaign. High-quality marketing firms typically bring far more than their specific areas of expertise to the client. They usually look at the issues from a total marketing perspective and raise important questions regarding the institution's mission, objectives, strategies, and opportunities.

Also, the LTC administrator might retain a marketing consultant to conduct a comprehensive audit of the problems and opportunities facing the organization. The consultant ought to be chosen on the basis of proposals submitted by at least three candidates, and there should be a written contract that specifies the objectives, the time frame, the research plan, and the billing. A liaison person from the LTC institution's staff should be assigned to work with the consultant, arrange interviews, read and comment on the emerging reports, and make arrangements for the final presentation and implementation of proposals.

After the completion of one or more of these implementation steps, the LTC administrator might become convinced of the need to appoint a full-time director of marketing. This decision requires the development of a formal job description specifying to whom this person reports, the scope of the position, and the functions and responsibilities of the position. (See Appendix S for a sample director of marketing job description.)

The relationship of the new position to kindred functions within the organization must be defined with special care. For example, in larger LTC institutions, the director of marketing is usually located within the planning office and reports to the vice president of planning. In smaller LTC institutions, the director of marketing usually reports to the LTC administrator. Whatever the size of the institution, or whether it is chartered for-profit or nonprofit, it rarely makes sense for the director of marketing to report to the head of public relations or fund raising, for this severely limits the use that can be made of the strategic marketing perspective.

THE PUBLIC RELATIONS FUNCTION

Whereas the marketing function defines strategic objectives, the public relations function provides the tools by which those objectives can be accomplished. Therefore, public relations is and should be considered a part of marketing within the LTC organizational structure.

In larger LTC institutions, the staffing of both positions—director of marketing and director of public relations—may be warranted. (See Appendix T for a sample director of public relations job description.) In smaller LTC institutions, where marketing is performed as a group exercise by members of the administrative staff or by the LTC administrator, public relations duties can be handled by the LTC administrator or can be assigned to a staff member in addition to his or her normal job responsibilities.

Whatever the level of organizational complexity, the obligation of the public relations person (or department) is the same. It is to earn understanding and acceptance for the LTC institution among its various external and internal constituencies. Among other things, these constituencies are

- potential sources of resident referrals (e.g., social service agencies, physicians, area hospitals, elderly affairs councils, other LTC institutions, and families of past and present residents)
- potential sources of employee and volunteer referrals (e.g., current employees and their families, applicants who are on the waiting list for admission to residence, local and state employment offices, institutions of higher education, church groups, charitable organizations, and the general public)
- potential sources of friction (e.g., local government officials and agencies, community action groups, and neighborhood associations)

Sometimes the public relations function involves fighting "fires" that may flare from time to time (see "How to Deal with the News Media" and "Coping with Crisis: Risk Management Strategies" below). Mostly it is a process of building credibility by accretion, day by day, in various public forums and among targeted groups.[8]

HOW TO DEAL WITH THE NEWS MEDIA

Like most managers everywhere, LTC administrators tend to be fearful or at the least extremely cautious when dealing with representatives of the print or electronic media. Their every instinct tells them that the reporter standing ready with microphone or note pad in hand likely harbors some antibusiness bias or, worse yet, some bias against those who would reduce the task of caring for the infirm elderly to a business. The prospect of talking to such a person, whose reportage will be read or seen or heard by thousands of people, becomes daunting, and LTC administrators can scarcely be blamed if their quick assessment of the risk-benefit ratio comes down entirely on the side of unacceptable risk.

While such trepidation is understandable, it ought not to be decisive, for the news media can be extremely helpful to LTC institutions in executing their marketing and public relations programs. "The man who would most effectively transmit his message to the public must be alert to make use of all the means of propaganda," wrote Edward Bernays, the guiding spirit of the new science of public relations, in the year 1928.[9] Bernays' admonition is no less apt today. Over the last 10 or 15 years, universities have become much more skilled at public and media relations, a logical and necessary response to spiraling costs, shrinking demographics, and a growing awareness of the need to improve fund-raising techniques. For much the same set of reasons, acute care hospitals have also increased the level of sophistication of their public relations efforts. Now it is the turn of LTC institutions to recognize the strategic value of promoting good relations with the press.

Of course, consorting with the news media can never be a 100 percent safe activity. Media bias does sometimes rear its ugly head, especially when the facts are ambiguous or must be interpreted or when decisions are made as to what is newsworthy and what is not. Which is only to suggest that dealing with the press represents an important managerial challenge for the LTC administrator or the marketing and public relations staff. The main concern should be to reap the benefit of favorable public exposure while minimizing the risk of adverse consequences.[10]

There are two general sets of circumstances that may occur. In one, the LTC administrator or designated spokesperson takes the initiative and approaches the news media with a request for coverage of some event, program, or point of view.

In the other, the LTC administrator or spokesperson is approached by the news media for details or a perspective on a developing story that may or may not directly involve the institution itself.

The observations that follow address both sets of circumstances.

The object of communicating with the press is not to influence its opinion of the institution or program but to influence public opinion. It is easy to lose sight of this distinction and to proceed as if the press constituted the audience. It does not. Rather, the press is a *medium*—a go-between, an intermediary, a means for conveying a message to the public.

In order to establish a linkage with the electronic or print media and use its power to influence public opinion in positive ways, it is necessary to understand how journalists instinctively respond to solicitations from interested parties. To be sure, journalists are individuals and differ a great deal from one another. But most, perhaps due to some self-selection process or the nature of their professional training, tend to think of themselves as advocates for the public interest somehow defined, and so they tend to filter what is told to them through the lens of their public interest advocacy.

As a consequence, when an organization approaches the news media with a viewpoint or the description of an event it wishes to have publicized, the immediate instinct of the journalist is to assume that the interest of the organization is somehow at odds with the interest of the community at large. This very healthy skepticism was no doubt anticipated by the Founding Fathers when they wrote the guarantee of freedom of the press into the First Amendment to the Constitution.

Therefore, when approaching the press, the LTC administrator (or public relations person) must acknowledge that this instinctive skepticism of journalists exists and then turn it to his or her advantage. How? By taking great pains to articulate the message in terms that specifically address how and why the situation or viewpoint being described is consistent with the public interest. The LTC administrator, in doing this, must not insist that the interests of the LTC institution and the public interest are one and the same, because they are not. Rather, the administrator should (a) point to the institution's reputation for integrity in caring for the infirm elderly, (b) indicate that in the specific circumstances being described the interests of the institution and the interests of the public are quite compatible, and (c) explain why, clearly and succinctly.

It is important to recognize that the press has needs, which derive both from the nature of its task and from its self-image as a public interest advocate. Some of the press's needs are basic. One is speed. All reporters work on a deadline. Television crews may have just a matter of minutes to get videotape and copy back to the station in time to make the evening news. Print reporters may have three or four deadlines per issue and must deal with late-breaking developments quickly. The competition to be first with a story, or even with a fact within a story, is intense.

All of this is common knowledge to any layperson. Yet such understanding often evaporates when the subject of the interview is caught in the midst of the reporter's haste to gather up the facts and meet the deadline.

Two adverse outcomes are typical.

In one situation, the reporter asks for information regarding some potentially negative subject, and the staff person receiving the inquiry takes two days to find the right person to talk to, gather data, and respond. In the meantime, the reporter runs the story, saying that the institution has failed to return repeated calls. A local television station, which relies on the print media for most of its story leads, airs its version of the events, also full of unsubstantiated data.

In another situation, the interviewee stands exposed before the news media. Feeling out of control, worried that editorial snips of words or phrases will distort well-thought-out positions, the interviewee concludes that the situation is extremely dangerous and that the reporter is resorting to high-pressure tactics in order to catch him or her off guard. The result is a botched interview, full of equivocation, lacking in authoritativeness, and failing to show the institution or its spokesperson in anything resembling a favorable light.

Another of the press's needs is for clarity. Reporters want to speak with someone who can make sense to a layperson. When dealing with technical matters—such as medical treatment of the elderly, nursing home economics, or legal and ethical issues—reporters know that if a source does not help them comprehend the subject, they will never be able to communicate it succinctly to the public. A reporter can become extremely frustrated, therefore, when a spokesperson takes refuge in professional jargon, whether out of nervousness or a heightened sense of circumspection. The reporter begs for a layperson's description; the LTC administrator considers this a request for superficiality. The result, almost always, is a thwarting of communication and another lost opportunity for favorable publicity for the institution.

Another of the press's needs is for honesty. Even a hint of skirting the issue is a red flag to good reporters, a signal to dig deeper to uncover facts that the source may be trying to hide. In the face of such inquisitiveness, interviewees often lose the distinction between honesty and discretion. Instead of saying, "I cannot comment on that matter because we have not yet made a decision," which is forthright and true, they equivocate, a posture that almost always exposes them and the institution to a series of more probing and potentially embarrassing questions.

Given that the press has needs, it is almost always in the LTC institution's best interest to accommodate them. The key to the effective management of media relations is responsiveness. This means giving top priority to every media request.

It means being cooperative to the point of exhausting all possible sources of information. It means making available whomever the press wants to talk to, whether it be the public relations director, the controller, the attending physician, the head nurse, or the LTC administrator.

Responsiveness is an especially useful tactic when the press is pounding on the door and already has one slant on a rapidly developing story. One example was discussed in Chapter 7: The disappearance of Zelda Z. from an LTC institution and the discovery of her body 22 days later in a firebreak corridor of the main library downtown. In that instance, the LTC institution was forthright to the press, and although several stories in the metropolitan dailies mentioned it as the place of Zelda Z.'s residence, the focus was almost entirely on the failure of systems and procedures in the library where she was found.

Another example, which received national attention, illustrates the point even more clearly. In 1980, the Madeira School, located in McLean, Virginia, had a problem. Its headmistress, Jean Harris, had just traveled to Scarsdale, New York, where, either by accident or premeditation, she shot and killed her lover, a physician and the celebrity author of the Scarsdale diet, Dr. Herman Tarnower, who she knew was having an affair with another woman. Subsequently, Jean Harris was tried and found guilty of murder.

One need not be an expert in public relations damage control to recognize that the shooting and all of the attendant publicity presented a sizable problem for the institution that employed Jean Harris. To be sure, the school was old, elite, and monied, acting as mentor and guardian to some of the most privileged young women in America. To be sure, it enjoyed a fine academic reputation, regularly placing its graduates in the finest colleges and universities in the land. To be sure, it was located in the most bucolic of settings, a vast sylvan dell surrounded by hundreds of acres of prime Virginia woodlands just across the Potomac from Washington, D.C.

But many other private schools (several of them in the Washington, D.C., area) possessed exactly those same impressive qualifications and serviced exactly the same clientele as the Madeira School, and none of these others had a headmistress whose name was on the evening news and on virtually every front page in the country. There was no guarantee, that is to say, that the Madeira School was going to emerge unscathed, or even survive.

So when the press descended on the campus immediately after the shooting, the problem facing the school's administrators and board of trustees was quite clear: How to react?

They might have chosen to be rigid, aloof, and unsympathetic. (In fact, this was the posture adopted by Jean Harris during her trial, and it probably contributed to the jury's guilty verdict.) Instead, the school's officials chose a different course. They recognized that this was a story that the press was going to investigate thoroughly and that the school—in fact and in symbol—was an intimate part of it. They recognized the importance of being credible, concerned, and, above all, accommodating. So, as part of its public stance, the Madeira School granted the press full access to its grounds, its faculty, its administrators, its students. It answered questions promptly. It was polite and considerate of the reporters' needs.

The result was that in its coverage of the story the press had unflattering things to say about Jean Harris but it said nothing damaging about the Madeira School. Quite the contrary. The school received a wealth of favorable publicity. As a consequence, there was an increase in the number of applications received, in dollars raised by fund raising, and in involvement of alumnae and their families. What might have been a public relations disaster for the institution had been turned into a strategic advantage.[11]

COPING WITH CRISIS: RISK MANAGEMENT STRATEGIES

There are thousands of possible events that could negatively impact the relationship of a long-term care institution to its outside constituencies. Fire. The deranged actions of an employee or visitor. A failure to follow established procedures that leads to death or extreme discomfort to residents. The sudden disclosure of unethical or illegal business activities. Malicious rumor.

Enumeration of possibilities aside, it is safe to say that if an event interferes with the flow of normal business operations, jeopardizes the institution's image and public standing, produces a higher than normal level of scrutiny by government agencies, or results in the news media wanting to talk to someone on the scene about it, that event qualifies as a full-blown crisis.

Unlike many companies, which invest large amounts of time and energy assessing their unique areas of vulnerability and preparing for the worst, long-term care institutions typically do little planning with regard to how to respond to the public implications of a crisis situation. This is an approach that is fraught with peril, for it virtually guarantees that when a crisis occurs, events will assume a life of their own and the effect on the institution and its various constituencies will be far more damaging than it otherwise might have been.

A large measure of control can be achieved if LTC management takes the time to prepare in advance a crisis communications plan. This document need not anticipate every dreadful event that might occur, nor even any event in particular. It must, however, reflect the organization's best thinking on how it intends to respond to a crisis situation, including (1) procedures for training a crisis management team of key employees, (2) assignment of responsibilities for gathering facts and preparing statements to the public, and (3) designation of the spokesperson(s) who will represent the institution to the press.

The objectives of the crisis communications plan are the same whatever the size or complexity of the institution. They are

- to enable the spokesperson(s) for the institution to communicate effectively under pressure
- to preserve the institution's reputation
- to ensure that the institution is able to compete in the marketplace after the crisis is resolved
- to ensure that all contacts with the news media are handled in a consistent and professional manner.

How to accomplish these objectives? Several principles apply universally.[12]

Find out the truth. When a crisis occurs, management must actively commit itself to finding out what caused the problem and take steps to prevent it from happening again. This commitment to action must be articulated as part of the crisis communications plan. Otherwise, the possibility exists that, in the midst of a stressful situation, management will blur the distinction between the reality of effects and the community's perception of them and will assume that good public relations is the solution to the actual problem as well as to the perception problem.

Gather the facts. Assign responsibility for assembling the facts for public distribution. Prepare the facts in a bullet list—who, what, why, where, when, and how. Get whatever approvals are necessary from legal counsel, the board of trustees, and so on, and do so quickly. Release the approved written statement to journalists when they ask for information.

Designate the spokesperson. Although any employee is fair game for an interview in a crisis situation, those persons at the highest levels of the organization have the greatest credibility, and the press will generally gravitate to them for statements. So, as part of the crisis communications plan, management should designate a high-ranking individual to be available 24 hours a day to speak to the press on behalf of the institution. Usually, this person is the LTC administrator, although under special circumstances it may be someone who has superior knowledge of the institution's procedures or safety measures or the steps being taken to avoid future problems.

Whoever is designated as spokesperson, he or she should be willing, not reluctant, to take on the responsibility. Credibility is the key attribute. Do not, therefore, select as spokesperson for an institution in crisis anyone with the title of "legal counsel" or "director of public relations" or anyone whose job description suggests professional training in obfuscation.

Train the crisis management team. Training is extremely important, because in a crisis situation the rules of the game with regard to media coverage change dramatically. Coverage of the event will occur on two levels. The first level concerns what happened and the reaction of participants and bystanders to what happened. The second level concerns how the institution itself reacts to the event. At this level, the news media will usually hand out grades, doing so either openly, saying things like "the management of the XYZ nursing home generally gets high marks for its handling of the crisis," or tacitly, implying in its reportage that the XYZ nursing home has so far been less than exemplary in its response to media inquiry.

So here again reality and the perception of reality converge and become blurred. Consequently, the crisis management team must recognize its twofold obligation: (1) to respond to the event itself, fully and completely, and (2) to ensure that its response is perceived by the institution's constituencies as the proper way to handle such a crisis.

In articulating the institution's position, the LTC administrator or other designated spokesperson will probably find him- or herself in the communications trenches face to face with a reporter armed with microphone or note pad. Following are some suggestions for turning the situation into a positive, or at least a balanced, media opportunity.[13]

Establish credibility.

Be prepared. Do your homework. If the situation mandates, prepare a written statement. If time permits, submit the statement to your legal counsel or board of trustees for approval. It is all right to read a prepared statement to the reporter.

Always tell the truth. Do not bluff or lie, even about seemingly inconsequential matters.

When you promise to get back to a reporter with further information, be sure to do so promptly.

Avoid industry jargon. Use easily understood words and simple, not convoluted, sentences. Remember, a large segment of the public is immediately distrustful of anyone who appears to be pontificating.

Never ask a reporter for story approval. You are not entitled to it, and your credibility as a spokesperson is severely diminished by asking.

Be forthright but not effusive.

Take care always to position the institution as the problem solver, never as the cause of the problem. Focus on the positive. What did you do to rectify the situation? How did your emergency plan work? What did you learn from the crisis?

Listen carefully to the reporter's question. Think. Then respond. Most mistakes, in talking to the news media as elsewhere, occur when people speak before thinking.

Keep your answers short and to the point, especially for broadcast news interviews. Long answers will be edited severely, sometimes to the detriment of content.

If you have been advised not to answer a question, tell the reporter why you cannot (e.g., "The case is in litigation right now, and it would be inappropriate for me to speculate on the outcome").

Never say "no comment." It is a stonewalling tactic and a virtual admission that you have something to hide. Instead, say something like "I don't know, but we are investigating the situation and we'll have a statement as soon as all the facts are known."

Never say anything "off the record." If you do not want it attributed to you or the institution, do not say it.

Do not offer your personal opinion on the crisis if it differs in any respect from the institution's official position. To the reporter doing the interview, you are the spokesperson, and the spokesperson and institution are one. Any attempt to dissociate yourself from the unity of that relationship will either be misunderstood or purposely ignored.

Confine your remarks to the LTC institution only. Do not, under any circumstances, say anything critical of residents, families, current employees, former employees, or competitors.

Watch for tricks.

Agree in advance about the subject of the interview. If the reporter changes subjects during the interview, say, "I was prepared to talk about topic A. If you want to talk about topic B, I'll need some additional time to prepare, so let's reschedule."

If you do not understand the reporter's question, ask for an explanation. If necessary, ask again. Keep asking until the thrust of the question is entirely clear.

Challenge any negative implication in the reporter's question. Then, politely but firmly turn it into a positive. For example:

> *Reporter:* We all know you don't provide quality care. It is also generally agreed that you don't take care of your employees. How can you expect to survive?
>
> *Spokesperson:* I don't agree with your assumptions. There is a lot of misunderstanding about us, and that's why we are here. We are an excellent provider of long-term care services, primarily because we care deeply about the quality of life of our residents. We value our employees greatly and we give them an excellent place to work.

Do not allow the reporter to dictate your answer by framing the question as a choice between A and B. For example:

> *Reporter:* It would seem that the reason for the outbreak of influenza in the institution is either inadequate sanitation or lack of contingency planning. Which is the more likely?

Spokesperson: In fact, neither. Our record for maintaining a clean, safe environment for our residents is well known. As you are no doubt aware, the elderly are particularly susceptible to upper respiratory infections, which have been plaguing the entire region this winter. To minimize the possibility of exposure, we are asking families of residents to postpone visits if they have any flu-like symptoms and requesting our employees to remain at home until they are completely well.

Do not respond to remarks attributed to others. For example:

Reporter: John Smith is reported as saying that . . . . What do you think about his comments?
Spokesperson: I don't know how John Smith feels. But I will tell you what I know. . . .

Do not respond to what-if questions. When you engage in speculation about improbable circumstances, you validate them as a possibility and run the risk of having your speculation reported as a contingency for which you have been actively planning.

Do not respond to editorial comments. Make the reporter ask a question.

Do not let a reporter interrupt your reply. Politely but firmly say, "Excuse me, I have something more to say in answer to your question."

Do not feel compelled to fill pregnant pauses in a reporter's statement with the sound of your own voice. Respond only to questions.

Beware of "turned off" microphones and cameras. Do not say anything in their presence that you do not wish to be recorded.

Cultivate your image.

Never argue with a reporter.

Never suggest to a reporter or editor that a favorable story or slant will be rewarded by the institution with advertising revenues.

Be pleasant and smile.

Express genuine concern for injuries, death, or other human tragedy.

Do not become emotional. Do not lose your temper.

Do not address a reporter as "Sir" or "Ms." Your conversation with any reporter should be as an adult to an adult, not as a child to its parent.

Be aware of your appearance and your grooming. Dress in a conservative, businesslike fashion whatever the circumstances.

Be conscious of your body language, whether on camera or not. Do not cross your arms across your chest, roll your eyes, grimace, and so on. These gestures are fair game for interpretation.

Maintain eye contact with the reporter. Shifting eyes suggest that you may have something to hide and therefore might be cause for more probing questions.

Talk to the camera as if it were a person.

End interviews with a smile, a handshake, and a thank-you.

Above all, instruct your crisis management team to view matters from the point of view of the public. Try to anticipate the social impact of events (i.e., their seriousness to your community, your employees, and your industry). The impulse of management will be to view events from the perspective of insiders and therefore to downplay their importance. Beware of this predictable response. It is far safer for the institution to err on the side of caution and take the events too seriously than to underestimate their newsworthiness and suffer the consequences when the press begins a thorough investigation.

GOVERNMENT RELATIONS

In previous chapters, it was advocated that the LTC administrator take a very aggressive stance vis-a-vis the regulatory apparatus—to confront rather than acquiesce when questionable rulings are made on funding, delivery of services, allocation of resources, internal procedures, and so on. The issue, as was suggested, is who shall be in charge of the operation of the institution—the regulators or the LTC administrator?

Yet with regard to those persons and agencies of government responsible for enacting legislation, passing ordinances, and otherwise affecting the external environment in which the institution functions, the recommendation is quite different. Here the watchwords are, or ought to be, accommodation and persuasion.

Every LTC institution, like virtually every business of any sort, has multiple relations with government. Government is local; it is state; it is federal. In each of these jurisdictions it has enormous power, which can either be set against the interests of the institution or be deployed in its behalf. The LTC administrator must, therefore, acknowledge the power of government from the outset and involve the institution in public debates on zoning, traffic, taxes, public transportation, housing, roads, and any other matter that could conceivably affect competitive position.

Establishing a relationship with government is, in one sense, very simple. Officials maintain offices in public buildings, and there is seldom any difficulty in getting an appointment.

Establishing an effective relationship, however, is somewhat more complicated. The idea is to create a favorable climate for discussion based on a mutual awareness of each other's interests so that over time any problems can be resolved as part of a natural process of accommodation.

How to accomplish this? Several suggestions may be useful.

Maintain continuous communication with government at all levels. The key word here is "continuous." Too many LTC administrators look upon government relations as something to be cultivated only in times of crisis. This makes as much sense as demanding instantaneous service from a vendor with whom one has had no contact for years.

There are many easy and natural ways to keep in touch with elected public officials and other important government figures. One is the informal luncheon date. You will be astonished at how eagerly the mayor, members of the town council, or state representatives will accept your invitation. Yet it should not be surprising, for it is their business to meet with community leaders. Your status as a employer and your responsibility for the care and well-being of large numbers of the infirm elderly, most of whom have family members who vote, qualify you as a person well worth listening to.

Another way to maintain contact is to send to the mayor, local legislator, or government contact person a copy of your institution's most recent annual report, progress report, or similar in-house publication. Do not send it "cold," for it will likely be tossed aside. Instead, attach a personal letter containing the substance of the report and any particular messages that may be appropriate. Personal letters are *always* read, even if the accompanying material is not.

Letters to elected officials need not be sent only at annual report time. There may be other occasions during the year when your institution has some important information to impart. When it does, send the information promptly. Local government officials do not like to be caught unawares, and they greatly appreciate being informed of an impending change before it becomes general knowledge.

Sometimes the smallest gestures are the most important. All legislators and municipal officials are plagued by complaints. They very seldom hear any favorable comments. So one of the best ways to make a lasting impression on a legislator or public official is to write a note when you are particularly pleased with something that the individual did, whether your institution was affected or not. Sales departments call this tactic "customer cultivation."

Make it your business to know what is going on in your locality and in your state. More than one LTC administrator has awakened after years of disinterest in government processes to discover the institution's neighborhood has deteriorated so much it is no longer suitable as a location. Or to discover the existence of adverse zoning ordinances that are preventing a logical and necessary building expansion. Or to discover congested roads that are adding hours to the weekly commute and so encouraging a large number of the institution's employees to seek jobs elsewhere.

The admonition, therefore, is to be alert to proposed changes in your neighborhood, city, and state. Read the local newspapers and the bulletins of the local chamber of commerce. When there is a hearing at the town hall on a matter that impacts your institution, be sure that it is represented and that its viewpoint is heard. Join your trade association. Review the information it sends you, let it know of your needs and aspirations, and contribute time and energy to its political action campaigns.

Encourage your employees to participate in local politics and government affairs. Many companies actively discourage their employees from participating in politics, believing that it will be too distracting and too time consuming. LTC institutions often take a position one step further. They tend to believe that political involvement is somehow unsavory and therefore contrary to the institution's public image as caregiver.

This is a shortsighted policy for two reasons. First, no enterprise can hope to be adequately represented in the give and take of political discussion if those who know it best are forbidden to participate. That is why the LTC administrator will, if asked, generally accept an invitation to testify at state or congressional hearings on matters relating to long-term care of the infirm elderly.

Second, the LTC institution itself has a great deal to gain when its employees assume strategic posts in the local government structure.

Local offices may be either elected or appointed. In smaller towns especially, much of governance is done by boards and commissions staffed by unpaid or almost unpaid volunteers, and the persons who perform these quasi-legislative or quasi-judicial functions wield considerable power. Local political organizations are also generally run by volunteers, and there is always room for an energetic partisan to achieve a position of influence. In either instance, the LTC institution can only benefit if one of its trusted employees attains a position of local authority.

COMMUNITY INVOLVEMENT

There is a necessary precondition for the success of any community outreach program, however well conceived: The LTC institution must earn the respect and approval of the community by assiduously following an enlightened code of corporate conduct.

- It must be a good employer of local labor, grant all applicants a fair, tactful, and courteous interview, and manage the business in a way that maximizes stability of employment.
- It must be a good housekeeper, keeping its buildings in excellent repair and its grounds well tended.

- It must be a buyer of local goods and services to the fullest extent possible.
- It must be a good taxpayer, demanding justice but not special favors.
- It must be a generous, but not paternalistic, contributor to local charities and capital fund drives.

Which is only to say that to be perceived as a good neighbor, one must be a good neighbor.

Beyond that, certain types of programs and activities may be helpful to the LTC institution in enhancing its reputation and solidifying its position as an asset to the community. The following recommendations are worth keeping in mind.

Build a cooperative relationship with the gerontology faculty of a local university, medical school, or school of nursing. Such an affiliation can provide several important benefits to the LTC institution and the educational institution:[14]

- In-service training and workshops conducted by the faculty will expose LTC staff to new information about specific skills relating to caring for the elderly as well as to new theoretical developments in understanding how the elderly interact. LTC staff will be encouraged to question and to learn, and their increased knowledge should translate into improved quality of care for residents.

- The LTC administrator and staff will be in a position to influence the current content of teaching and the future course of research at the school or university by helping faculty to interpret new information. Specifically, they will be able to ask pointedly, and from their unique perspective, what the research findings mean and how can they be made useful to those engaged in the day-to-day delivery of care to the infirm elderly.

- The recruitment of nurses and other key staff by the LTC institution will be facilitated, often as a direct result of relationships formed during the course of the program.

- The public's perception of the LTC institution will be enhanced as a result of the cooperative venture, mirroring the reality of the matter, which is that the school or university would not risk its own prestige by attaching itself to an institution that did not provide excellent care.

To be sure, several caveats apply when considering an affiliation with an educational institution. One involves the issue of control, especially as regards teaching nursing home programs. As a physician at New York University's Bellevue Medical Centers wrote,

> There is a danger that inappropriate or excessively invasive diagnostic and therapeutic maneuvers will be undertaken purely for the sake of

learning. The philosophy of the traditional nursing home has emphasized making the patient comfortable, limiting invasive maneuvers,
and allowing the very elderly or critically ill patient to die peacefully
if nonheroic measures prove inadequate. The increased presence of
academic physicians will undoubtedly—and happily—shed new light
on medical problems neglected in the nursing home, but the academic
thrust will introduce a risk that the practices of gentle care and
nonintervention may be altered.[15]

The "danger" that the modus operandi of the LTC institution may be under-
mined does not mean that it will be. However, there is clearly a need for each
side, at the earliest possible stage of negotiation, to gain a complete understanding
of what the other side expects from the relationship. It is not necessary, or likely,
that the sets of expectations will match. The LTC institution may be primarily
interested in participating in the education of future LTC administrators and other
professionals in the field, whereas the school or university may be primarily
interested in exposing its faculty and students to the practical aspects and problems
of working with the institutionalized infirm elderly. But it is necessary that a
common ground of understanding be reached and that mechanisms for resolving
any conflict that may arise be formalized before the program is allowed to begin.

Another caveat is legal. Where students from the school or university actively
participate in the care of residents, there are inevitable concerns about liability for
injuries caused by students, about possible substandard care, about confidentiality,
about supervisory responsibilities, and about informed consent. None of these
issues should unduly inhibit either the educational process or the delivery of
resident care. Indeed, in the opinion of one attorney specializing in risk management in the long-term care setting, "in the overwhelming percentage of cases
where the student performs appropriately assigned functions in a non-negligent
manner under adequate clinical supervision, no danger of legal liability exists."[16]
Nevertheless, some specific recommendations should be considered:[17]

- The LTC institution and affiliated school should provide training sessions
  on the ethical considerations and obligations owed by students to the
  residents they serve.
- The LTC institution must always regard students as trainees, not as substitutes who can make decisions and take actions that are the exclusive province
  of its staff. It must resist the temptation to utilize students only as an
  attractive source of free labor to compensate for shortcomings in its recruitment of qualified physicians and nurses.
- When a student has taken part in a resident's care, the clinical records of the
  LTC institution should clearly indicate the degree of faculty supervision that
  existed. An accurate and complete record documenting who did what

concerning the resident's treatment is ethically proper and also practically advantageous if a supervisor or the LTC institution is subsequently accused of malpractice.

- The LTC institution should incorporate into its standard admission contract a clause indicating the possibility that some resident care may be rendered by students. This contingency should be fully explained to entering residents and their families.

Since many other legal considerations may apply in the individual instance, the LTC administrator should consider seeking the advice of experienced counsel before commencing an affiliation with a school or university.

Develop a mailing list of civic leaders and decision makers, that is, all identifiable members of the local power structure. The list is used to distribute periodic communications from the institution regarding its mission, current status, and recent accomplishments. For example, a one- or two-page bulletin published bimonthly or quarterly might detail the number of jobs provided by the institution, the demographics of its resident population, any planned building expansions, the dollar amount of purchases made from local vendors, taxes paid, upcoming open house events, affiliations with local colleges or universities, and the like.

Invest in local newspaper advertising. Some LTC institutions publish an annual report for their neighbors in the community in the form of a full-page newspaper advertisement. With a headline such as "Here Is What the XYZ Nursing Home and Its 75 Employees Meant to the Community Last Year," the report might detail (in words and graphics) the size of the annual payroll, the economic impact of the LTC institution on the community, the number of residents and families served now and in the recent past, the levels of care provided, the relationships that have been forged with local hospitals, and the involvement of local citizenry in volunteer programs.

Through newspaper advertisements, the LTC institution might also announce a series of lectures by members of the medical or social services staff and invite the general public to attend. Advertising can also be used to recruit new employees or volunteers or to deliver a series of public service articles on how the latest changes in Medicare or Medicaid regulations will affect long-term care of the infirm elderly.

Whatever the thrust of the LTC institution's advertising program, the advertisements should be initiated during normal times and appear in the local press on a regular basis. In this way credibility among the public is slowly built, and any announcements made by the institution in a time of crisis will be given that much more credence.

Finally, in all matters relating to government and community relations, the critical component, as always, is awareness of constituencies. This is especially true if the LTC institution or management happens to find itself in a situation that seems important enough to fight about. At such times, remember who your natural allies are. They are your employees. They are your residents' families. They are your suppliers. They are the local medical establishment. They are the local clergy.

In a time of conflict, if a program of government and community relations has been carefully administered over the past months and years, the community itself or powerful individuals and segments within it will likely rally to the institution's side. When that happens, any political opposition that is not extremely well focused will dissipate. There is an old adage about doing battle with city hall that applies here: The easiest way to convince politicians of the essential wisdom of your point of view is first to convince their constituents of the rightness of your position, and then to convince the politicians that their constituents have been convinced.

NOTES

1. Theodore Levitt, *The Marketing Imagination* (New York: The Free Press, 1983), 99. See also idem, "Marketing Success through Differentiation—of Anything," *Harvard Business Review* 58 (January-February 1980): 83–91.

2. See, for example, Philip Kotler, "From Sales Obsession to Marketing Effectiveness," *Harvard Business Review* 55 (November-December 1977): 67–75; David V. Hass, "Marketing: A Tool for Long Term Care Administration," *American Health Care Association Journal* 6 (March 1980): 4–14.

3. See, for example, Philip Kotler, *Marketing Management: Analysis, Planning, and Control*, 5th ed. (Englewood Cliffs, N.J.: Prentice-Hall, 1984); idem, *Marketing for Nonprofit Organizations*, 2d ed. (Englewood Cliffs, N.J.: Prentice-Hall, 1982); Stephen W. Brown, Anne-Marie Nelson, and Steven D. Wood, "Marketing's Creative Response to Change in the Long-Term Care Industry," *Journal of Long-Term Care Administration* 15 (Winter 1987): 5–9; Christopher H. Lovelock, "Concepts and Strategies for Health Marketers," *Hospital and Health Services Administration* 22 (Fall 1977): 50–62. On acute care hospitals as competitors, see Donald E.L. Johnson, "Hospitals Expected to Acquire Larger Share of Long-Term Care," *Modern Healthcare*, August 15, 1986, 94–96; Edward W. Campion, Axel Bang, and Maurice I. May, "Why Acute-Care Hospitals Must Undertake Long-Term Care," *New England Journal of Medicine* 308 (1983): 71–75.

4. On the legal implications of admitting into residence anyone with needs the institution is not equipped to handle, see Marshall B. Kapp, "Hospital Reimbursement by Diagnosis-related Groups: Legal and Ethical Implications for Nursing Homes," *Journal of Long-Term Care Administration* 14 (Fall 1986): 20–26.

5. See, for example, the several articles composing the special section on marketing in *Modern Healthcare*, September 27, 1985, 79–96.

6. "Life's Basic Problems Are Still Top Concern in the Nursing Homes," *New York Times*, January 19, 1989, B14.

7. On using the trust division of large metropolitan banks as a source of LTC referrals, see Susan Goldsmith, "A Social Worker Gets the Job Done," *Trusts and Estates* 120 (October 1981): 52–54.

8. See, for example, James R. DeNoyer, "Planning the Public Relations Program," in *The Health Care Facility's Public Relations Handbook*, edited by Lew Riggs (Gaithersburg, Md.: Aspen Publishers, 1982), 9–21; Lew Riggs, "Organizing the Public Relations Function," in ibid., 23–52; J. David Pincus, "Public Relations: Prescription for an Ailing Public Image," *Journal of Long-Term Care Administration* 14 (Spring 1986): 3–6.

9. Edward Bernays, *Propaganda* (New York: Horace Liveright, 1928), 158.

10. See, for example, Fred J. Evans, *Managing the Media: Proactive Strategy for Better Press Relations* (New York: Quorum Books, 1987); Kenneth G. Trester, "The Management Approach to Media Relations," in Riggs, *Health Care Facility's Public Relations Handbook*, 83–106.

11. Shana Alexander, *Very Much a Lady: The Untold Story of Jean Harris and Dr. Herman Tarnower* (Boston: Little, Brown, 1983); interview with Karl Wolf, Boston, April 18, 1990.

12. See, for example, Thomas F. Garbett, *How to Build a Corporation's Identity and Project Its Image* (Lexington, Mass.: Lexington Books, 1988), esp. 153–72.

13. See also Dorothy Wiley, "Crisis Communications and the Long-Term Care Administrator," *Journal of Long-Term Care Administration* 16 (Fall 1988): 34–36.

14. See, for example, Timothy H. Brubaker, "Enhancing Long-Term Care Education by Building Relationships between University Faculty and Administrators," *Journal of Long-Term Care Administration* 11 (Summer 1983): 14–18; William Ciferri and Renae Baker, "A Nursing Home/University Exchange Program: An Alternative Model for Teaching Nursing Homes," *Journal of Long-Term Care Administration* 13 (Spring 1985): 27–30; Mildred Seltzer, "Update: Partnerships with Educational Institutions," *Journal of Long-Term Care Administration* 13 (Summer 1985): 45–46; Helen Everett and Bettie Hooks, "The Nursing Home: A Setting for Student Learning," *Geriatric Nursing* 6 (January-February 1985): 32–35.

15. Judith C. Ahronheim, "Pitfalls of the Teaching Nursing Home: A Case for Balanced Geriatric Education," *New England Journal of Medicine* 308 (1983): 335–36.

16. Marshall B. Kapp, "Nursing Homes as Teaching Institutions: Legal Issues," *The Gerontologist* 24 (1984): 59.

17. Kapp, "Nursing Homes as Teaching Institutions," 55–60. For further information on the teaching nursing home, see Robert N. Butler, "The Teaching Nursing Home," *JAMA* 245 (1981): 1435–37; Edward L. Schneider, Marcia Ory, and Maybelle L. Aung, "Teaching Nursing Homes Revisited: Survey of Affiliations between American Medical Schools and Long-Term Care Facilities," *JAMA* 257 (1987): 2771–75; Don Riesenberg, "The Teaching Nursing Home: A Golden Annex to the Ivory Tower," *JAMA* 257 (1987): 3119–20.

Functional Assessment Case Examples: Mobility

Case Example A1: Ambulates with walker to main dining room for all three meals and to another unit for daily visits with wife.

> Mobility Score:
> *Independent*

Case Example A2: Ambulates around unit with cane. Independently wheels herself in wheelchair to leisure activities, to main dining room, and to clinics, all of which are located on a lower floor.

> Mobility Score:
> *Independent*

Case Example A3: Ambulates independently to main dining room for all meals every day. About twice a week, requires staff assistance in order to get to main dining room for dinner.

> Mobility Score:
> *Some Assistance*

Case Example A4: Independently finds way to main dining room for all meals and to the chapel for daily services. Needs staff assistance to get to areas that are unfamiliar to him.

> Mobility Score:
> *Some Assistance*

Case Example A5: Ambulates independently around the Center by pushing a wheelchair. Because she is afraid at night, requires staff assistance several times nightly for transfers and ambulation to the bathroom.

Mobility Score:
Substantial Assistance

Case Example A6: Ambulates independently in supervised areas. Due to cognitive impairment, is unable to leave his unit unless accompanied by staff member.

Mobility Score:
Daily Light Assistance

Case Example A7: Ambulates slowly about the unit with a walker. Stops to rest every 10 to 15 feet. Must always be pushed in a wheelchair when leaving the unit.

Mobility Score:
Daily Light Assistance

Case Example A8: Ambulates with a four-pronged cane. Able to cover long distances. Always requires staff assistance to find the unit dining room, the bathroom, and his room.

Mobility Score:
Substantial Assistance

Case Example A9: Needs to be lifted by two people during transfers from bed to wheelchair several times a day. Able to push himself in wheelchair anywhere in Center.

Mobility Score:
Dependent

Case Example A10: Ambulates independently. Is terrified of elevators and crowds. Takes the back staircase to the lower level for most meals and leisure activities.

Mobility Score:
Independent

Case Example A11: Walks short distances with physical assistance of two people. Spends most of waking hours in a wheelchair. Is dependent on staff for wheelchair mobility.

Mobility Score:
Dependent

Case Example A12: Walks short distances independently using a walker but requires verbal cueing for transfers and finding his way around the unit.

Mobility Score:
Substantial Assistance

Case Example A13: Can safely negotiate his way around his room and bathroom without assistance but requires staff assistance when moving around the unit.

Mobility Score:
Substantial Assistance

Case Example A14: Is transferred from bed to wheelchair via Hoyer lift. Requires staff assistance for wheelchair mobility. Is repositioned every two hours when in bed.

Mobility Score:
Dependent

Case Example A15: Requires verbal cueing and supervision for repositioning in bed, transfers, and walking.

Mobility Score:
Substantial Assistance

Functional Assessment Case Examples: Dining

Case Example B1: Arises after 9 A.M. and skips breakfast. Eats lunch and dinner in main dining room.

Dining Score:
Independent

Case Example B2: Would like to gain 10 pounds. Eats meals in main dining room and takes dietary supplements or snacks of her choosing on the unit between meals.

Dining Score:
Independent

Case Example B3: Eats all meals in main dining room. Tires in late afternoon and so, several times a week, requires the evening meal in the unit dining area.

Dining Score:
Some Assistance

Case Example B4: Dines in the main dining room for all meals. Staff must provide and encourage her to take a daily snack on the unit at 3 P.M. and at bedtime.

Dining Score:
Some Assistance

Case Example B5: Is brought to main dining room for lunch every day. Eats breakfast and dinner in the unit dining area.

Dining Score:
Daily Light Assistance

Case Example B6: Eats all meals in the unit dining area. Eats independently once he is brought to meals, his tray has been organized, and he is instructed to eat.

Dining Score:
Daily Light Assistance

Case Example B7: Eats independently as long as only one food item is placed in front of him at a time. As each item is given to him, requires orientation as to the type of food it is and must be given correct utensil to use.

Dining Score:
Substantial Assistance

Case Example B8: Independently eats finger foods but needs verbal cueing for fluids and foods requiring utensils.

Dining Score:
Substantial Assistance

Case Example B9: Refuses to eat with others. Carries his tray from unit dining area to his room, where he dines independently and watches the news on television.

Dining Score:
Daily Light Assistance

Case Example B10: Requires staff assistance to organize tray, but eats independently. Requires staff supervision during meals to stop her from eating food from other residents' trays.

Dining Score:
Substantial Assistance

Case Example B11: Needs reminders to come to meals. Eats independently once tray is organized. Wanders off during meals and requires constant staff coaxing to ensure that meal is eaten.

Dining Score:
Substantial Assistance

Case Example B12: Is capable of giving herself her own gastric tube feeding with staff setup and supervision.

Dining Score:
Substantial Assistance

Case Example B13: Independently feeds herself in the unit dining area at breakfast and lunch once tray is set up. Tires late in day and must be fed at dinner time.

Dining Score:
Dependent

Case Example B14: Eats soft solid foods independently. Receives fluids via tube from staff.

Dining Score:
Dependent

Case Example B15: Eats independently but requires verbal cueing throughout the meal in order to eat at a slower pace to prevent choking.

Dining Score:
Substantial Assistance

Functional Assessment Case Examples: Dressing and Hygiene

Case Example C1: Selects own clothes. Dresses, bathes, and grooms independently.

Dressing and Hygiene Score:
Independent

Case Example C2: Refuses baths and showers. Independently takes a "birdbath" every night in her own room. Owns minimal changes of clothing but keeps clothes clean. Dresses and grooms independently.

Dressing and Hygiene Score:
Independent

Case Example C3: Dresses and grooms herself. Has a tendency to layer her clothing and thinks she looks great. Adamantly refuses to wear clothes pre-selected by staff or to change when staff make suggestions. Accepts assistance with weekly bath.

Dressing and Hygiene Score:
Some Assistance

Case Example C4: Likes to choose own clothes but requires staff assistance to retrieve the items she selects from closets and drawers. Dresses independently except for donning and removing elastic stockings and shoes. Needs help with tub bathing.

Dressing and Hygiene Score:
Daily Light Assistance

Case Example C5: Selects clothing. Requires daily assistance with bra straps, buttons, zippers, and tying shoes. Staff clean her dentures. Otherwise, grooms and dresses herself. Needs assistance with weekly bath.

Dressing and Hygiene Score:
Daily Light Assistance

Case Example C6: Capable of bathing, grooming, and dressing himself with daily cueing by staff to do so.

Dressing and Hygiene Score:
Daily Light Assistance

Case Example C7: Needs daily help with retrieving, care, and donning of wig, applying makeup and jewelry, and pulling garments over her head. Clothes laid out daily. Independent in other areas of dressing. Assistance with bath twice a week.

Dressing and Hygiene Score:
Daily Light Assistance

Case Example C8: Usually dresses, bathes, and grooms herself. Because of unstable heart condition, may need total staff help several times a week.

Dressing and Hygiene Score:
Substantial Assistance

Case Example C9: Requires total assistance with dressing and bathing every morning. Grooms himself. Feels better as the day progresses and only requires staff assistance to pull shirt off over head in the evening. Does remainder of undressing independently.

Dressing and Hygiene Score:
Substantial Assistance

Case Example C10: Likes to sleep in his clothes just in case there is a fire at night. Changes clothes about three times a week. Looks neat. Grooms himself. Independently takes showers when he changes his clothes.

Dressing and Hygiene Score:
Independent

Case Example C11: Requires total staff help in applying and removing back brace and leg brace as well as shoes and stockings. Assistance with weekly bath.

Dressing and Hygiene Score:
Substantial Assistance

Case Example C12: Requires total assistance but can participate in small tasks such as washing face and brushing teeth.

Dressing and Hygiene Score:
Dependent

Functional Assessment Case Examples: Toileting

Case Example D1: Continent. Self-care of colostomy.

> Toileting Score:
> *Independent*

Case Example D2: Incontinent of a large amount of urine approximately twice a week. Cleans and redresses himself.

> Toileting Score:
> *Independent*

Case Example D3: Dribbles urine on the way to the bathroom every morning. Independent in self care. Needs staff assistance to wipe up spills.

> Toileting Score:
> *Daily Light Assistance*

Case Example D4: Requires periodic reminders to toilet.

> Toileting Score:
> *Some Assistance*

Case Example D5: Refuses to get out of bed to toilet at night. Requires bedpan about three times a night. Independent and continent when out of bed.

> Toileting Score:
> *Daily Light Assistance*

Case Example D6: Self-care. Empties and cleanses own colostomy bag twice a shift. Staff changes ostomy appliance twice a week and as necessary.

Toileting Score:
Some Assistance

Case Example D7: Continent. Verbalizes toileting needs. Requires staff help with hygiene in the toileting room.

Toileting Score:
Daily Light Assistance

Case Example D8: Usually remembers to toilet. Incontinent of urine approximately twice a week, requiring staff assistance.

Toileting Score:
Some Assistance

Case Example D9: Continent of urine. Staff changes ileostomy bag on a daily basis.

Toileting Score:
Daily Light Assistance

Case Example D10: Resident is toileted every two hours. Usually continent while awake. Incontinent several times a night, requiring staff assistance with hygiene.

Toileting Score:
Substantial Assistance

Case Example D11: Continent. Has a ureterostoma. Requires staff help to empty bag every two hours. Total ostomy care daily, including skin care.

Toileting Score:
Substantial Assistance

Case Example D12: Has an indwelling Foley catheter that requires daily irrigation by a nurse. Continent of bowel while on a daily toileting program.

Toileting Score:
Daily Light Assistance or Substantial Assistance

Case Example D13: Incontinent of bowel and bladder. Wears an external catheter, which is applied and maintained by staff.

Toileting Score:
Dependent

Case Example D14: Urinates in inappropriate receptacles such as wastebaskets, plants, and drawers. This occurs no more than twice a week, so long as staff brings him to the toileting room every few hours.

Toileting Score:
Daily Light Assistance

Functional Assessment Case Examples: Mental Status

Case Example E1: Is able to correctly state the name of the facility, the name of her unit, and her room number. Knows her roommate's name, her daughter's telephone number, and her own former address and telephone number. Knows nursing staff by name and is quite articulate in verbalizing her needs. Arises at 7:00 A.M. and then spends most of the day off the unit in recreational or other activities, returning only at 11:00 A.M. and 2:00 P.M. for her medication.

Mental Status Score:
Normal

Case Example E2: Unable to speak. Maintains a large calendar in her room where she writes her daily schedule of activities so that staff and visitors will know where to find her. Independent in Center activities. Is an active participant in her newly developed interests of ceramics and art history. Since admission six months ago, she has continued to pursue her commitment as officer of the ladies auxiliary of her former place of worship, corresponding with the membership by mail.

Mental Status Score:
Normal

Case Example E3: Unable to remember the name of the Center. Although he is not sure just what month or day it is, he knows that it is winter and dresses himself appropriately. He is an active Boston Celtics basketball fan and enjoys relating highlights of their latest victories to staff. He has put together a scrap book of Celtics memorabilia for his great-grandson. Independent in his daily activities but occasionally needs reminders when it is his bath day or when to get a haircut.

Mental Status Score:
Mild Impairment

Case Example E4:   Independent in getting herself organized every day. Knows the names, dosages, and times of her medications. As she often forgets what day it is, she needs reminders for daily activities programs and is terribly disappointed when she misses her favorite ones. She has been able to make her needs known, and so one or more of her many friends usually reminds her to go along to an activity. In addition to group activities, she loves reading Harlequin romances and keeps her dining companions enthralled discussing the heroines' latest escapades.

Mental Status Score:
Mild Impairment

Case Example E5: Knows she is in a nice place where old people live but is unable to name the facility. Upon admission three months ago, she wandered into other people's rooms regularly for several days until she learned which room was hers. Recognizes her roommate and enjoys her company but forgets her name. Independent in dressing and hygiene. Is able to get herself to meals and activities on her unit by relying on a schedule of daily activities posted in her room by staff. Although she has difficulty finding the right words to say what she wants, she is still able to convey her needs and feelings.

Mental Status Score:
Moderate Impairment

Case Example E6: Knows the name of the facility as well as his old address. Has difficulty finding his way around the unit and requires verbal cueing from staff. Remembers his children's names but not his grandchildren's, whom he sees infrequently. Recognizes staff but only remembers the names of his favorites. Knows the month and the year but needs reminders for the day and date. Enjoys socializing with both staff and fellow residents but is repetitive in his story telling. Is able to participate and succeed in many activities programs as long as there is plenty of structuring on the part of the therapist. Performs best in small group activities.

Mental Status Score:
Moderate Impairment

Case Example E7: Has forgotten her married name and responds only to her first name. Oblivious to place and time. Quiet most of the time. Totally dependent on staff for personal care. Every morning after breakfast she is brought to a seat opposite the nurses' station, where she stays until she is brought to programs on the unit. She does not know the names or recognize the faces of her caregivers but is able to differentiate staff from other residents. She feels safe when she is sitting across from the nurses' station and usually leaves her programs in the dining room to resume her seat.

Mental Status Score:
Severe Impairment

Case Example E8: Knows she is not in her own home but does not know where she is. Every day, usually in the late afternoon, she will stop any passers-by to ask them to take her home as her mother is waiting for her for dinner. Is able to dress herself with staff supervision and verbal cueing. Otherwise, she dresses inappropriately. Has a limited attention span and therefore has difficulty participating in activities programs. Enjoys eating and "helping" people.

Mental Status Score:
Severe Impairment

Functional Assessment Case Examples: Behavior

Case Example F1: A frail woman has several medical problems that cause disability and irritating symptoms that are not life-threatening. She spends the day in her room, frequently moaning and calling for help. These cries are audible up and down the hall and occur on all shifts. At night they awaken residents in neighboring rooms, who do not complain. Neither a behavioral modification program nor medication has been successful in calming or quieting the resident.

Behavioral Status Score:
Noisy (5); Agitated (5)

Case Example F2: A manic depressive woman talks in a loud voice. During her manic episodes, which occur about once every three months and last about two weeks, her voice becomes especially loud. Other times she can be heard muttering to herself as she sits in the day room. Other residents sometimes tell her to quiet down when she loudly interrupts a group, but they do not seem to mind her muttering.

Behavioral Status Score:
No Severe Behavior Dysfunction

Case Example F3: A demented woman is confined to a geri chair because of her inability to walk without assistance. She often dozes, but several times during the day and evening shift she awakens with a start and calls loudly for help and bangs her table. Various tranquilizers were tried, but they caused her to become oversedated and were not helpful. When agitated, she hits staff members who try to soothe her. The episodes subside spontaneously in a few minutes.

Behavioral Status Score:
Noisy (5); Physically Abusive (4)

Case Example F4: An anxious woman lives with her husband, who is disabled with Parkinson's disease. She manages most of his care. Once or twice a week she becomes frustrated and can be heard shouting loudly at him to get moving and help her because she is tired. When staff respond and reassure her that she is doing a good job, she becomes calm and quiet.

Behavioral Status Score:
Noisy (2)

Case Example F5: A reclusive man actively shuns company and spends most of his time in his room, which he occupies alone. While in the room he mutters constantly to himself and can be heard in the hall just outside. When he comes for meals on the floor, he stops muttering. He is considered odd by other residents, who do not complain about his noise.

Behavioral Status Score:
Noisy (5)

Case Example F6: A demented man is quiet and cooperative. He is on a toileting schedule and is usually continent. About three times a week he becomes confused while in his room and urinates in a wastebasket. On about half of these occasions, he forgets to zip his fly and wanders into the hall, exposing himself. Staff have learned to respond quickly, and these episodes cause no one distress.

Behavioral Status Score:
Bizarre (2)

Case Example F7: A woman has chronic bronchitis and a chronic cough productive of large amounts of sputum. She uses at least two large boxes of tissue per day and carries around a large plastic bag into which she puts the tissue after blowing her nose. Several of the other residents find this offensive and occasionally complain to the nurse.

Behavioral Status Score:
No Severe Behavior Dysfunction

Case Example F8: A paranoid woman refuses to put on clothes because she fears that they have been washed in poison. She will wear only a johnny, which she refuses to tie, so that it is always open at the back. She paces up and down the hall peering into rooms but does not enter them.

Behavioral Status Score:
Bizarre (5); Agitated (4)

Case Example F9: A woman has a chronic cough productive of large amounts of sputum. She spits on the floor wherever she is sitting. When asked not to do this, she becomes angry, denying that she did it and saying that she has no cough.

Behavioral Status Score:
Bizarre (5)

Case Example F10: A chronically angry and demanding woman insists on sleeping nude. Occasionally she kicks off the covers at night while asleep, and her roommate sees her while on the way to the bathroom. When this happens, her roommate becomes angry and shouts that she is a whore.

Behavioral Status Score:
No Severe Behavior Dysfunction

Case Example F11: A demented woman is confined to a geri chair. When she has nothing to do, she becomes agitated and scratches at a mole on her nose, causing it to bleed. Staff have learned that she is happy and calm when her hands are occupied, and so they give her yarn, which she happily winds into balls all day. About once a day a ball of yarn falls onto the floor, and she becomes agitated and picks at herself. When given back her ball, she soon becomes calm again.

Behavioral Status Score:
Bizarre (3); Agitated (3)

Case Example F12: An ambulatory man lives with his demented wife and manages most of her care, frequently becoming fatigued and irritable. On three occasions in the six months he has lived at the Center, someone has pushed him in the elevator and he has responded by punching them, on one occasion giving a woman a black eye. Psychiatry has been working with him, and he has not punched anyone in about six weeks. He is a large man. Other residents and some staff are afraid of him.

Behavioral Status Score:
No Severe Behavior Dysfunction

Case Example F13: A woman is fully ambulatory in a wheelchair. She is cognitively intact but lives on a Pattern III unit because of activities of daily living needs. She is very impatient, particularly around mealtime. When her way into the dining room is blocked by a slow-moving resident with a walker, she runs into the other person. This occurs about twice a week. Also about twice a week, a demented resident wanders into "her" place in the dining hall, at which time she screams, curses, and tries to push the other person out of the way. Once in the last three months she scratched another resident doing this.

Behavioral Status Score:
Physically Abusive (5); Verbally Abusive (2)

Case Example F14: A mildly demented woman is able to do most of her activities of daily living with some cueing. About three times a day she approaches the desk and asks, with fear in her voice, where she is and what she should do. When pointed to an activity, she becomes calm and can participate with pleasure. She hates baths and resists her weekly bath, screaming and scratching. Twice in the last month aides have been scratched while attempting to bathe her.

Behavioral Status Score:
Noisy (2); Physically Abusive (2); Agitated (4)

Case Example F15: A woman lives with a demented roommate who tries to get into bed with her during naps. This enrages her, and on one occasion she threw the demented resident on the floor, dislocating her shoulder. She has never before been physically violent.

Behavioral Status Score:
No Severe Behavior Dysfunction

Case Example F16: A schizophrenic woman spends most of her time in bed. She is totally dependent in activities of daily living. When staff come to care for her, she mutters "go to hell" in a quiet voice and tries to pull away from them. Staff do not find her threatening and are amused by her behavior.

Behavior Status Score:
No Severe Behavior Dysfunction

Case Example F17: A cognitively intact woman requires only routine dressing changes for a healing skin ulcer, but she is convinced that she is seriously ill. About twice a shift, she approaches the desk and demands to see the doctor for a variety of complaints, insisting that there is an emergency. About once a month, she meets with administration to complain about her care. Whenever there is a float nurse whom she does not know (i.e., about twice a week), she accuses her loudly of doing her dressing wrong, tells her she is no good, and demands that "her" nurse ("the only one who knows how to do it right") care for her. She is well known in the institution, and nurses ask not to float to her floor.

Behavior Status Score:
Noisy (2); Verbally Abusive (2); Agitated (4)

Case Example F18: A demented woman cannot find her room. Staff bring her back and forth, but about twice a week she gets lost and enters a room not her own. When asked to leave, she apologizes and does so.

Behavior Status Score:
Wandering (2)

Case Example F19: A demented man is fully ambulatory. He appears anxious and worried, and he spends the entire day pacing up and down the halls looking for his wife, who still lives in the community. When told to sit still, he becomes yet more anxious and soon resumes his pacing. Twice a day he wanders through the day room, disrupting activities if not steered away. About once a week he attempts to leave the floor. On one occasion, about a month ago, he got onto the elevator and was found wandering in the parking lot. Since then staff have been more aware of him, and he has not left the Center.

Behavior Status Score:
Wandering (4); Agitated (5)

Case Example F20: A demented man is convinced that he has business in New York, where he once lived. Every day he tries to get onto the elevator and leave the Center. Staff are vigilant, but on one occasion he did leave and was able to get onto a bus. He was found in a town 15 miles distant asking for directions to the D train.

Behavior Status Score:
Wandering (5)

Case Example F21: A likeable man is dementing quietly in a Pattern II unit. Twice a day, he forgets where his room is and needs to be intercepted by staff on his way down the hall to the adjacent unit. About once a week he does wander onto the adjacent unit and is brought back by staff, who know him and are fond of him.

Behavior Status Score:
Wandering (4)

Case Example F22: An ambulatory woman is obviously anxious and speaks in a whining and querulous voice. She is not, however, particularly demanding and usually goes quietly about her business. When she is sick, she becomes frightened and sits at the desk, frequently and insistently asking for help. This happened about a week ago for three days when she had a bad cold, but she has since resumed her usual quiet behavior. A float nurse who saw her during this period suggested strongly that she be transferred to a Pattern III unit.

Behavior Status Score:
No Severe Behavior Dysfunction

Case Example F23: A cognitively intact woman is able to manage most of her activities of daily living despite very severe heart and lung disease, which makes her chronically short of breath. She gets several treatments and eight different medicines. She is extremely compulsive about these and insists that they must be given at exactly the same time each day. When they do not come at these times, she complains to the nurse. She seems to have at least one such complaint each day, and on bad days, which occur about twice a week, she has several.

Behavior Status Score:
Agitated (4)

Case Example F24: A quiet woman has spent most of her life in a state hospital with a diagnosis of schizophrenia. She is seclusive and refuses to attend any activities other than meals. She is cooperative with treatments when necessary, but she does need reassurance. When asked, she states that she hears two men talking loudly outside her window and that this sometimes keeps her awake at night. Her roommate, who says she is a nice, quiet woman, does not hear this.

Behavior Status Score:
No Severe Behavior Dysfunction

Case Example F25: A frail woman seems chronically unhappy. Although not demanding, whenever asked, she weeps and states that she is extremely sick and wishes she were dead. Despite this, she has a routine in which she participates without complaint. She eats well, although she doesn't like the food, and has not lost weight. She looks forward to family visits, but she spends much of the time with her family weeping because she is so glad they took the time to see her.

Behavior Status Score:
Depressed (3)

Case Example F26: A cognitively intact woman is fully ambulatory but spends most of her time in her room. She frequently tells her nurse that she wishes she were dead, and when she sees her doctor, she asks him for poison. She attends some activities, sitting on the outside of the group and not participating. Her family say that she is always unhappy when they visit, and they ask if they made the right choice in encouraging her admission.

Behavior Status Score:
Depressed (5)

Functional Assessment Patterning System: Case Studies

Case Study G1

Albert is nonambulatory. Each day one person pivots him into a geri chair with a tray. He requires close supervision and coaxing at mealtimes because past refusals to eat or drink have resulted in fluid imbalance. Staff dress him. He is incontinent, and this aggravates his areas of skin breakdown. Nurses are involved in special decubitus care and dressing changes once a shift. Evening and night nurses position him every one to two hours to prevent further breakdown. At times, two nurses are required because he is resistant and assaultive.

He usually does not vocalize. When he does, his speech is garbled. His communication skills are further limited by his profound hearing loss, for which he has refused a hearing aid.

He is very demented and is aphasic. He does not recognize staff or family members. He constantly tries to bang his hands on the tray of his geri chair and cannot be stopped. He grabs at others whenever they come near, and often it requires two staff members to loosen his grip.

Scoring

Mobility:	Dependent
Dining:	Substantial Assistance
Dressing and Hygiene:	Dependent
Toileting:	Dependent
Health:	Not Applicable
Mental Status:	Severe Impairment
Behavior	
Noisy:	Serious and Unresponsive

Bizarre: Not Present
Physically Abusive: Serious and Unresponsive
Verbally Abusive: Not Present
Wandering: Not Present
Depressed: Not Present
Agitated: Not Present

Pattern: IIIE

Case Study G2

Beatrice is an 87-year-old woman who ambulates readily around the unit. She transfers independently but always requires a guide when leaving the unit. All meals are eaten on the nursing unit with the assistance of staff in organizing her tray. Her dressing and hygiene needs are totally taken care of by staff. She has no ability to recognize her own needs. She is continent during the day with a bowel and bladder program, but she becomes incontinent after sundown. Her medical status is stable, but her memory is severely impaired. She does not recognize family or staff. She is a quiet woman who does not make any demands on staff.

Scoring

Mobility: Daily Light Assistance
Dining: Daily Light Assistance
Dressing and Hygiene: Dependent
Toileting: Substantial Assistance
Health: Not Applicable
Mental Status: Severe Impairment
Behavior
  Noisy: Not Present
  Bizarre: Not Present
  Physically Abusive: Not Present
  Verbally Abusive: Not Present
  Wandering: Not Present
  Depressed: Not Present
  Agitated: Not Present

Pattern: IIID

Case Study G3

Clara is an alert and oriented 84-year-old married woman who resides with her husband. Her medical problems consist of angina pectoris, diabetes mellitus, peripheral vascular disease, glaucoma, and a history of thrombophlebitis, for which she requires limited nursing supervision to maintain a stable status.

Due to her cardiac condition, Clara requires a wheelchair for mobility. She receives assistance or supervision transferring to the wheelchair from her husband or a nurse's aide. She attends two meals in the main dining room but requires assistance if making additional trips, such as to the clinics. She cares for herself in dressing and hygiene, except for help with minor tasks such as tying her shoes. She dribbles urine on occasion but is otherwise independent in toileting.

Clara is a sociable woman, participating with others in programs on and off the unit. Her relationship with her husband is tense and conflictive at times.

Scoring

Mobility:	Daily Light Assistance
Dining:	Some Assistance
Dressing and Hygiene:	Some Assistance
Toileting:	Independent
Health:	Not Applicable
Mental Status:	Normal
Behavior	
Noisy:	Not Present
Bizarre:	Not Present
Physically Abusive:	Not Present
Verbally Abusive:	Not Present
Wandering:	Not Present
Depressed:	Not Present
Agitated:	Not Present

Pattern: II

Case Study G4

Dora is a 91-year-old woman who ambulates independently. Presenting herself in neat, clean attire, she dresses and toilets herself independently. All meals are eaten in the main dining room.

She participates in Center activities. She has a hearing problem but refuses to wear a hearing aid. Her medical status is stable, and she receives a Vitamin B_{12} injection once a month. Her blood pressure is checked once every two weeks.

Dora is well organized, alert, and oriented to time, place, and person. This past month she was transferred to another unit due to roommate incompatibility. She presents herself as a calm, quiet individual who expresses her happiness over this transfer, saying that she now has a roommate with whom she can communicate and develop a comradeship.

Scoring

Mobility:	Independent
Dining:	Independent
Dressing and Hygiene:	Independent
Toileting:	Independent
Health:	Light Care
Mental Status:	Normal
Behavior	
Noisy:	Not Present
Bizarre:	Not Present
Physically Abusive:	Not Present
Verbally Abusive:	Not Present
Wandering:	Not Present
Depressed:	Not Present
Agitated:	Not Present

Pattern: I

Case Study G5

Edna is a frail 93-year-old woman with rheumatoid arthritis, anemia, and diverticulosis. She has unstable congestive heart failure. Two months ago she suffered an attack of acute cholecystitis, which was treated with antibiotics and IV fluids but not with surgery because of her extremely frail condition.

She is wheelchairbound but is able to assist with transfers, which require the aid of one staff person. Once in the wheelchair, she is able to propel herself short distances but becomes tired if required to make more than two trips a day between her room and the common area on her floor. She never leaves the floor without assistance but does enjoy trips in the car with her family, who are able to get her in and out of the car and take a wheelchair along so that she may go into restaurants.

She is unable to achieve a sitting position in bed because of weakness and deformed joints secondary to her arthritis. She assists with dressing, putting her arms through the sleeves, etc., but is unable to dress herself. She is able to wash her hands and mouth if given a washcloth but is unable to manipulate the faucet herself and so requires an attendant. She is able to hold a specially designed toothbrush, which was obtained for her by occupational therapy, and to use it appropriately. She has very little hair and wears a wig, which must be prepared for her carefully by the staff, as she is quite vain about her appearance.

She is able to perceive a need to urinate. However, when she does, she must be taken to the toilet quickly or she is incontinent of urine (about three times a week) and of stool (about once a week). She is able to feed herself using special implements to compensate for her arthritis, but she requires that food either be blenderized or cut up for her by someone.

Although she knows her family and all of the nurses by name, she is occasionally forgetful, which causes her considerable unhappiness. About once a week she misplaces some of her belongings, at which time she becomes quite agitated and often accuses staff or other residents of stealing. She tends to be meddlesome with other residents and is occasionally verbally abusive when people do not appreciate what she perceives as efforts in their behalf. Staff are usually able to reason with her, but occasionally she must be isolated in her room for short periods of time after one of these outbursts.

Because of her congestive heart failure, her weight is monitored daily and she receives daily doses of diuretics depending on her weight. She has a chronic cough and has had many bouts of wheezing and bronchitis. At such times, she requires twice daily respiratory therapy to mobilize her secretions, also occasional suctioning and oral and inhaled medication every four hours. On three occasions in the last year she has developed pulmonary edema quite suddenly, once in the middle of the night. She has an ongoing occupational therapy and physical therapy program to maintain her ability to transfer and her limited use of her hands.

Despite her many disabilities, she is cheerful as long as she feels cared for, and she gets along well with the staff most of the time. She is a very anxious woman and requests reassurance approximately twice a week regarding her fear that one of her several diseases is progressing.

Scoring

Mobility:	Substantial Assistance
Dining:	Daily Light Assistance
Dressing and Hygiene:	Dependent
Toileting:	Substantial Assistance
Health:	Light Care
Mental Status:	Mild Impairment
Behavior	
Noisy:	Not Present

Bizarre:	Not Present
Physically Abusive:	Not Present
Verbally Abusive:	Less Than Once a Day
Wandering:	Not Present
Depressed:	Less Than Once a Day
Agitated:	Less Than Once a Day

Pattern: IIIA

Case Study G6

Frank is ambulatory with a stable gait and is able to move about the floor at will without fatigue. He does, however, become lost several times daily on his way from his room to the dining area on the floor and requires a staff person to point him in the direction of his room. When he eats, he requires constant coaxing throughout the meal. He is somewhat sloppy in eating and occasionally needs to be changed (or the table needs to be cleaned) following meals.

He is able to dress himself but requires someone else to lay out the clothes for him, as he dresses with many layers of clothes and inappropriate garments when left to choose his own. He is able to go to the toilet by himself but is incontinent of urine about twice a week.

He has mild hypertension and adult onset diabetes, which is stable on oral medication. He requires monthly monitoring of his weight. His blood and urine are tested once a week. He has moderately severe senile dementia, is able to identify all of the staff, but forgets their names about half the time. He is disoriented to place but knows that he is among friends and is being cared for. When in the dining area or in his room, he frequently becomes confused, asking staff what he should do or where he should go. He never goes into other people's rooms, nor does he attempt to leave the Center. When oriented and directed, he does what he is told cheerfully and gratefully.

He occasionally talks loudly or makes requests for orientation in a loud and disturbing voice but is easily quieted. Staff and other residents seem to like him.

Scoring

Mobility:	Substantial Assistance
Dining:	Substantial Assistance
Dressing and Hygiene:	Daily Light Assistance
Toileting:	Some Assistance
Health:	Not Applicable
Mental Status:	Moderate Impairment

Behavior
    Noisy: Less Than Once a Day
    Bizarre: Not Present
    Physically Abusive: Not Present
    Verbally Abusive: Not Present
    Wandering: Not Present
    Depressed: Not Present
    Agitated: Not Present

Pattern: IIIB

Case Study G7

George is ambulatory with a cane. He is able to negotiate his way around the unit with verbal cues from staff. He always requires a guide when leaving the unit.

He takes his meals in the dining area on the floor. He is a picky eater but is capable of feeding himself once his tray has been organized. In order to maintain his nutritional status, the nurses maintain a calorie count of his intake and give him diet supplements between meals.

George requires total assistance from staff for bathing, grooming, and dressing. He is petrified of taking showers and will occasionally swear at and hit staff during shower time. During such outbursts, he responds well to a calm, gentle approach by staff.

He is totally incontinent of urine and stool despite a structured toileting program. He presents himself as an alert gentleman who is disoriented to time and place. He is a gentle, sociable man who enjoys participating in leisure activity programs on the unit and biweekly visits with his family.

Scoring

Mobility: Substantial Assistance
Dining: Daily Light Assistance
Dressing and Hygiene: Dependent
Toileting: Dependent
Health: Not Applicable
Mental Status: Moderate Impairment
Behavior
    Noisy: Not Present
    Bizarre: Not Present
    Physically Abusive: Less Than Once a Day

Verbally Abusive: Less Than Once a Day
Wandering: Not Present
Depressed: Not Present
Agitated: Not Present

Pattern: IIIC

Case Study G8

Helen is an 86-year-old former piano teacher who has senile dementia of the Alzheimer's type. Her health is relatively stable.

She has been living in a private room at the Center for the past two years. She keeps her room neat and clean but has a habit of misplacing some of her prized possessions, specifically a photograph book of her family and friends and her favorite sheet music. Whenever she loses these items, which usually occurs several times a day, she rummages through her neighbor's dresses in an attempt to locate them. Often she becomes very agitated and verbally abusive and accuses staff of stealing her treasures. She threatens to call the FBI if the items are not returned. She usually responds to one-on-one interaction with a familiar staff member, who helps her to locate her belongings in her room. On those occasions when she becomes extremely agitated, staff have difficulty calming her down.

Helen is a sociable woman who loves music. She attends the weekly concerts at the Center as well as sing-alongs on the unit. Although her memory is poor for independent functioning, she is able to remember the words of her favorite songs and takes pride in entertaining others during the sing-alongs.

She needs minor assistance in dressing and hygiene in the way of reminders and the laying out of clean clothes. She is continent of urine and toilets herself. She is fully ambulatory and full of energy and has a tendency to pace about the unit. She does not tolerate having her path obstructed by others, and on occasion she will push other residents aside. Sometimes she will tell wheelchairbound residents to get up and get out of her way. In the past month, she has wandered off the unit on three occasions and has been found in various locations looking for her office.

She takes her meals in the dining area on the floor and is able to feed herself. When she is finished eating, she enjoys helping the staff clean the dining room by clearing trays and wiping tables. She likes to feel useful on the unit, and staff try to engage her in such activities as much as possible. She does, however, need a lot of verbal cueing in order to be able to complete the tasks. The staff believe that the effort is worthwhile, for when Helen feels useful she has less of a tendency to wander.

Scoring

Mobility:	Daily Light Assistance
Dining:	Daily Light Assistance
Dressing and Hygiene:	Daily Light Assistance
Toileting:	Independent
Health:	Not Applicable
Mental Status:	Moderate Impairment
Behavior	
Noisy:	Not Present
Bizarre:	Not Present
Physically Abusive:	Serious and Unresponsive
Verbally Abusive:	More Than Once a Day
Wandering:	More Than Once a Day
Depressed:	Not Present
Agitated:	More Than Once a Day

Pattern : IIIF

Identifying Characteristics: Patterns I, II, and III

	Percentage in a Typical Resident Population							
Identifying Characteristic	*PI*	*PII*	*PIIIA*	*PIIIB*	*PIIIC*	*PIIID*	*PIIIE*	*PIIIF*
Requires help in ambulation	6	47	73	85	92	89	85	45
Requires help in dressing	7	50	87	91	100	100	100	100
Requires help in eating	1	28	70	91	100	100	100	100
Requires help in bathing	61	99	98	100	100	100	100	100
Continent (bladder)	97	75	34	26	0	19	5	24
Continent (bowel)	100	87	47	37	15	22	5	45
Mentally oriented	92	57	62	0	8	0	0	0
Mild or no behavior problems	87	45	30	28	38	36	0	0
Severe behavior problems	0	18	43	46	31	52	95	97

Employee Opinion and Attitude Survey Questionnaire

1. In your opinion, what do your fellow employees think about this center as a place to work?

_____Excellent
_____Good
_____Average
_____Fair
_____Poor

2. In general, is there a friendly feeling among the employees?

_____Yes
_____No

3. How do you feel the people who work here are treated as compared with other hospitals or nursing homes?

_____Much better
_____Somewhat better
_____About the same
_____Somewhat worse
_____Much worse

4. In your opinion, the care of residents here is:

_____ Excellent
_____ Good
_____ Adequate
_____ Poor
_____ Very bad

5. In your opinion, the pay here, compared with other hospitals or nursing homes, is:

_____ Much better
_____ Somewhat better
_____ About the same
_____ Somewhat worse
_____ Much worse

6. Compared with other hospitals or nursing homes, employee benefits here are:

_____ Much better
_____ Somewhat better
_____ About the same
_____ Somewhat worse
_____ Much worse

7. The administration really tries to satisfy employees.

_____ Agree
_____ Disagree

8. In general, does the management keep employees in the dark about things?

_____ Most of the time
_____ Some of the time
_____ Almost never

9. Does long service really mean something at this center?

_____ Yes
_____ No

10. Do people who get promotions here usually deserve them?

_____ Yes
_____ No

11. Do you feel there is cooperation between the various departments?

_____ Most of the time
_____ Some of the time
_____ Almost never

12. Is there a team feeling among the people with whom you work?

_____ Most of the time
_____ Some of the time
_____ Almost never

13. Do you feel your department is usually given proper recognition?

_____ Yes
_____ No

14. Have you been made aware of what the center's employee benefit programs provide?

_____ Very aware
_____ Somewhat aware
_____ Unaware

15. In general, does the management keep you informed on matters you need to know about?

_____ Most of the time
_____ Some of the time
_____ Almost never

16. Do you think the center does enough in its training and development of employees?

_____ Yes
_____ No

17. Do you feel that your personal property is safe at the center?

_____ Yes
_____ No

18. Are there any conditions concerning your job that could be improved?

_____ Many
_____ Some
_____ Very few
_____ None

19. Do you feel physically safe when you are working at the center?

_____ Yes
_____ No

20. Do you usually have adequate supplies and equipment to do your job?

_____ Yes
_____ No

21. If you have a problem or complaint, do you feel that you can talk to your supervisor and receive fair consideration?

_____Most of the time
_____Some of the time
_____Almost never

22. In general, your supervisor really tries to get your ideas and suggestions for improvement.

_____Agree
_____Disagree

23. When you have a problem about how to get your work done, are you able to talk to your supervisor when you want to?

_____Most of the time
_____Some of the time
_____Almost never

24. In general, your supervisor lets you know what is expected of you.

_____Agree
_____Disagree

25. In general, is your supervisor fair with respect to discipline?

_____Yes
_____No

26. In general, your supervisor gives you credit and praise for work well done.

_____Agree
_____Disagree

27. Do you feel your supervisor shows reasonable concern for you when you are absent from work?

_____ Yes
_____ No

28. Your supervisor doesn't really understand the problems you face on the job.

_____ Agree
_____ Disagree

29. Does your supervisor provide you with learning opportunities and the chance to broaden your knowledge?

_____ Yes
_____ No

30. In general, center supervisors and managers really care about the welfare of employees.

_____ Agree
_____ Disagree

31. In general, your supervisor really listens to and takes action on your suggestions for work improvement (or explains if no action can be taken).

_____ Agree
_____ Disagree

32. In general, your supervisor lets you know what she or he thinks of your job performance.

_____ Agree
_____ Disagree

33. In general, if your supervisor is not satisfied with your work, she or he will tell you how you can improve.

_____Agree
_____Disagree

34. Your supervisor usually lives up to commitments.

_____Agree
_____Disagree

35. Do you have freedom on the job to use your own judgment?

_____Most of the time
_____Some of the time
_____Almost never

36. Do you think the administration is trying to improve relations with employees?

_____Most of the time
_____Some of the time
_____Almost never

37. Do you feel that you are treated with dignity and respect at the center?

_____Most of the time
_____Some of the time
_____Almost never

38. If you have a complaint to make, do you feel free to talk to someone in a higher position?

_____Most of the time
_____Some of the time
_____Almost never

39. In dealing with other departments, are work assignments well coordinated?

_____ Most of the time
_____ Some of the time
_____ Almost never

40. You are proud to work for the center.

_____ Agree
_____ Disagree

41. It really bothers you when you make a serious error on the job.

_____ Agree
_____ Disagree

42. Do you really feel part of the center?

_____ Yes
_____ No

43. Do you like to have your friends know where you work?

_____ Yes
_____ No

44. Do you feel a sense of accomplishment in your work?

_____ Most of the time
_____ Some of the time
_____ Almost never

45. Is your job interesting enough to keep you from getting bored?

_____Most of the time
_____Some of the time
_____Almost never

46. Do you think you are really doing something worthwhile in your job?

_____Yes
_____No

47. Do you have to force yourself to go to work?

_____Most of the time
_____Some of the time
_____Almost never

48. Do you get a sense of satisfaction working directly or indirectly to improve the welfare of the residents?

_____Yes
_____No

49. An important part of working here is getting to know the residents.

_____Agree
_____Disagree

50. You prefer doing jobs that require little contact with the residents.

_____Agree
_____Disagree

51. You would like to talk to the residents more than you do now.

_____ Agree
_____ Disagree

52. In general, do you feel the employees' council has been effective?

_____ Yes
_____ No

53. In general, do you feel the employees' council has been helpful in improving wages?

_____ Yes
_____ No

54. In general, do you feel the employees' council has been helpful in improving benefits?

_____ Yes
_____ No

55. In general, do you feel the employees' council has been helpful in improving working conditions?

_____ Yes
_____ No

56. In general, do you feel the employees' council has been helpful in improving employee relations?

_____ Yes
_____ No

57. In general, do you feel the employees' council has been helpful in improving personnel policies?

_____ Yes
_____ No

58. In general, do you feel the employees' council has been helpful in improving communications?

_____ Yes
_____ No

59. Have you yourself thought about retirement matters in the last year or so?

_____ Yes
_____ No

60. Where employees are allowed to work as long as they are capable, do you think this restricts advancement opportunities?

_____ Yes
_____ No

61. How good a job do you believe the center is now doing in helping employees plan for retirement?

_____ Excellent
_____ Good
_____ Adequate
_____ Poor
_____ Very poor

62. Have you personally considered how the center might help you with pre-retirement planning?

_____ Yes
_____ No

63. Given your responsibilities, do you feel that you usually spend too much time, too little time, or about the right amount of time talking to your immediate supervisor about residents, especially their needs and problems?

_____ Too much time
_____ Too little time
_____ Right amount of time

64. Given your responsibilities, do you feel that you usually spend too much time, too little time, or about the right amount of time talking to other people in your department about residents, especially their needs and problems?

_____ Too much time
_____ Too little time
_____ Right amount of time

65. Given your responsibilities, do you feel that you usually spend too much time, too little time, or about the right amount of time attending interdepartmental resident care conferences?

_____ Too much time
_____ Too little time
_____ Right amount of time

66. Given your responsibilities, do you feel that you usually spend too much time, too little time, or about the right amount of time developing resident care plans?

_____ Too much time
_____ Too little time
_____ Right amount of time

67. Given your responsibilities, do you feel that you usually spend too much time, too little time, or about the right amount of time providing direct resident care?

_____Too much time
_____Too little time
_____Right amount of time

68. Given your responsibilities, do you feel that you usually spend too much time, too little time, or about the right amount of time evaluating resident conditions?

_____Too much time
_____Too little time
_____Right amount of time

69. Given your responsibilities, do you feel that you usually spend too much time, too little time, or about the right amount of time making notes on resident charts?

_____Too much time
_____Too little time
_____Right amount of time

70. You do not have much opportunity to use your abilities at the center.

_____Agree
_____Disagree

71. Do you think you should be given more opportunity to use your judgment on the job?

_____Yes
_____No

72. Do you avoid taking on extra duties and responsibilities?

_____ Yes
_____ No

73. Does it seem to you that all you do is clean up after residents?

_____ Yes
_____ No

74. Residents always ask staff to do the things they could do themselves.

_____ Agree
_____ Disagree

75. There are many things that should be improved here, but nothing will ever be done about them.

_____ Agree
_____ Disagree

76. The manner in which the center manages excessive absenteeism and tardiness is:

_____ Too strict
_____ Not strict enough
_____ Appropriate

77. Do you believe the use of sick time at the center is abused?

_____ Yes
_____ No

78. Does absenteeism have a negative effect on the operations of the center and your fellow employees?

_____Yes
_____No

79. In your opinion, your supervisor:

_____Is too strict
_____Maintains proper discipline
_____Is too lenient

80. Have you been made aware of the center's grievance procedure for handling problems?

_____Yes
_____No

81. Employees are to follow strict operating procedures at all times.

_____Agree
_____Disagree

82. Whatever situation arises, the center has procedures to follow in dealing with it.

_____Agree
_____Disagree

83. In general, the center takes reasonable precautions to prevent accidents at work.

_____Agree
_____Disagree

84. Would you use the grievance procedure?

_____ Yes
_____ No

85. Are you personally willing to help the center look clean by taking care of minor spills or picking up debris?

_____ Yes
_____ No

Source: Hebrew Rehabilitation Center for Aged, 1200 Centre Street, Boston, MA 02131.

Bylaws of the Employees' Council

I. PURPOSE

    A. To assist in improving communications between employees and management by making suggestions that pertain to issues involving Center employees and by expressing employees' reactions to Center policies and programs.

    B. To encourage closer cooperation among all Center employees.

II. NAME

    A. This body shall be known as the Employees' Council.

III. MEMBERSHIP

    A. Section 1: Eligibility and Representation

        1. Election to the Council shall be open to all Center employees who have completed one year of employment.

        2. Each department or combination of departments shall be represented on the Council by an elected member.

        3. An elected member shall normally represent 50 employees from a single department or 50 employees from a combination of smaller departments.

    B. Section 2: Elections

        1. Elections of representatives and alternates shall be held every year by secret ballot within the department or combination of departments. Elections shall take place prior to the first meeting of the Council in January.

        2. Nominations and election of Council officers shall occur in January.

        3. Election of officers shall be by majority vote, using secret ballot.

    C. Section 3: Terms of Membership
1. Each elected member of the Council shall, at the pleasure of the department or combination of departments he or she represents, serve a term of one year beginning with the first meeting in January of the year he or she is elected.
2. Officers will be elected for a one-year term.
3. A vacancy created by termination of employment or resignation from the Council of an elected representative shall be filled by the elected alternate. A replacement for the alternate shall be elected by the department or combination of departments for the remainder of the unexpired term.
4. In the event of a vacancy in the office of Chairperson, the Vice-Chairperson shall fill the position for the remainder of the unexpired term.
5. In the event any official position, other than Chairperson, is vacated, nominations are open within the Council, first to the representatives, then to the alternates. If no Council member wishes to serve as an officer, it shall be the responsibility of the Chairperson to appoint a member of the Council to fill this vacated post for the remainder of the unexpired term.

    D. Section 4: Ex-Officio Members
1. A member of the Personnel Department, at the pleasure of the Council, shall attend Council meetings as an ex-officio member.

IV. DUTIES AND RIGHTS OF COUNCIL MEMBERS
    A. A member shall be expected to attend meetings regularly, and in his or her expected absence the elected alternate should be requested by the representative to attend.
    B. Voting by proxy shall not be allowed.
    C. Ex-officio members shall have use of the floor but shall enjoy no voting privileges.
    D. Ex-officio members shall not act as chairpersons of committees or subcommittees.

V. OFFICERS
    A. The officers of the Council shall be:
1. Chairperson
2. Vice-Chairperson
3. Recording Secretary
4. Corresponding Secretary

VI. DUTIES OF OFFICERS

   A. Chairperson
      1. The Chairperson shall call and preside at all meetings of the Council and shall be responsible for setting the agenda.
      2. The Chairperson shall appoint committees and their chairpersons to deal with such issues as may arise.
      3. The Chairperson shall call emergency meetings when he or she deems it necessary.
      4. The Chairperson shall enjoy no veto power.
   B. Vice-Chairperson
      1. The Vice-Chairperson shall assume the office and duties of the Chairperson in the event of the latter's absence, resignation, or inability to continue in office.
   C. Recording Secretary
      1. The Recording Secretary shall take the minutes at each meeting and be responsible for distributing copies of the minutes to each Council member as soon as possible after each scheduled meeting. Voting on each resolution by each representative shall be reflected in the minutes. The minutes shall be reviewed by the Chairperson before distribution. The Secretary shall also keep a record of all the Council members present or absent at all meetings and shall incorporate this record into the minutes.
   D. Corresponding Secretary
      1. The Corresponding Secretary shall be responsible for all correspondence between the Council and other organizations and individuals.

VII. RESOLUTIONS

   A. Eight Council members shall represent a quorum.
   B. A resolution shall be adopted by a two-thirds vote of all members present and voting.

VIII. AMENDMENTS

   A. Any member of the Council proposing an amendment to the bylaws shall present the proposal to the Chairperson, who shall then appoint a bylaws committee to study the proposal and present its recommendations to the Council.
   B. Proposed amendments shall be included in the Council minutes at least one month prior to a vote upon them by the Council members.
   C. A vote of two-thirds of the Council membership shall be required to ratify an amendment.

Preapplication Inquiry

Telephoned: _____ Personal Visit: _____ Mail: _____

Inquiry/Need

Age:
Interested in Residence:
Immediate Placement:
Medical Need:
Future Placement:
Reference Only:
Further Discussion:
General Information:

Projected Pattern:
Follow-up (month):
No Follow-up:
Family Not Interested:
Other:

Questionnaire Sent (date):

Medical Records Release Cards Enclosed (yes/no):

Date:
Inquirer:
Address:
Telephone:
Regarding:
Address:
Age:
Relationship:

Notes:

Social Worker:_____Date: _____

Application and Admission Policies

Need and Age

Any man or woman 65 years of age or older who is chronically ill and judged to require long-term nursing for the rest of his or her life shall be eligible to apply for admission.

The existence of financial need must be substantiated.

Residence

Applicants living within an approximate 20 mile radius of the center shall be eligible to apply.

New Residents

A resident new to the community shall have at least 1 year of residence before applying for admission.

Former Residents

Former residents of the community shall be eligible to apply provided they have at least 5 years of residence cumulative over the previous 20 years.

Involvement of Applicant

An application shall be accepted only when a qualified staff member determines that the applicant knows or has been made aware of the application and wishes this type of care.

Conditions Precluding Application

Regarding the following known conditions, no application on persons shall be taken until such time as referrals and full medical data have been received from medical care institutions and/or attending physicians indicating that there may be potential for admission. These known conditions are:

1. active communicable disease
2. alcoholism (active)
3. psychiatric problems requiring hospitalization
4. management problems
    a. uncontrollable wandering
    b. assaultive behavior
    c. suicidal tendencies
    d. disruptive or dangerous personal habits (e.g., uncontrollable spitting, dangerous smoking habits, bizarre behavior with urine or feces)

Chronological Order

Applicants shall be admitted in chronological order as of the date a determination is made by qualified staff members that the application is acceptable.

Nonadministrative Priority

Those applicants who are completely alone, with no one able or willing to provide the necessary supervision, shall be given a nonadministrative priority. Applicants with a nonadministrative priority shall, as a general rule, be admitted as soon as possible after a minimum wait of 3 months from date of application.

Administrative Priority

The following are eligible for administrative priority consideration:

1. volunteers who have worked more than 1,000 hours and are on the current volunteer list as maintained by the Volunteer Coordinator
2. employees who have been employed for at least 1 year or 2,080 hours
3. trustees who have been on the Board for at least 1 year
4. members of the President's Council who have served for at least 2 years

In addition, the following relatives of the above-specified volunteers, employees, trustees, and council members are eligible for administrative priority consideration:

1. their spouses
2. parents and parents-in-law
3. siblings and siblings-in-law
4. grandparents and grandparents-in-law
5. aunts and aunts-in-law; uncles and uncles-in-law
6. parents-in-law of children of Board members
7. grandparents-in-law of children of Board members

Administrative priorities will not exceed 12 in a calendar year.

Preapplication Questionnaire

Name: _____

Date: _____

This questionnaire, to be answered by potential applicants, is not an application.

1. What is your need for admission to this center ?
   _____
   _____
   _____

2. Are you at present in a hospital or recuperative center?
   Yes _____ No _____

3. Do you live in a nursing home? Yes _____ No _____
   If yes, where? _____

4. If you are not in a nursing home, what is your address?
   Street _____
   City _____ State _____ Zip _____
   Telephone No. _____

5. How many years have you lived at this address? _____

6. With whom do you live? (Check one)
Alone____Husband/wife_____ Son/daughter _____ Brother/sister_____
Grandchild _____ Other _____

7. What was your previous address?
Street_____
City_____ State _____ Zip _____
How long did you live there?_____

8. What is your marital status?_____
Name of husband/wife _____

9. What is your date of birth?_____ Age? _____
Birthplace?_____

10. Who should the center contact for an appointment?
Name _____
Address_____
Home phone_____Business phone _____

11. If there is a cancellation, could you accept an appointment on short notice?
Yes _____ No _____

Signature: _____

Witnessed by: _____

Relationship: _____

Date Signed: _____

RETURN QUESTIONNAIRE BY THIS DATE _____

Preapplication Questionnaire Cover Letter

[Date]

Mr. William Green
780 Boylston Street, Apt. 19
Boston, MA 02199

Dear Mr. Green:

Thank you for your interest regarding possible application to [name of long-term care institution].

Enclosed please find a questionnaire that should be completed and personally signed. Please then return the questionnaire to us in the enclosed envelope.

We will review your completed questionnaire and be in contact with you regarding an appointment time.

Sincerely,

Intake Interview

Applicant: _____

Age:_____ Marital Status: _____

Social Worker: _____

Place of Interview: _____ Date: _____

Appearance and Personality (clothing and affect):

Presenting Problem (including reason for application and attitude of applicant
and family toward center):

Family Situation and Relationship:

Intake Dictation

Social History (including marriages, losses, education, work history, and interests aside from family and work):

Languages:

Health:
    A. Physical

    B. Mental

    C. Emotional (including reaction to stress)

    D. Functional (including ADL)

Conferences or Consultations with Other Professional Personnel:

Financial Planning:

Interim Planning:

Projected Pattern of Care:

Projected Waiting Period:

Withdrawal Letter

[Date]

Mrs. Carol Smith
18 South Street
Newton, MA 02158

Re: William Green

Dear Mrs. Smith:

This is in confirmation of your conversation with Ellen Harris, Social Worker, on this date, wherein you have decided to have your father remain in his present surroundings and not follow through with his application for residence at this time.

Therefore, we have removed his name from the waiting list.

If at some time in the future it is determined that he would like to be considered again for admission, we will review the situation. If it seems appropriate, we will then begin the process of preparing a new application.

Please feel free to call us at 617-555-5555, extension 123, if you have any questions.

Sincerely,

Letter of Condolence

[Date]

Mr. John Mann
20 Atlantic Street
Wellesley, MA 02181

Re: Helen Mann

Dear Mr. Mann:

I was so sorry to learn of the recent death of your mother. Please accept our sincerest condolences to you and your family.

With deepest sympathy,

Medical Release Request

[Date]

Beth Israel Hospital
330 Brookline Avenue
Boston, MA 02215

Attention: Medical Records Department

To Whom It May Concern:

We would appreciate receiving summaries of all your medical records, including Outpatient Department records, of a patient applying for admission here.

Patient's Name: _____
Current Address: _____
_____
Former Address: _____
_____
Age:_____Birth date: _____ Birthplace: _____
Marital Status:_____ Spouse: _____

Thank you very much.

Very truly yours,

Enclosed: Medical Release Card

Job Description: Director of Marketing

Position Title: Director of marketing.

Reports to: LTC administrator or designate.

Scope: Institutionwide.

Position Concept: The director of marketing is responsible for providing marketing guidance and services to the LTC administrator, executive staff, department heads, and other agents of the institution.

Functions: The director of marketing will:

1. Contribute a marketing perspective to the deliberations of executive management in their planning of the institution's future.

2. Prepare data that might be needed by the LTC administrator or any member of the executive staff on a particular market's size, segments, trends, and behavioral dynamics.

3. Conduct studies of the needs, perceptions, preferences, and satisfactions of particular markets.

4. Participate in the planning, promotion, and launching of new programs.

5. Supervise the development of communication and promotion campaigns and materials.

6. Advise on pricing questions.

7. Advise on fund raising.

Responsibilities: The director of marketing will:

1. Contact individual members of the executive staff, department heads, and small groups within the institution to explain services and solicit problems.

2. Prioritize the various requests for services according to their long-run impact, cost-saving potential, time requirements, ease of accomplishment, cost, and urgency.

3. Select projects of high priority and set quantifiable accomplishment goals for the year.

4. Prepare a budget request to support the anticipated work.

5. Prepare an annual report on the major accomplishments of the office.

Minimum Qualifications: Master of Business Administration degree or equivalent. Minimum five years marketing experience, preferably in health care or related field. Proven ability to analyze market needs and to participate in the creation and implementation of a strategic marketing program. Excellent interpersonal and supervisory skills. Ability to interact smoothly with all levels of executive management and staff.

Job Description: Director of Public Relations

Position Title: Director of public relations.

Reports to: Director of marketing.

Scope: Institutionwide.

Position Concept: The director of public relations is responsible for creating a favorable perception of the institution among its external constituencies and for advising management on all matters relating to public relations.

Functions: The director of public relations will:

1. Interpret the viewpoints of the institution's external constituencies to the director of marketing, and recommend appropriate programs and action.

2. Promote good relations with local radio and television outlets, periodical and newspaper publishers, and other media organizations.

Responsibilities: The director of public relations will:

1. Establish and operate a film library, photographic library, and speakers' bureau.

2. Prepare, publish, and distribute a monthly newsletter of institution activities for distribution to residents, families of residents, and external constituencies.

3. Maintain an up-to-date fact file for use by management and staff.

4. Periodically evaluate the effectiveness of the public relations program and offer suggestions for its improvement.

Minimum Qualifications: Baccalaureate degree or equivalent. Minimum three years public relations experience, preferably in health care or related field. Knowledge of media requirements and public relations techniques, procedures, and resources. Ability to write clearly and convincingly and to conduct elementary public relations research with accuracy and thoroughness.

Index

About the Authors

MAURICE I. MAY has been President of Hebrew Rehabilitation Center for Aged since 1963. He is a past president of the National Association of Jewish Homes and Housing for the Aging, the Massachusetts Health Council, the Association of Massachusetts Homes for the Aging, and the Massachusetts Public Health Association. He served as the only representative from a nonprofit institution on the National Academy of Sciences Commission that studied nursing home regulations for the U.S. Congress. He holds a B.A. in government from Columbia College and an M.S. in hospital administration from Columbia University.

EDVARDAS KAMINSKAS is Physician-in-Chief at Hebrew Rehabilitation Center for Aged, a position he has held since 1981. He is also associate professor of medicine at Harvard Medical School and a physician at Beth Israel Hospital. His research interests include DNA damage and repair and Alzheimer's disease. He is a graduate of Yale University School of Medicine, was trained in internal medicine and hematology, and pursued further research and training in molecular biology at Massachusetts Institute of Technology.

JACK KASTEN is lecturer on health services at Harvard School of Public Health and an Adjunct Professor in the Department of Public Health at Boston University. From 1970 to 1988, he was leader of the health care management activities of Arthur D. Little, Inc., and was a vice president of the company. Previously, he was Director of Clinical Services and Associate Director of Beth Israel Hospital. He holds an M.P.H. from the University of Michigan and a J.D. from Boston College.

DAVID ALLAN LEVINE is a management consultant and writer. He has served on the corporate staff of Augat Inc., and before that he was a member of the faculty of Wayne State University, where he taught American history. He is the author of *Internal Combustion: The Races in Detroit, 1915–1926*, published by Greenwood Press. He holds a B.A. in American civilization from Brandeis University and a Ph.D. in history from the University of Chicago.